Coauthoring with Undergraduates
in Writing Studies

Coauthoring with Undergraduates in Writing Studies

Revising Identities and Institutions

Edited by
LAURIE GROBMAN AND JANE GREER

UTAH STATE UNIVERSITY PRESS
Logan

© 2025 by University Press of Colorado

Published by Utah State University Press
An imprint of University Press of Colorado
1580 North Logan Street, Suite 660
PMB 39883
Denver, Colorado 80203-1942

All rights reserved

　The University Press of Colorado is a proud member of
Association of University Presses.

The University Press of Colorado is a cooperative publishing enterprise supported, in part, by Adams State University, Colorado School of Mines, Colorado State University, Fort Lewis College, Metropolitan State University of Denver, University of Alaska Fairbanks, University of Colorado, University of Denver, University of Northern Colorado, University of Wyoming, Utah State University, and Western Colorado University.

ISBN: 978-1-64642-777-2 (hardcover)
ISBN: 978-1-64642-778-9 (paperback)
ISBN: 978-1-64642-779-6 (ebook)
https://doi.org/10.7330/9781646427796

Library of Congress Cataloging-in-Publication Data

Names: Grobman, Laurie, 1962– editor. | Greer, Jane, 1964– editor.
Title: Coauthoring with undergraduates in writing studies : revising identities and institutions / edited by Laurie Grobman and Jane Greer.
Description: Logan : Utah State University Press, [2025] | Includes bibliographical references and index.
Identifiers: LCCN 2025016632 (print) | LCCN 2025016633 (ebook) | ISBN 9781646427772 (hardcover) | ISBN 9781646427789 (paperback) | ISBN 9781646427796 (ebook)
Subjects: LCSH: English language—Rhetoric—Study and teaching (Higher) | Authorship—Collaboration. | Academic writing—Study and teaching (Higher)
Classification: LCC PE1404 .C547 2025 (print) | LCC PE1404 (ebook) | DDC 808.042/0711—dc23/eng/20250709
LC record available at https://lccn.loc.gov/2025016632
LC ebook record available at https://lccn.loc.gov/2025016633

Cover illustration by Mari Dein/Shuttertock.

Contents

Introduction
Jane Greer and Laurie Grobman   3

Section I: Spaces and Places of Coauthoring

1. Situating Faculty-Student Coauthoring in a Department of English
   Joyce Kinkead and Shane Graham   31

2. Lingering, Listening, and Cocreating: Undergraduate Writing Center Researchers and the Ethics of Coauthoring
   Steven J. Corbett, Annette Vara, and Katherine Villarreal   49

3. Coauthoring the Writing Studies Curriculum: An Ongoing Student-Faculty Partnership
   Heather Thomson-Bunn and Mía Zendejas   64

4. Cultivating Boundary Dwellers: Coauthoring Collaborative Relationships with Undergraduates in Community Engagement
   Tina Le and Rachael Shah   78

Section II: Models and Methods of Coauthoring

5. Nested Coauthorship: A Framework for Building Productive Undergraduate Research Experiences
   Teresa Contino, Isabella Gomez, Leah Senatro, and Amy Lueck   95

6. Feminist Pedagogy and Coauthorship: Decentering Meaning-Making and Valuing Students' Authentic Voices
   Letizia Guglielmo   112

7. Collaborative Coauthorship among Graduate and Undergraduate Students: A Horizontal, Mutual Mentorship Model for Writing Projects
   Jennifer Burke Reifman, Mik Penarroyo-Smith, Mikenna Modesto, and Loren Torres   127

8. Archives as Sites of Collaboration: "Side-by-Side" Coauthoring
   Lynée Lewis Gaillet   143

9. Scenes from behind the Scenes: Fostering Reciprocal Faculty-Undergraduate Coauthorships via Feminist Communities of Practice
   Vanessa Kraemer Sohan, Jennifer Peña, Xuan Jiang, and Giovanna Rodriguez   159

Section III: Consequences of and Reflections on Coauthoring

10. Destabilizing and Restabilizing Hierarchies in Faculty-Undergraduate Coauthoring
    Abby M. Dubisar   177

11. Telling Our Own Stories: Coauthoring with Students to Advance DEI Pedagogy
    Lauren S. Cardon and Brandy Martinez   193

12. Charting a Pathway from First-Year Composition to Academic Publishing
    Shirley E. Faulkner-Springfield, Kayla Moore, and Charity Riddick-Mullen   207

13. Creative-Critical Coauthoring: Definition and Demonstration
    Sandy Feinstein, Nicolas Fay, Faith Iseman, Ashley Offenback, Christian D. Brendel, Rachel Jensen, and Jennifer Muret-Bate   222

    Index   241
    About the Authors   251

COAUTHORING WITH UNDERGRADUATES
IN WRITING STUDIES

Introduction

JANE GREER AND LAURIE GROBMAN

In 2012, Joseph Harris published a trenchant call in *Journal of Advanced Composition (JAC)* for scholars in the field of writing studies to attend carefully to how students and their texts enter our professional discourse. Taking as his corpus some 448 articles published in *College Composition and Communication (CCC)* between 1987 and 2009, Harris argues that although "working with student writing is indeed one of the defining moves of our field, we too often use student texts in a quotidian fashion as mere examples for arguments already made" (686). Harris's analysis reveals an abundance of *CCC* articles in which a student and their writing is introduced in an essay to frame a conundrum about teaching or as an example or evidence to substantiate an argument being made by the article's author.

As an alternative to such uses of student texts, Harris poses a tantalizing possibility: "One strategy to bring students more fully into the discourse of our field is to invite them to become our coauthors" (683). He points to four publications coauthored by postsecondary faculty and undergraduates in *CCC* from 1987 to 2009, including Jenn Fishman, Andrea Lunsford, Beth McGregor, and Mark Otuteye's "Performing Writing, Performing Literacy," which subsequently won the 2006 Braddock Award for best article published in *CCC*. The other coauthored texts in *CCC* to which Harris calls attention are the work of other well-established scholars (Susan Miller, Cynthia Selfe and Gail Hawisher, Beverly Lyon Clark) who also collaborated with undergraduates. Harris concludes, though, that while coauthoring with undergraduates would be "a welcome move," it is "not one . . . we yet know how to make with confidence" (683).

Coauthoring with Undergraduates in Writing Studies: Revising Identities and Institutions takes up the important questions raised by Harris and initiates further conversation about what happens when postsecondary teachers and students write together and circulate their coauthored texts in academic publications, to institutional audiences, and outward to wider communities. In moving through the thirteen essays that compose this volume, readers will encounter faculty and undergraduates describing and theorizing about their coauthoring experiences within a variety of institutional contexts, including land-grant universities, historically Black colleges and universities (HBCUs), Hispanic-serving institutions (HSIs), religiously affiliated research universities, and regional campuses of statewide higher education systems. Readers will also find that the relationships between undergraduates and faculty that lead to coauthoring opportunities develop in a range of courses—first-year writing classes; courses that meet general educational requirements for students in a variety of disciplines; upper-level offerings for English majors (both online and in person)—as well as in other institutional spaces, such as writing centers, community engagement initiatives, and assessment offices. Coauthoring with undergraduates is by no means a niche practice available only to writing studies faculty who work within particular curricular structures, with selected student populations, or at a narrow range of institutions.

The contributors to this volume and the coauthoring endeavors they have undertaken are part of long-standing, though perhaps not fully appreciated and explored, traditions of faculty/undergraduate publication in writing studies. In our research for this volume, we combed through the online archives of *CCC* and *College English*. The earliest example of a faculty member and undergraduate coauthoring that we pinpointed in these flagship journals was in a 1962 issue of *CCC*.[1] Professor Warren French and undergraduate Marc Rosenberg coauthored a review of James Purdy's 1959 novel *Malcolm*. The coauthored text provides Rosenberg with an opportunity to offer his insight into the novel and how it might be received by his peers and also demonstrates how French's perspectives on the novel are shaped by Rosenberg's reactions.

French and Rosenberg's review has been followed by dozens of other publications coauthored by faculty and undergraduates on diverse topics. Some are in-depth research articles, such as David Wallace and Annissa Bell's article on systemic racism and the experiences of Black men at a large research university (*College English*, 1999) and Jordynn Jack and Lucy Massagee's study of the rhetoric of women's interracial cooperation in the 1930s in the South (*Rhetoric of Public Affairs*, 2011). Other coauthored publications are shorter, reflective essays on classroom practices and students' educational experiences (Herzl-Betz and Virrueta; Toth et al.; Bradley et al.), persuasion briefs (Davis and Dubisar), and a range of digital and multimodal publications (Tulley et al.; Balzhizer et al.; Halbritter et al.; Canzeroni et al.). Faculty and undergraduate students have also coauthored museum exhibits, reports and documents for community partners, and other texts that circulate beyond the citational economy of the academy.

Our own interests in and commitment to coauthoring with undergraduates are long standing and wide ranging. Laurie first began considering what it means to "author-ize" students in a 2009 *CCC* article, urging "members of our discipline to see *all* scholarly authorship in composition on a *continuum* that extends from novice to expert, and is fluid: scholarly authorship is not an all or nothing proposition but a matter of degree, and student scholarly authorship creates opportunities for varied modes and arenas of expertise" (W179). Though Laurie had long supported undergraduate students in claiming academic authority and circulating their work, her experiences of coauthoring with undergraduates began in 2015. Teaching a capstone class in professional writing, Laurie jumped on a call for proposals (CFP) in *Composition Studies* calling for faculty and undergraduates to write about the progress of undergraduate writing majors and concentrations, acknowledging students as a "necessary but so far under-represented component" of these disciplinary conversations. She was hooked. Over the next eight years, Laurie coauthored and published with several undergraduates about community writing projects in *Community Literacy Journal* (2015), *Reflections: A Journal of Public Rhetoric, Civic Writing, and Service-Learning* (2017), and *College English* (2022).

Jane's first effort at coauthoring with undergraduates arose from a class project to create an exhibit about the history of rhetorical education in western Missouri and eastern Kansas. All twenty-three students in the class were credited as authors (or curators) of the exhibit, along with Jane and a graphic designer who collaborated with the students to create twelve stand-up banners that were installed in the Kansas City convention center in 2018 during the Conference on College Composition and Communication (CCCC). The exhibit was subsequently displayed on campus and at a local cultural center dedicated to preserving Black history in the metropolitan area. Since then,

Jane has curated another digital exhibit with undergraduates and coauthored an article with two students that appeared in *College English* in 2020 (Crawford et al.).

We are keenly aware, though, that simply examining the texts that we have coauthored with students does not begin to tell the full story of our work with undergraduate coauthors, or the work of other faculty who have coauthored with undergraduates. Focusing only on the texts produced by faculty and undergraduate coauthors short circuits important questions about the intellectual and affective labor of the collaborative research and writing process that leads, ultimately, to *coauthorship* of a text that moves out into the world. As Kami Day and Michele Eodice point out in their landmark study *(First Person)*[2]: *A Study of Co-Authoring in the Academy* (2001), "There are lacunae in the body of research concerning collaboration in the academy: few studies examine co-authoring in academia, and even fewer are looking at co-authoring in the humanities, despite the increase of multiply authored publications" (15).

Like the writers interviewed by Day and Eodice, coauthoring with undergraduates has for us been far more than the products—textual and otherwise—that we produced. In coauthoring with undergraduates, we have connected with new communities and developed new partnerships; reconsidered our own habits as teachers, researchers, and writers; and assumed new roles, both formally and informally, within the institutions that serve as our professional homes. And while the processes of coauthoring are never easy or straightforward, we believe our students have benefitted in myriad ways from their experiences as coauthors as well. For some of them, coauthoring has exposed them to processes of academic publication and public writing and prepared them for a variety of career paths. For others, coauthoring has served as an opportunity to demystify the recursive processes of writing and revision that are difficult for even experienced authors. For still others, coauthoring with faculty has primarily provided them with a platform to circulate ideas and insights in which they are deeply invested.

In pulling back the curtain on the processes and outcomes of their own coauthoring experiences, the work of our contributors is vitally important. They take readers behind the scenes of coauthoring, reflecting on the processes and evaluating the consequences of the varied texts they have composed and published. Years ago, Ken Gale and Jonathan Wyatt asked, "How might collaborative writing take us—and the academy—somewhere different? Where might we as a scholarly community take collaborative writing?" (Gale and Wyatt, qtd in Duffy 146). The authors in this collection ask and answer similar questions about coauthoring, a specific type of collaborative writing, one that necessarily involves the concept of authorship. While our hope is that the chapters assembled here might result in more faculty making the "welcome move" to coauthor with undergraduates "more confidently" (Harris 683), we also believe that faculty and undergraduates who write together can revise their own intellectual lives and take academia in exciting new directions. Taken collectively, the thirteen chapters that compose *Coauthoring with Undergraduates in Writing Studies* seek to accomplish three important goals: (1) complicate understandings of the identities and relationships of faculty and undergraduates when they become coproducers of knowledge, (2) highlight the promise of bringing in underrepresented voices into these disciplinary conversations, and (3) interrogate embedded practices and policies in higher education institutions. Ultimately, this collection demonstrates the potential of coauthoring relationships involving faculty and undergraduates to make the academy a more just, diverse, and inclusive space.

Stabilizing (Temporarily) Unstable Terms: Coauthor and Undergraduate

Recognizing that the terms *coauthor* and *undergraduate* can be unstable, some clarification about definitions and the parameters of this volume will be helpful. We begin with "coauthor." The Committee on Publication Ethics (COPE) offers a simple yet elegant definition of coauthorship that focuses on two critical elements: a coauthor makes a "substantial contribution to the work" and "is accountable for the work and its published form." Across disciplines, though, what constitutes being named a "coauthor" can vary widely (Helgesson; Helgesson and Eriksson; Osborne and Holland; Jabbehdari and Walsh; Wren et al.). Within English studies, professional organizations such as the Conference on College Composition and Communication (CCCC) and the Modern Language Association (MLA) have sought to parse out what constitutes coauthorship and how various forms of authorial labor should be represented in bylines, in tenure and promotion guidelines, and in other forms of professional documentation. But as William Duffy has argued, "[E]ven the most articulated guidelines for accounting for and crediting collaboration often raise more questions than they answer" (20). Indeed, in working on this volume, we have as coeditors often debated and disagreed on what constitutes coauthorship, the varied forms of labor that can land someone's name in the byline of a publication, and what the order of authorial names on a publication might signify. We ultimately determined that, like Day and Eodice, coauthoring must of necessity be defined "polytypically" (23), and we have allowed contributors to this volume to determine who counts as an author and how authorship credit will be distributed. Indeed, each essay in this volume reveals nuanced kairotic details about institutional context, social connections and affective relationships among writing partners, genre and audience, access to technology, and complex work lives and diverse demands upon people's time—all factors that shape the work of faculty and students who coauthor together.

Despite the rich diversity of coauthorial labor described and represented in these thirteen chapters, the common thread of "consequential publicness" runs through them all. As Doug Downs, Laurie McMillan, Megan Schoettler, and Patricia Roberts-Miller note, such consequential publicness certainly includes traditional academic publishing in the form of journal articles and book chapters, but it can also involve the creation of exhibits, presentations and reports for institutional stakeholders, publications intended for a community audience or campus stakeholders, or contributions to databases, online catalogs, and digital repositories (98). The crucial move to go public with a collaboratively written text can transform students' sense of their own authorial agency and responsibility while also representing to the intended audiences the complex, collaborative intellectual work that unfolds in various spaces on college campuses.

Beyond establishing the parameters of the types of coauthorship explored by our contributors, it is also important to recognize that an individual's status as an undergraduate may be far less self-evident than one would assume. The term *undergraduate* is for most individuals a short-lived moniker, reflecting their academic identity during an interlude of a few years when they are pursuing a first postsecondary degree. An undergraduate student may well begin coauthoring with a more established scholar, but by the time the project is finished, submitted for publication, reviewed, revised, prepared for production, and finally circulated, the undergraduate may have finished their associate or baccalaureate studies and be pursuing any number of professional goals. For example, it is difficult to parse Sonja Weidenhaupt's professional status in the *CCC* article she coauthored in 1992 with Beverly Lyon Clark. Harris points to the article as an example of student-faculty coauthorship, and it focuses on Weidenhaupt's struggles with writer's block as she completed her senior honors thesis. The essay opens with a sentence that creates immediacy and seems to reflect Weidenhaupt's perspective as an undergraduate writer: "I would like to give you insight into what I went through trying to write this thesis over the last year and a half" (55). The article then consists of a series of passages or exchanges—presented in different typographical fonts—between Clark and Weidenhaupt about the factors that contribute to a writer feeling blocked and possible solutions as well about the roles faculty might play in supporting students. As the exchange unfolds, though, Weidenhaupt discloses, "Now, in graduate school, I try to do hour blocks of work" (59), and in the article's penultimate paragraph, Clark triumphantly announces "Sonja is now in graduate school, where she has written several 20-page papers, not without pain, but successfully" (71). In the biographical note accompanying the essay, Weidenhaupt's professional trajectory is further extended: "Sonja Weidenhaupt has completed an MA in Developmental Psychology at Teachers College."

Like Weidenhaupt, other undergraduate coauthors may choose to be identified by new professional identities they have assumed at the time of publication or they may be identified in the biographical notes commonly included in scholarly publications in other ways, such as "student," "undergraduate," "recent graduate," and "alumnus." Indeed, the limited temporality of an author's identity as an undergraduate makes it nearly impossible to search current scholarly databases or use academic analytics to locate publications coauthored by undergraduates in writing studies.

In moving through *Coauthoring with Undergraduates in Writing Studies*, readers will encounter contributors who at the time of publication identify as undergraduates; who began collaboratively writing with faculty during their undergraduate studies but have now become alumni working in a variety of professions; who have moved on to graduate school in various disciplines; and who have taken staff positions at their alma maters. Tina Le, for example, characterizes herself as "a former undergraduate turned community partner" in the essay she has coauthored for this volume with faculty member Rachael Shah (chapter 4). Likewise, Katherine Villarreal, one of the three coauthors of chapter 2, began collaborating with faculty member Steven J. Corbett as a first-year college student and writing center tutor at Texas A&M University, Kingsville, but she is now a fifth-grade teacher. *Coauthoring with Undergraduates in Writing Studies* is thus centered on exploring the complexities of coauthoring for faculty and collaborators who identify as undergraduates during the conception, composition, and/or publicly consequential circulation of their shared project.

Conversations About Coauthorship

Each individual chapter in *Coauthoring with Undergraduates in Writing Studies* offers insights into the under-researched and under-theorized topic of coauthoring between postsecondary educators and undergraduate students. The authors approach coauthoring from varying perspectives, theories, and areas of scholarship, for example, "nested coauthorship" (Contino, Gomez, Senatro, and Lueck, chapter 5), critical race theory (Cardon and Martinez, chapter 11), feminist pedagogy (Guglielmo, chapter 6), students as partners (Thomson-Bunn and Zendejas, chapter 3), explorations of the "boundary zone" between academic/community and undergraduate/faculty (Le and Shah, chapter 4), and communities of practice (Sohan, Peña, Jiang, and Rodriguez, chapter 9).

At the same time, the sections below illustrate the important ways these diverse chapters speak to one another, demonstrating three primary ways that coauthoring between post-secondary educators and undergraduates work toward justice, in both writing studies and the academy more broadly. These include (1) challenging long-standing negative representations of undergraduate writers through expanding the available range of representational identities and relationships available to both teacher/researchers and students, (2) advancing DEI practices by creating opportunities for students from underrepresented groups to view themselves as writers and academics, claim authorship, and affirm the value of the linguistic diversity of their cultures, and (3) interrogating and potentially shifting embedded institutional policies and practices impacting both students and faculty.

NEW IDENTITIES: REDEFINING FACULTY AND STUDENTS AS COPRODUCERS OF KNOWLEDGE

Like Harris, several scholars have long called for careful attention to how undergraduate students have entered into professional conversations in writing studies. Students are too often represented as "young beginner[s] . . . presexual, preeconomic, prepolitical people" (Miller 87); as "doltish figure[s], usually quite lazy and verbally stunted" (Helmers 19); as "remedial—deficient in grammatical and creative skills and political awareness" (Bastian and Harkness 101); and as "novices, . . . as being supported by teachers, . . . as entering unfamiliar cultures, and . . . as ideologically or cognitively limited" (Johnson 418). Lulu C. H. Sun characterizes representations of students in research published by their teachers as a "pervasive and problematic discourse of Othering . . . a discourse of the colonizer and the colonized, the missionary and the heathen" (46). As Lynn Z. Bloom notes, perhaps the most positive representations of students occur in composition textbooks when they are presented as "writers-in-process" who serve as models for other students (68). In none of these characterizations are undergraduates considered scholars who might contribute to the discipline with new insights and perspectives or carefully researched arguments.

The growing presence of undergraduate research across the higher education landscape in the twenty-first century has helped to shift perceptions of students' abilities as researchers and scholars who can contribute to disciplinary conversations. The Boyer Commission (1998); George Kuh's use of the National Survey of Student Engagement to identify "high impact educational practices," including undergraduate research (2008); Laurie Grobman and Joyce Kinkead's landmark volume *Undergraduate Research in English Studies* (2010); and the CCCC Position Statement on Undergraduate Research in Writing (2017)—all have urged faculty to refigure educational opportunities to emphasize inquiry and knowledge production and provided faculty with important strategies and tools for supporting students as undergraduate researchers.

Not surprisingly, several scholarly journals have emerged so that undergraduates might have access to national and even international audiences for the research they were producing. Such journals include the *Oswald Review* (1999), *Xchanges* (2001), *Young Scholars in Writing* (2003), *The Jump+* (2010), and *Queen City Writers* (2012). Other journals, including *Kairos* (2011), *Writing Center Journal* (2012), *Pedagogy* (2022), and *College English* (2022), have published special issues featuring the work of undergraduate researchers, and the Undergraduate Research Poster Session at the Conference on College Composition and Communication was launched in 2012, under the leadership of Jessie Moore. Focused on *Young Scholars in Writing* as one of the earliest "undergraduate only" journals, Amy Robillard argues that such publications stand "as evidence that students are able and willing to contribute to composition studies' disciplinary knowledge about writing and rhetoric" (262).

Along with undergraduate research, students as partners (SaP) initiatives have helped counter limiting conceptions of undergraduate students and their capabilities. Citing work done in the first decades of the twenty-first century, Alison Cook-Sather and her coauthors note that "[t]he term 'students as partners' emerged in response to a felt need to name students as colleagues—to call into presence and action a constituency in higher education traditionally considered the recipient, not the producer, of knowledge" (2). For Mick Healey, Abbi Flint, and Kathy Harrington, "partnership works to counter a deficit model where staff take on the role of enablers of disempowered students, implicit in some forms of student engagement, aiming instead to acknowledge differentials of power while valuing individual contributions from students and staff in a shared process of reciprocal learning and working" (Healy et al. 15). The Students as Learners and Teachers (SaLT) program at Bryn Mawr and Haverford College is "one of the longest standing pedagogical partnership programs in the world" ("SaLT"). It was originally focused on linking faculty members with student consultants of color "to support the development of more culturally sustaining practices" ("SaLT"). Building on the work of SaLT, numerous colleges and universities in the US and around the world have developed programs that place trained student-consultants in classrooms where they observe, write reflection reports, and engage faculty in dialogue about pedagogical practices and classroom dynamics. Other examples of SaP initiatives include teams of students and faculty designing and assessing curriculum; creating, implementing, and evaluating online, open-access textbooks (Hanley et al.); and building sustainable partnerships between postsecondary educational institutions and a range of community partners.

In the spirit of partnership, such initiatives may result in coauthored publications and other consequential, public texts. But Lucy Mercer-Mapstone and her colleagues note in their systematic literature review of scholarship and research on the SaP initiatives published between 1968 and 2016 that the principle of reciprocity that undergirds such efforts "does not always translate into co-authorship" (28). Indeed, Mercer-Mapstone et al. found that nearly ninety percent of articles on SaP listed faculty or staff as first author and only one-third listed a student as a coauthor (28). Reviewing the list of contributors to Mercer-Mapstone and Abbot's more recent *The Power of Partnership: Students, Staff, and Faculty Revolutionizing Higher Education* (2020) affirms these numbers: approximately two-thirds of the authors include staff/faculty appointments or doctoral study in their biographies. While SaP initiatives certainly help supplant unproductive and unflattering representations of students, the paucity of coauthored publications suggests missed opportunities for the ongoing revision of student and faculty identities.

Indeed, when faculty voices dominate professional conversations that occur through articles, book chapters, and other publicly consequential texts and undergraduate voices are largely accessible in journals devoted to undergraduate research, it leaves intact representations of faculty as experts and authorities who mentor novices and serve as exemplary role models of professionalism and field-specific norms. We believe that when faculty and undergraduates engage in coauthorship they extend the available range of representational identities and relationships available to both teacher/researchers and students at postsecondary institutions. For example, in chapter 6, Letizia Guglielmo describes how she and undergraduate coauthors with whom she has previously published recorded and transcribed their online conversations as a deliberate part of the writing and revision process, enabling "generative conversation" and "collective meaning-making." By restructuring the essay that they published in a volume on feminist collaboration as a "dialogue among the four of us," the coauthors "create[d] space for more authentic student voices" in writing studies scholarship.

To be sure, a faculty member who coauthors with undergraduates may continue to act as a guide or mentor, especially in terms of making explicit the norms and practices of professional publication. But as our contributors make apparent, faculty are often guided and taught by students, whose contributions as coauthors are central to the finished work. In chapter 10, Abby M. Dubisar describes coauthoring with Sara Davis to publish a persuasion brief in *Rhetoric of Health and Medicine* on the gendered communication surrounding elective sterilization procedures. Davis's own experiences in seeking elective sterilization informed the project, and she assumed the role of guide as she and Dubisar worked through patient information brochures she had collected. Similarly, Lynée Lewis Gaillet (chapter 8) and Tina Le and Rachael Shah (chapter 4) describe in their essays how undergraduates mentor their faculty coauthors on engaging with community archives or partnering with community organizations. Gaillet emphasizes the students' innate understandings of the stakeholders and community members represented by the archives, arguing that "none of the coauthors could produce this chapter individually, and intergenerational mentoring/coauthoring enriches the project by providing broader and more inclusive perspectives." Likewise, Le and Shah, adopting the term *boundary dweller* to characterize students' status in the academy and in wider communities, emphasize the importance of valuing different forms of expertise and types of authorial tasks individual coauthors can take on, particularly within the context of community partnerships. Jennifer Burke Reifman, Mik Penarroyo-Smith, Mikenna Modesto, and Loren Torres (chapter 7) also emphasize the value of undergraduate coauthors' perspectives by explicitly modeling "horizontal, mutual mentoring" and argue that such an approach to coauthoring can "dismantle notions of expertise and perceived power."

Beyond realigning authority and expertise so that it is not solely ascribed to faculty, coauthoring can also lead to richer, more nuanced understandings of individuals' needs and vulnerabilities. In chapter 3, faculty member Heather Thomson-Bunn describes her feelings of vulnerability after sustaining a concussion because she "was the one in need of extra time, in need of understanding and grace from someone who was counting on me." Mía Zendejas responded with generosity, recalling how Heather had shown her empathy during her struggles as a student in class—"Now she was coming to me, and I could empathize with her."

There are times, though, when despite everyone's best efforts, some hierarchies hold firm. For undergraduate coauthors Kayla Moore and Charity Riddick-Mullen (chapter 12), being asked by Shirley Faulkner-Springfield to critique her writing as part of the team's revision process went too far. When they "finally divulged our secret [to Shirley] that it was difficult to collapse the hierarchy even after applying our authorial voices and executing authority in all other matters related to revising this chapter," they realized that they needed space to "work together without constant faculty guidance." Faculty member Abby M. Dubisar (chapter 10) was unable to break down power structures when she fielded inquiries from journalists seeking expert commentary on women's access to reproductive health care. Though undergraduate Sara Davis was listed as first author of the persuasion brief they published in *Rhetoric of Health and Medicine*, journalists opted to contact Dubisar for her "expert" opinion.

While hierarchical understandings of academic identities and authority may at times resist recalibration, Day and Eodice note that participants in their study—faculty who collaborated with other faculty and occasionally with graduate students—were all "receptive to other insights and perspectives because they are teachable and because of their respect for and trust in their co-authors" (82). Day and Eodice saw the coauthors they studied as embracing Iris Marion Young's theory of "asymmetrical reciprocity," which depends less on unity and equality and more on valuing diversity (93). In committing to the creation and publicly consequential circulation of a coauthored text, faculty and undergraduate coauthors whose work is represented in this volume embrace the unique forms of experience and expertise they bring to the project as partners contributing to and taking responsibility for their shared work.

DIVERSITY, EQUITY, AND INCLUSION: AMPLIFYING STUDENTS' VOICES

As this volume attests, opportunities to coauthor with faculty demonstrate promise in increasing access to meaningful research experiences for undergraduates from communities that have historically been underserved in higher education and to create more inclusive learning environments.[2] For several student coauthors in this volume, viewing themselves as writers and academics as well as claiming authorship has been a defining feature of their coauthoring.

In chapter 2, undergraduate Annette Vara describes how intimidated and insecure she'd initially felt about coauthoring with writing center director Steven Corbett but how she pushed through it by finding support not only from Corbett and her sister, coauthor Katherine Villarreal, but other Hispanic tutors she met at the 2022 National Conference of Peer Tutors in Writing. Villarreal adds that once Corbett began to show her some of what Corbett called "the tricks of the trade" for applying for and participating in conferences, "it opened a realm of futures that I never thought could be opened to a minority as well as a woman in academia. With this information, I feel this kind of practice needed to be shared ethically with my peers, who were predominantly Hispanic." Similarly, undergraduate coauthor Charity Mullin (chapter 12) confirms that she had "persistent doubts . . . about whether [she] was the right choice" to coauthor with her professor, Shirley Faulkner-Springfield, but reflecting on the authoring experience writing this chapter, Charity claims she has become a more confident "writer and justice activist" and hopes the published chapter will "inspir[e] African American female students to conduct scholarly research and coauthor with their professors." This is precisely why Faulkner-Springfield deliberately invites her students at HBCUs to coauthor with her, because "many students did not self-identify as writers who possessed the wherewithal to produce a scholarly product." Faulkner-Springfield seeks broader change, arguing that the discipline "should carefully define the term 'writer' because many students, particularly students of color, have not been conditioned to self-identify as writers."

For several of the undergraduate coauthors in this volume, coauthoring with faculty has affirmed the value of their cultures' linguistic diversity. Coauthoring with faculty member Heather Thomson-Bunn through a SaP initiative at Pepperdine University led Mía Zendejas (chapter 3) to recognize that her practice of code-switching was "a valid linguistic and rhetorical device," and she was able to bring her *perspectiva latinoamericana* to the curriculum they created together and shared with institutional stakeholders (chapter 3). Likewise, Vanessa Sohan, Jennifer Peña, Xuan Jiang, and Giovanna Rodriguez (chapter 9) point out the significance of "the diverse linguistic, cultural, and social resources [undergraduates] bring to our collaborations." And Isabella Gomez, the high school senior applying for college in chapter 5, has also learned the power of her writerly voice, "with the end product being the ability to highlight community values." By including her Tribal Land Acknowledgment in her and Amy Lueck's article in *CCC*, Isabella acknowledges how the land her "people have tended to and built memories on since time immemorial" should "be a space where my people are able to thrive in any manner, especially in higher education."

To be sure, students' voices and perspectives might be coopted or overwritten when they collaborate with faculty coauthors, particularly students whose paths through higher education are often strewn with microaggressions and systemic barriers to success. In chapter 11, Brandy Martinez and Lauren Cardon address that possibility, suggesting that both faculty and undergraduates must be mindful of power differentials, ensuring that the student feels comfortable asserting their desires, including walking away from the project. We concur with Day and Eodice, who argue that "successful co-authoring invites voices that might never have been heard at all otherwise, especially less powerful voices that might have been drowned out in a hierarchy" (35). They go on to suggest that "[a]s we work with others, our individual voices may be enlarged, reaccented, and modulated, but need not be lost" (36). The faculty/undergraduate coauthorships described in this volume emphasize such conversation, collaboration, shared goals, and unique perspectives. Thomson-Bunn and Zendejas (chapter 3), for example, abandoned "traditional student-faculty research dynamics" and worked together to choose specific diversity topics. Neither recalls "who first mentioned neurodiversity" because they "pursued ideas regardless of their originator" and established "the 'we'" of their coauthorship. Through such shared work, the power of authorship as ownership and its links to racialized identities of privilege and authority begins to recede, allowing new visions of textual labor to come to the fore and new, more diverse authorial identities to emerge.

NEW POSSIBILITIES: INTERROGATING OUR INSTITUTIONS

Beyond their emergent roles as reciprocal knowledge-makers, faculty and undergraduate coauthors have potent opportunities for interrogating the entrenched practices and policies that shape postsecondary institutions. Many extant examples of scholarship that have been coauthored by undergraduates and faculty explicitly address how such shared work serves as a site for investigating and disrupting academic norms. In their 2007 article in *Writing Center Journal*, Renee Brown, Brian Fallon, Jessica Lott, Elizabeth Mathews, and Elizabeth Mintie shared their collaborative research on Turnitin.com, calling for faculty across the disciplines to educate themselves about how plagiarism-detection software functions and suggesting strategies writing center tutors might use to ameliorate its effects on students' sense of themselves as writers. More recently, Gregory J. Palermo, Qianqian Zhang-Wu, Devon Skylar Regan, and Mya Poe have written about their efforts to develop more nuanced forms of writing program assessment to meet the needs of linguistically diverse students. They argue for the value of "multigenerational mentoring," that brings together faculty, graduate students, and undergraduate students to renegotiate "the terms and methods that comprise disciplinary boundary work" (92). As an undergraduate English major and member of the research team, Regan writes, "Activists and scholars alike have critiqued academia's disinterest in critically examining its own practices," but she notes that her engagement with her coauthors involved a process of "concurrent learning and unlearning" about "elitism and other forms of colonial gatekeeping in educational spaces" (103). By questioning institutional norms and imagining new kinds of roles for students, such coauthored publications align with the goals espoused by advocates of SaP. Cook-Sather, Bovill, and Felten note that partnering with students can affirm pedagogical practices and institutional structures that are working well, but also that taking into account students' perspectives and insights can also mean "following where students lead, perhaps to places we may not have imagined or been to before" as educators (9).

Several essays in this volume speak to faculty-student coauthorship and the publications that serve as vehicles for institutional critique and for imagining new possibilities. For example, in chapter 6, Letizia Guglielmo describes her long-standing commitment to coauthoring with undergraduates across a range of disciplines, which has resulted in the publication of multiple peer-reviewed articles. As Guglielmo notes, the work of coauthorship can "engage students as change-agents." In chapter 11, Lauren Cardon and Brandi Martinez challenge business as usual in DEI research and scholarly publishing, and they view their coauthored essay as an intervention that addresses "the dearth of student input on inclusive practices in the college classroom." In sharing her "counterstory," Martinez challenges her faculty coauthor as well as readers of this volume to step into new roles and to be open to shifts in tone and style as they "listen, learn, and trust" when students share their experiences. Ultimately, Cardon and Martinez hope to "stimulate conversations about student-professor relationships in the college setting" with the goal of "making pedagogy more inclusive and equitable." Similarly, Isabella Gomez, a tribal leader among Muwekma Ohlone youth, was preparing to enroll at Santa Clara University (SCU) as she was coauthoring chapter 5 with her faculty mentor, Amy Lueck, and current undergraduates at SCU. Through a year-long internship with Lueck, Gomez was able to design and develop a cultural camp for young people in her tribe. Upon her matriculation to SCU, Gomez will be "entering the campus space on her homelands prepared to talk back to it and transform it." As these and other chapters in this volume demonstrate, coauthoring with undergraduates can and, we would argue, should involve far more than simply inculcating undergraduates into norms of academic publication and the practices of circulating their work in consequential ways. Faculty-undergraduate coauthoring makes space to raise important questions about pedagogies and policies that limit the ways students might imagine their roles as participants in higher education.

The myriad ways that undergraduate coauthors leverage their shared work with faculty to interrogate the colleges and universities they attend and to posit new possibilities for themselves and their fellow students runs as a conversational thread through the thirteen essays that compose this volume. But an equally important theme threaded throughout this collection involves how coauthoring with undergraduates also allows faculty to (re)write their professional lives and counteract institutional structures that would define their work in limiting ways. In chapter 10, Abby M. Dubisar, a tenured professor at an R1 university, documents how coauthoring with undergraduates has on multiple occasions allowed her to insist on the visibility of her work as *both* a researcher and a teacher at her institution. She notes that the faculty-evaluation process at her university does not value her work in- and outside of the classroom to mentor undergraduate researchers, but that this privileging of faculty research over teaching is "a hierarchy I subvert by writing and publishing with students." In chapter 9, Vanessa Sohan, Jennifer Peña, Xuan Jiang, and Giovanna Rodriguez argue for many important outcomes from their work as coauthors within a feminist community of practice (CoP). As a writing center administrator and contingent faculty member, Xuan Jiang notes how coauthoring with undergraduates has added important nuances to her professional identity. Having worked with Jennifer Peña over multiple semesters, Xuan was invited to Jennifer's master's thesis defense and was introduced as her "research mentor" by Jennifer, even as Vanessa Sohan directed her thesis. As a contingent faculty member and unofficial mentor of a graduate student, Xuan, having heard Jennifer's introduction, felt more legitimate and motivated to continue with her mentorship and coauthorship with students. Jennifer and Xuan's reciprocal, collaborative coauthorship indicates that there can be a synergistic impact for faculty with a wide range of institutional identities.

Not only do faculty find themselves revising their academic and institutional identities when they coauthor with undergraduates, they also have opportunities to explore new genres of writing and to work against the constraints of much academic discourse. Joyce Kinkead and Shane Graham's opening chapter provides a rich catalog of "diversified scholarly production" resulting from their university's long-standing commitment to supporting undergraduate research and faculty-student coauthorship. In chapter 8, Lynée Lewis Gaillet troubles the genre of the textbook and how coauthoring portions of instructional texts with undergraduates creates new possibilities for teaching and learning. And indeed, so many of the chapters in this volume are themselves stretching the boundaries of the academic essay in fruitful, exciting ways, standing as complex and creative multivoiced dialogues that demand nimble readers. The final chapter of the volume, authored by Sandy Feinstein, Nicholas Fay, Faith Iseman, Ashley Offenback, Christian D. Brendel, Rachael Jensen, and Jennifer Muret-Bate, exemplifies the power of coauthoring to give rise to new ways of writing and reading. In demonstrating the power of their "creative-critical" approach to coauthoring, their chapter stands as "An Eptalogue, A Post-Modern Symposium."

In sum, we believe—and the contributors to this volume demonstrate—that when faculty and undergraduates coauthor publicly consequential texts, they can create unique opportunities to interrogate institutional structures as well as to imagine new possibilities for teaching, learning, and being in relationship with others.

Overview of Chapters

Organized into three sections, this volume provides researchers, teachers, and writers with opportunities to consider the places and spaces in academia and beyond that often give rise to coauthoring opportunities with undergraduates, to explore models and methods for carrying out the work of coauthoring, and to reflect on the consequences and impacts when postsecondary teachers coauthor with undergraduates. Across these three sections, readers will encounter the voices of faculty and undergraduates as they share their coauthoring experiences in a wide range of educational contexts and trace both the practical and theoretical implications of their shared work.

The timing of CFPs and publication deadlines, though, do not always align with the temporal horizons of potential undergraduate collaborators, and coauthoring with undergraduates can be as serendipitous as other scholarly projects, depending on teaching schedules, student interest, the needs of community partners, and other factors. Several faculty members with deep experience in coauthoring are thus sharing work in this collection that they composed without an undergraduate partner or partners. Joyce Kinkead and Shane Graham (chapter 1), Letizia Guglielmo (chapter 6), Lynée Lewis Gaillet (chapter 8) and Abby M. Dubisar (chapter 10) have all coauthored multiple consequentially public texts with undergraduates, including articles in peer-reviewed journals, book chapters, digital publications, and contributions to anthologies and textbooks. Writing without undergraduate coauthors for this volume, these contributors are able to chart how coauthorship with undergraduates has impacted their institutional lives as faculty members in higher education across years and even decades, and they offer insights about diverse pedagogical approaches that they have developed and are continually revising in order to extend and expand the possibilities for coauthoring with undergraduates.

In Section I, "Spaces and Places of Coauthoring," readers are invited to consider a range of sites—English departments, writing centers, students as partners (SaP) programs, and community engagement initiatives—that have proved to be fruitful ground for faculty and undergraduates to become coauthors. This section opens with Joyce Kinkead and Shane Graham's essay that describes and interrogates the institutional culture of the English Department at Utah State University, where numerous faculty/undergraduate partnerships have resulted in coauthored scholarly monographs and edited collections of primary documents, articles in regional and national academic journals, exhibitions and historical markers, institutional reports and digital resources for students across campus, and other types of texts. In chapter 2, Steven J. Corbett, Annette Vara, and Katherine Villarreal bring forward writing centers as sites that invite the kind of "lingering, listening, and co-creation of knowledge" that can lead postsecondary teachers and researchers to coauthor with undergraduates. Heather Thomson-Bunn and Mía Zendejas position their work at the intersection of the students as partners (SaP) approach to pedagogy and institutional reform and diversity, equity and inclusion (DEI) efforts at their university, chronicling how their work as coauthors in this space underscores how both faculty and undergraduates negotiate moments of power and vulnerability. Tina Le and Rachael Shah's "Cultivating Boundary Dwellers" takes readers beyond the university and considers the opportunities for coauthoring with undergraduates in community spaces, arguing that successful coauthoring in such boundary zones accrue from healthier relationships among people with varied positionalities more so than published papers or widely circulated documents.

Section II, "Models and Methods of Coauthoring," offers readers opportunities to consider various models and ways of conceptualizing the work that unfolds when faculty and undergraduates coauthor a range of texts. Teresa Contino, Isabella Gomez, Leah Senatro, and Amy Lueck open this section with their essay "Nested Coauthorship: A Framework for Building Productive Undergraduate Research Experiences." The image of a nest—built over time and with intent, assembled from diverse materials at hand—serves as a useful way to frame their experiences of coauthoring and can help to bring forward diverse voices and validate capacious forms of knowledge-making and sharing.

Framing coauthorship in light of feminist pedagogy and the principles of writing across the curriculum, Letizia Guglielmo's essay offers a flexible conceptualization of the generative work that leads students to coauthor with faculty. Guglielmo demonstrates how opportunities for dialogic meaning-making, reflection, and meta-analysis in the required discussion boards of interdisciplinary, online courses and high-impact practices (HIPs), such as undergraduate research projects and internships, have led to undergraduates coauthoring conference presentations and chapters in edited collections with her.

Jennifer Burke Reifman, Mik Penarroyo-Smith, Mikenna Modesto, and Loren Torres promote a "horizontal, mutual mentorship model" for characterizing coauthorship with undergraduates, enabling all coauthors to ask questions, share insights, and develop new relationships to writing, regardless of the varied positions each of them occupy within the academy. Turning to the archives as a generative site for research that leads undergraduates to coauthor with faculty, Lynée Lewis Gaillet proposes a model of "side-by-side" coauthoring, an extension of Lunsford and Ede's foundational work on collaborative writing and coauthoring. Such a model opens a range of publishing opportunities while also raising provocative and important questions about attribution and the blurry boundaries of coauthorship when students collaborate with faculty to produce elements contained in textbooks. Vanessa Sohan, Jennifer Peña, Xuan Jiang, and Giovanna Rodriguez's "Scenes from behind the Scenes: Fostering Reciprocal Faculty-Undergraduate Coauthorships at a Hispanic-Serving Institution" draws on Wenger's concept of communities of practice as a heuristic that allows undergraduates and faculty to tap into their everyday lived experiences as learners and their intersectional identities, troubling the presumed expertise of particular positionalities within colleges and universities; of coauthors as colearners; and of continuous conversations about the intellectual, affective, and embodied processes of collaboration.

Section III, "Consequences of and Reflections on Coauthoring," features four essays that allow readers to trace the impacts of coauthoring on teachers, students, and institutions. In "Destabilizing and Restabilizing Hierarchies in Faculty-Undergraduate Coauthoring," Abby M. Dubisar considers three occasions on which she coauthored articles with undergraduates and the resulting publications in national, peer-reviewed journals. With clear-eyed self-reflection, Dubisar considers the benefits and responsibilities that flow to diversely circumstanced writers from each of her coauthoring experiences and the subsequent publications and how academic authorship becomes a continual process of destabilization and restabilization when faculty and undergraduates coauthor a range of texts.

Powerful advocates for the processes and products of faculty and undergraduates who engage in coauthorship, Lauren S. Cardon and Brandy Martinez argue that scholarship on inclusive pedagogies and equity initiatives should include the voices of students as fully empowered contributors to such critical conversations. Students who coauthor with faculty can more fully represent their intersectional identities and counter the tokenization that can occur when their lives and learning are simply described by faculty. Shirley Faulkner-Springfield, Kayla Moore, and Charity Riddick-Mullen draw upon their experiences at two HBCUs in North Carolina to boldly advance the position that writing studies faculty should coauthor with undergraduate students of color in order "to promote justice in academia, in the professions, and in the wider society." Weaving together all three of their voices and perspectives in their essay, "Creating a Pathway from First-Year Composition to Academic Publishing," Faulkner-Springfield, Kayla Moore, and Charity Riddick-Mullen reveal how each of them came to self-identify as a writer in personally meaningful ways and how coauthoring can provide a critically important pathway for students and faculty of color to claim agency in their lives in the academy and beyond.

Sandy Feinstein, Nicolas Fay, Faith Iseman, Ashley Offenback, Christian D. Brendel, Rachel Jensen, and Jennifer Muret-Bate close out this section with their essay, "Creative-critical Coauthoring: Definition and Demonstration." Coauthoring with students for nearly three decades, Feinstein describes the ways her longstanding "pedagogic experiments involving creative constructions as critical acts" led to coauthoring with undergraduates. Feinstein's six coauthors reflect upon their experiences as a student in Feinstein's class and their original experience of coauthoring with her and how those experiences have impacted their lives as graduate students, for some, and in academic and nonacademic careers, for others. Together, the coauthors enact creative critical coauthorship by presenting their chapter as an Eptalogue.

Conclusion

Scholars of collaborative writing and coauthorship have long trumpeted its potential to "transform academia into a place that nurtures intellectually, spiritually, and emotionally" (Day and Eodice 184). Characterizing dialogic collaboration as "loosely structured," "fluid," and "multivoiced and multivalent," Lunsford and Ede posit that such work can be "deeply subversive," disrupting entrenched hierarchies and giving rise to more empowering relationships (133). Our hope is that this volume contributes to the work of destabilizing and reconfiguring authorship in more equitable, exciting ways. By mapping the contexts that support and enable coauthoring and by sharing nuanced stories of the processes, consequences, and range of outcomes, we can continue to work on creating a robust intellectual sphere where the status of author can be claimed by a variety of people and where authorship can be a tool for future engagement and equity.

Beyond these vital changes, we want to end on a lighter but important topic. Both of us view our coauthoring experiences with undergraduates with great fondness. For Laurie, coauthoring with seven seniors in a classroom setting was both very stressful and very exciting (Bradley et al.). Managing students' varying interests and skill levels within the semester time frame was daunting at times but was counterbalanced by the students' excitement about joining the scholarly conversation about *their* major in professional writing. After diving into the research and reflecting on their own experiences, the students had a lot to say. For Jane, the process of coauthoring with undergraduates has similarly been a (mostly) joyful experience. When students in a junior/senior-level course on rhetorics of public memory were told their curatorial work would be fabricated on standing banners and displayed in our city's convention center during a national conference, their excitement and investment in the course was palpable. When the exhibit was moved to campus, parents and other members of students' support networks came to share in and celebrate their accomplishment. And the process of collaborating with just two students to coauthor an article for *College English* about the experience of researching our city and creating the exhibit began with several long meetings in a campus conference room after the semester ended, but those conversations were thoughtful, generative, and intellectually satisfying. With Dubisar (chapter 10), we encourage readers to seek out opportunities to coauthor with undergraduates and to "Embrace fun amidst the complexities."

Notes

1. We are grateful for the assistance of UMKC student Faith McLeod, who helped review issues of *College English* and *College Composition and Communication* to identify articles coauthored by undergraduates.
2. Numerous scholars in writing studies have noted the importance of making undergraduate research opportunities more accessible. For example, Alexandria Lockett, D. Alexis Hart, and Rebecca Babcock have written eloquently about the importance of "multiple pathways" to and through undergraduate research opportunities, including paid research positions for undergraduates who assist faculty on research, opportunities to conduct substantive research within courses and valuing a wide array of research methods and research questions that are relevant to students' lives. Angela Rounsaville, Esther Milu, and Joel Schneier have taken an "equity and access-oriented approach" to first-year writing courses by building undergraduate research on linguistic diversity and language justice into the curriculum at Central Florida University, newly designated as HSI (520).

Works Cited

Balzhizer, Deborah, Mandy Grover, Evelyn Lauer, Sarah McNeely, Jonathan D. Polk, and Jon Zmikly. "The Facebook Papers." *Kairos: A Journal of Rhetoric, Technology, and Pedagogy*, vol. 16, no. 1, 2011.

Bastian, Heather, and Lindsey Harkness. "When Peer Tutors Write about Writing: Literacy Narratives and Self-Reflection." *Young Scholars in Writing*, vol. 1, 2003, pp. 101–24.

Bloom, Lynn Z. "The Good, the Bad, and the Ugly: Ethical Principles for (Re)Presenting Students and Student Writing in Teachers' Publications." *Writing on the Edge*, vol. 13, no. 2, 2003, pp. 67–82.

Boyer Commission on Educating Undergraduates in the Research University. *Reinventing Undergraduate Education: A Blueprint for America's Research Universities*, 1998.

Bradley, Erin, Melissa Davis, Michelle Dierlof, Keith Dmochowski, John Gangi, Laurie Grobman, Kristy Offenback, and Melissa Wilk. "Coauthoring the Curriculum: Student Voices and the Writing Major." *Composition Studies*, vol. 43, no. 2, 2015, pp. 172–76.

Brown, Renee, Brian Fallon, Jessica Lott, Elizabeth Matthews, and Elizabeth Mintie. "Taking on Turnitin: Tutors Advocating Change." *Writing Center Journal*, vol. 27, no. 1, 2007, pp. 7–28.

Canzoneri, Julia, Brie Cronin, Iris Finkel, Melissa Harden, Wendy Hayden, Alex Kreichman, Dana Krugle, Rasha Reda, Sarah Parente, James Wheaton, and Christina Yim. "'Stronger Together': Open Pedagogy, Digital Scholarship, and Hillary Clinton's Rhetorical Appeal." *Kairos*, vol. 24, no. 2, Spring 2020. https://kairos.technorhetoric.net/24.2/praxis/canzoneri-et-al/index.html.

"CCCC Position Statement on Undergraduate Research in Writing: Principles and Best Practices." *NCTE*, March 2017. https://cccc.ncte.org/cccc/resources/positions/undergraduate-research.

Clark, Beverly Lyon, and Sonja Weidenhaupt. "On Blocking and Unblocking Sonja: A Case Study in Two Voices." *CCC*, vol. 43, no. 1, 1992, pp. 55–74.
Committee on Publication Ethics (COPE). "Discussion Document: Authorship." *Publication Ethics*, https://publicationethics.org/sites/default/files/COPE_DD_A4_Authorship_SEPT19_SCREEN_AW.pdf. Accessed 20 Nov. 2023.
Cook-Sather, Alison, Catherine Bovill, and Peter Felton. *Engaging Students as Partners in Learning and Teaching: A Guide for Faculty*. Jossey-Bass, 2014.
Cook-Sather, Alison, Kelly E. Matthews, Anita Ntem, and Sandra Leathwick. "What We Talk about When We Talk about Students as Partners." *International Journal for Students as Partners*, vol. 2. no. 2, 2018, pp. 1–9.
Crawford, Anne, Peyton Galloway, and Jane Greer. "Drawing Hope from Difficult History: Public Memory and Rhetorical Education in Kansas City." *College English*, vol. 82, no. 3, 2020, pp. 255–80.
Davis, Sara, and Abby M. Dubisar. "Communicating Elective Sterilization: A Feminist Perspective." *Rhetoric of Health and Medicine*, vol. 2, no. 1, 2019, pp. 88–113.
Day, Kami, and Michele Eodice. *(First Person)²: A Study of Co-Authoring in the Academy*. Utah State UP, 2001.
Downs, Doug, Laurie McMillan, Megan Schoettler, and Patricia Roberts-Miller. "Circulation: Undergraduate Research as Consequential Publicness." *The Naylor Report on Undergraduate Research in Writing Studies*, edited by Dominic DelliCarpini, Jenn Fishman, and Jane Greer, Parlor Press, 2020, pp. 94–105.
Duffy, William. *Beyond Conversation: Collaboration and the Production of Writing*. Utah State UP, 2020.
Fishman, Jenn, Andrea A. Lunsford, Beth McGregor, and Mark Otuteye. "Performing Writing, Performing Literacy." *College Composition and Communication*, vol. 57, no. 2, 2005, pp. 224–52.
French, Warren, and Marc Rosenberg. "The Beast that Devours Its Young." *College Composition and Communication*, vol. 13, no. 2, 1962, pp. 4–8.
Gomez, Isabella A., and Amy J. Lueck. "To Embrace Tension or Recoil Away from It: Navigating Complex Collaborations in Cultural Rhetorics Work." *College Composition and Communication*, vol. 75, no. 1, 2023, pp. 75–96.
Grobman, Laurie. "The Student Scholar: (Re)Negotiating Authorship and Authority." *College Composition and Communication*, vol. 61, no. 1, 2009, pp. W175–W196.
Grobman, Laurie, Elizabeth Kemmerer, and Meghan Zebertavage. "Counternarratives: Community Writing and Anti-Racist Narratives." *Reflections*, vol. 17, no. 2, 2017, pp. 43–68.
Grobman, Laurie, and Joyce Kinkead, editors. *Undergraduate Research in English Studies*, NCTE, 2010.
Grobman, Laurie, Nicholas Kopp, Elijah Schade, and Wyatt Conrad. "Anti-Racist Commemorative Intervention at the Hopewell Furnace National Historic Site." *College English*, vol. 85, no. 1, 2022, pp. 13–36.
Grobman, Laurie, Meeghan Orr, Chris Meagher, Cassandra Yatron, and Jonathan Shelton. "Collaborative Complexities: Co-Authorship, Voice, and African American

Rhetoric in Oral History Community Literacy Projects." *Community Literacy Journal*, vol. 9, no. 2, 2015, pp. 1–25.

Halbritter, Bump, Noah Blon, and Caron Creighton. "Big Questions, Small Works, Lots of Layers: Documentary Video Production and the Teaching of Academic Research and Writing." *Kairos: A Journal of Rhetoric, Technology, and Pedagogy*, vol. 16, no. 1, 2011. https://kairos.technorhetoric.net/16.1/praxis/halbritter/index.php.

Harris, Joseph. "Student Texts in Composition Scholarship." *JAC*, vol. 32, no. 3/4, 2012, pp. 667–94.

Hawisher, Gail E., and Cynthia L. Selfe, with Brittney Moraski and Melissa Pearson. "Becoming Literate in the Information Age: Cultural Ecologies and the Literacies of Technology." *CCC*, vol. 55, 2004, pp. 642–92.

Healey, Mick, Abbi Flint, and Kathy Harrington. *Engagement through Partnership: Students as Partners in Learning and Teaching in Higher Education*. The Higher Education Academy, 2014.

Helgesson, Gert. "Authorship Order and Effects of Changing Bibliometric Practices." *Research Ethics*, vol. 16, no. 2, 2020, pp. 1–7.

Helgesson, Gert, and Stefan Eriksson. "Authorship Order." *Learned Publishing*, vol. 32, no. 2, 2019, pp. 106–12.

Helmers, Marguerite H. *Writing Students: Composition Testimonials and Representations of Students*. State U of New York P, 1994.

Herzl-Betz, Rachel, and Hugo Virrueta. "Perdiendo mi persona: Negotiating Language and Identity at the Conference Door." *Pedagogy*, vol. 22, no. 1, 2022, pp. 169–72.

Jabbehdari, Sahra, and John P. Walsh. "Authorship Norms and Project Structures in Science." *Science Technology and Human Values*, vol. 42, no. 5, 2017, pp. 872–900.

Jack, Jordynn, and Lucy Massagee. "Ladies and Lynching: Southern Women, Civil Rights, and the Rhetoric of Interracial Cooperation." *Rhetoric & Public Affairs*, vol. 14, no. 3, 2011, pp. 493–510.

Johnson, Kristine. "Representations of Students in Composition Scholarship." *Pedagogy*, vol. 19, no. 3, 2019, pp. 405–31.

Kuh, George D. *High-Impact Educational Practices: What They Are, Who Has Access to Them, and Why They Matter*, Association of American Colleges and Universities, 2008.

Lockett, Alexandria, D. Alexis Hart, and Rebecca Babcock. "Access to Undergraduate Research in Writing Studies." *The Naylor Report on Undergraduate Research in Writing Studies*, edited by Dominic DelliCarpini et al., Parlor Press, 2020, pp. 113–31.

Lunsford, Andrea, and Lisa Ede. *Singular Texts/Plural Authors: Perspectives on Collaborative Writing*. Southern Illinois UP, 1990.

Mercer-Mapstone, Lucy, and Sophia Abbot, eds. *The Power of Partnership: Students, Staff, and Faculty Revolutionizing Higher Education*. Center for Engaged Learning, Elon University, 2020.

Mercer-Mapstone, Lucy, Sam Lucie Dvorakova, Kelly E. Matthews, Sophia Abbot, Breagh Cheng, Peter Felten, Kris Knorr, Elizabeth Marquis, Rafaella Shammas, Kelly Swaim. "A Systematic Literature Review of Students as Partners in Higher Education." *International Journal for Students as Partners*, vol. 1, no. 1, 2017, pp. 15–37.

Miller, Susan. *Textual Carnivals: The Politics of Composition*. Southern Illinois UP, 1991.
Osborne, Jason W., and Abigail Holland. "What is Authorship, and What Should it Be? A Survey of Prominent Guidelines for Determining Authorship in Scientific Publications." *Practical Assessment, Research & Evaluation*, vol. 14, no. 15, 2009.
Palermo, Gregory J., Qianqian Zhang-Wu, Devon Skyler Regan, and Mya Poe. "Building Research Trajectories through Mutual Multigenerational Mentoring in Writing Program Assessment." *Mentorship/Methodology: Reflections, Praxis, Futures*, edited by Leigh Gruwell and Charles N. Lesh, Utah State UP, 2024, pp. 91–108.
Robillard, Amy. "'Young Scholars' Affecting Composition: A Challenge to Disciplinary Citation Practices." *College English*, vol. 68, no. 3, 2006, pp. 253–70.
Rounsaville, Angela, Esther Milu, and Joel Schneier. "Contributive Knowledge Making and Critical Language Awareness: A Justice-Oriented Paradigm for Undergraduate Research at a Hispanic-Serving Institution." *College English*, vol. 84, no. 6, 2022, pp. 519–85.
"SaLT Programming at Bryn Mawr and Haverford Colleges." *Bryn Mawr*. https://tli-resources.digital.brynmawr.edu/programs-and-opportunities/.
Sharma, Tanya, Rini Lukose, Jessica E. Shiers-Hanley, Sanja Hinic-Frlog, and Simone Laughton. "Improving the Student Learning Experience through the Student-led Implementation of Interactive Features in an Online Open-Access Textbook." *International Journal for Students as Partners*, vol. 5, no. 2, 2021, 67–77.
Sun, Lulu C. H. "Presenting and Mispresenting Students: Constructing an Ethics of Representation in Composition Studies." *Writing on the Edge*, vol. 13, no. 2, 2003, pp. 45–55.
Toth, Christie, Mitchell Reber, and Aaron Clark. "Major Affordances: Collaborative Scholarship in a Department of Writing and Rhetoric Studies." *Composition Studies*, vol. 43, no. 2, 2015, pp. 197–200.
Tulley, Christine, Christine Brickner, Sarah Brown, Matthew Buttermore, Brittany Cottrill, Kathryn Foor, Wendee Hall, Dana LaPlant, Melanie McCory, and Elizabeth Shaffer. "Review of *What Video Games Have to Teach Us about Learning and Literacy* by James Paul Gee." *Computers and Composition Online*, Spring 2004.
Wallace, David L., and Annissa Bell. "Being Black at a Predominantly White University." *College English*, vol. 61, no. 3, 1999, pp. 307–27.
Wren, Johnathan, Katarzyna Z. Kozak, Kathryn R. Johnson, Sara J. Deakyne, Lisa M. Schilling, and Robert P. Dellavalle. "The Write Position: A Survey of Perceived Contributions to Papers Based on Byline Position and Number of Authors." *EMBO Reports*, vol. 8, no. 11, 2007, pp. 988–91.

SECTION I

Spaces and Places of Coauthoring

1
Situating Faculty-Student Coauthoring in a Department of English

JOYCE KINKEAD AND SHANE GRAHAM

Our focus draws on the conditions and situations that promote productive coauthoring relationships between students and faculty. The illustrations that we share are embedded in a culture of undergraduate research (UR) that is evident in our own department and that the larger institution has nurtured. This foundation has not only enabled coauthoring between faculty and students but also provided incentives and rewards, particularly significant in the humanities, in which sole authorship is typically considered the gold standard. Through coauthoring, faculty members have rethought pedagogical approaches, enhanced learning, provided models for student authors, diversified scholarly production, and created opportunities for meaningful relationships.

We are just two of several faculty members in our department who have engaged in coauthoring with our students. Shane arrived at Utah State University (USU) in 2005, specializing primarily in South African literature and culture but over the years branching out into publishing about African American and Caribbean literatures, particularly focusing on interconnections among authors from Africa, the Caribbean, and the US, drawing on massive archival materials. Joyce was hired at USU in 1982 to direct its Writing Center, which led to directing the overall writing program and positions in administration at the

https://doi.org/10.7330/9781646427796.c001

college and university level, including overseeing the institution's undergraduate research program. Although we have coauthored with undergraduates in the past, the two of us are authoring this particular work alone. The fact of the matter is that our students who appear in this chapter have moved on to their own careers. While we would have enjoyed revisiting coauthorship with them, they have their own busy professional and personal lives—and good for them. While they are not coauthors themselves, their collaborative spirits continue with us.

Building a Culture That Supports Coauthoring

We work in the Department of English housed within the College of Humanities and Social Sciences at a land-grant research university, founded in 1888. Utah State University enrolls 27,000 students on thirty sites around the state, including three residential campuses.

Undergraduate research has been a hallmark on campus since its establishment in 1975, making it the second oldest program in the nation, organized with the help of MIT's Margaret MacVicar. The program strives to help students find, fund, and present research. Over 1,500 grants have funded students from a central pool, and several colleges and departments have additional resources to support students. Notably, both students and faculty are eligible for recognition for outstanding work in undergraduate research. The Council on Undergraduate Research (CUR) acknowledged USU's Undergraduate Research Program as stellar with national recognition in 2021. A contributing factor to this award, according to Lindsay Currie, CUR executive officer, was "an impressive number of student-authored publications" (Hughes).

The bedrock program in student research offers multiple openings for students to pursue inquiry and for faculty to mentor them. These faculty members are aware of and willing to tap into a wide range of university programs and supports that foster coauthorship: a central research office, university and college-funded grants, undergraduate teaching fellows and tutors, interdisciplinary units, institutional assessment, and public relations and marketing.

The Department of English serves majors on the Logan main campus as well as statewide, offering baccalaureate, master's, and doctoral degrees. Undergraduates may choose among several emphasis areas: creative writing, English teaching, folklore, literature, and technical communication and rhetoric—in addition to an interdisciplinary major in American studies. Over four hundred students are enrolled as English majors. This chapter offers examples of coauthorship opportunities among these subfields that have arisen when faculty see a variety of situations in which they may partner with students. These may occur within the curriculum or in extracurricular sites. In short, USU English faculty value working with students on scholarly and research projects, and that work is rewarded by the department and larger institution. In this chapter, we will address aspects of the department and university that created this encouraging culture and offer examples of successful partnerships. We begin with a detailed example of a faculty and student who coedited a scholarly book, explicating the process of coauthorship. Additional instances of coauthorship that follow mirror much of the philosophy and practice of the collaboration that Shane describes here.

Coauthoring and Coediting a Scholarly Monograph: An Instructive Model

This culture of student inquiry has been influential on individual faculty members, including Shane. When he took a position as assistant professor of postcolonial literature at Utah State University in 2005, the discourse of undergraduate research in the humanities was new and unfamiliar to him, but he soon discovered it was an essential part of the culture of USU's English Department. Joyce Kinkead had been a pioneer in this field going back decades, authoring books on the subject and serving as the university's overseer of the UR program in the Office of Research. Colleagues in literature regularly organized courses around some public outlet for the students' scholarly work, such as presenting at the university's Student Research Symposium or curating an exhibit from our library drawing on its special collections.

In a previous job, Shane had served as faculty advisor to a chapter of Sigma Tau Delta, the International English Honor Society, and in that capacity accompanied students to the annual convention and helped them prepare their papers to present there. The benefits of USU's emphasis on helping students take their classroom work into a public setting was therefore immediately obvious to Shane, who later took on the role of faculty advisor to USU's own chapter of Sigma Tau Delta for several years, during which time he helped many other students present their ideas and their research at the convention.

What was less clear to Shane was how teachers of literature might mimic a model of undergraduate research that is common in the natural sciences and some social sciences, in which students participate in the faculty member's own research projects in roles ranging from lab assistants to coauthors. Literary scholars at some institutions might have research assistants, but scholarly production in the discipline is highly individualized and often driven by idiosyncratic preoccupations and personal interpretations. Coauthorship is not unheard of in literary studies, but it is far from the norm, and collaborating on journal articles even with graduate students is extremely rare, much less with undergraduates.

Nevertheless, when Shane began to plan an edited collection of correspondence, it occurred to him that editing might be one area where an undergraduate student's contributions could be substantive enough to be listed as coeditor, not just as a research assistant as Margaret Whitt and Matthew Henningsen describe in their collaboration. For a student with academic aspirations, moreover, the experience could offer invaluable opportunities to hone research skills and gain insight into the processes of compiling and publishing such a book. In this spirit, Shane recruited John Walters, an exceptionally bright and promising undergraduate who had excelled in three different classes on postcolonial literature that Shane had taught. Shane had an advance contract from a publisher but no funding to pay for an editorial assistant. John was in his last year at USU when they began working together on the project, and he had begun a doctoral program at Indiana University by the time they finished. Knowing that John was planning an academic career, Shane offered to recognize John's efforts with a percentage of the royalties for the book as well as the currency of the academic realm, copublication credit. The final product bore both of their names: a collection of letters between African American poet Langston Hughes and a group of young Black South African writers in the 1950s and 1960s, entitled *Langston Hughes and the South African Drum Generation: The Correspondence*, published by Palgrave Macmillan in 2010 (Graham and Walters).

From Shane's perspective, the collaboration with John was a great success. One key to that success was to set down clearly and in writing expectations regarding division of responsibilities, publication credit (specifying first author and second author, for example), and respective royalties. A simple memorandum of understanding signed by both parties sufficed, laying out who was responsible for writing the introduction, selecting and annotating the letters, and proofreading the copyedited manuscript. The memorandum also gave Shane the right to authorize any subsequent editions of the book, specified how the two editors would be listed on the cover page and book jacket, and specified how royalties would be divided.

Another key was arriving at a realistic understanding of what is and is not within the capabilities of an undergraduate. For example, Shane wrote the book's introduction alone. But in many other ways, John functioned as a true coeditor and partner in the process. Below we attempt to survey the scope of John's responsibilities, the value he added with each task, and the opportunities to learn that he derived from each.

At the outset of the collaboration, Shane had already traveled to Yale University to read the archived letters and came back with microfilm reproductions, which he then transcribed. The first stage of the collaboration, then, involved selecting the letters and preparing them for publication. In deciding which letters were worth including, it was useful to Shane to have John's perspective on the interest these letters held to someone not a specialist in the field. Once the letters were selected, John checked the transcriptions with the microfilm copies against the original letters for errors, omissions, and redundancies. Next, Shane and John compiled and divided up a list of the many references contained in the letters to people, places, events, and things that might not be familiar to twenty-first-century readers and researched and wrote explanatory footnotes. This was a time-consuming task, and Shane appreciated having a capable partner to split the work. For John's part, he was able to develop and practice skills at using the library's online and print resources to find reliable information—skills that served him well in his graduate studies.

Once the manuscript was ready for peer review, Shane submitted it to Palgrave Macmillan. While they awaited the publisher's decision, Shane and John began tracking down the surviving authors of the letters or curators of their estates to seek permissions to publish the correspondence. The coeditors also began compiling a list of topics discussed in the letters to be included in the index. This was perhaps the most difficult task to which John contributed in the whole process, and the task to which his contributions truly rose to the level of coauthorship: more than just a list of people and places, a good index tries to predict who the book's readers will be and what they will be reading for, and it helps make visible the patterns or themes in the book that the authors or editors want to showcase. Working together on this process therefore required careful and regular communication and collaboration. Once again, having John's perspective as a newcomer to the discipline and an outsider to the field gave Shane useful insights, while John gained experience that helped him, for example, understand how academic indexes work and how to use them to navigate dense monographs. John confirms by email: "[G]aining practice with research resources and with constructing and navigating an index helped me understand how to use and contribute to academic writing."

The indexing process continued once Palgrave delivered positive feedback from the peer review and agreed to publish the book. After receiving the typeset page proofs, Shane and John checked the text for accuracy and began matching index topics with page numbers. They divided the topics between themselves: as the more experienced scholar, Shane focused on more abstract topics or ones that might require specialized knowledge, while John covered names of people, places, or artworks that he recognized. Finally, John and Shane worked together to prepare the marketing and promotional materials requested by the publisher.

At each stage of this two-year process, Shane's overriding goal was ensuring that the collaboration was useful not just to himself as principal editor but also to the student partner. This meant making sure John was developing research and writing skills, getting a glimpse behind the scenes of the making of a book, and garnering an early publication credit to kickstart his future academic career.

What can one faculty member do to promote authentic student engagement as in this notable case? Obviously from Shane's example, the answer is a lot. Sites of opportunity for productive relationships exist in multiple areas in our department. Later in this chapter, we provide further examples of individual students working with faculty members as well as instances of how UR has been scaled up to provide access to more students and, in the process, stimulate further coauthoring partnerships. First, we investigate the atmosphere that led a faculty member like Shane to believe that coauthoring with a student was not only beneficial but desirable.

Coauthoring, Faculty Roles, and Rewards

Shane clearly illustrates the transition from his previous university to USU, a research university where inquiry permeates every field. Involving all students, not just graduate students, is an expectation. A research culture determines attitudes, behaviors, values, and norms for both students and faculty. USU's faculty roles and rewards clearly delineate how researchers' career paths can be influenced positively by interaction and collaboration with students. Across our campus, students engage in research, scholarly, and creative activity that is celebrated in public venues and splashed across banners on webpages from art and anthropology to wildlife biology and yoga studies. A standard course number (4900) is used for research experiences across disciplines, so important in counting student participation. Courses can be designated as research, scholarship, and creative inquiry (RSCI), much like writing intensive or quantitative intensive. Students can graduate with a transcript designation as an "Undergraduate Research Scholar."

In this conducive atmosphere, a key factor in coauthoring with students is faculty roles and rewards. Does such coauthorship "count" in advancement and merit? The language of USU's Faculty Code on tenure and promotion includes this statement on the role of teaching:

> Teaching includes but is not limited to all forms of instructional activities: classroom performance, broadcast and online instruction, *mentoring students inside and outside the classroom*, student advising and supervision, thesis and dissertation direction, and curriculum development. Documentation supporting teaching performance must include student and peer evaluations, and may include, but is not restricted to: proficiency in curriculum development as demonstrated through *imaginative or creative use of instructional materials* such as syllabi, instructional manuals, edited readings, case studies, media packages and computer programs; authorship of textbooks; teaching and/or advising awards; authorship of refereed articles on teaching; *success of students in post-graduate endeavors*; *evidence of mentoring inside and outside the classroom, including work with graduate or undergraduate researchers*, graduate instructors or undergraduate teaching fellows, applicants for major scholarships or grants, *implementation of high impact practices* such as community-engaged teaching, first-year seminars, or strategies that promote student retention, and Honors or other independent study work; recognition by peers of substantive contributions on graduate committees; service on professional committees, panels, and task forces; and invited lectures or panel participation. ("USU Policy," emphasis added)

Faculty who coauthor with students may "double count," applying the work to both teaching and research roles. They report these publications and presentations through annual reviews, tenure and promotion documents, and institutional repositories. Lists of faculty publications sent to the institutional board on a monthly basis are marked with either a * for undergraduate coauthor or ** for graduate student coauthor, emphasizing the important connection between research and teaching. Digital Measures, the electronic system whereby faculty record their accomplishments for annual review, includes a mechanism for noting student coauthors. This has also led to a databank that could be drawn upon for institutional research with information on student authors.

In terms of rewards, faculty are recognized with Outstanding Undergraduate Research Mentor awards. Since the inauguration of these awards by our

Research Office in 2003, over one hundred faculty members have received acclaim at a ceremony, notice in press releases, and monetary acknowledgment. Notably, many of these winners have coauthored with students. Additionally, annual reviews offer the possibility of merit remuneration for such work.

With institutional commitment in place, faculty members are more likely to feel supported in inviting students to partnerships in coauthoring. They have found multiple situations in which coauthoring with undergraduates arose organically or intentionally. In short, faculty are positioned to see coauthoring across diverse genres and instances of public humanities as a respected activity. We turn now to further examples to illustrate the wide range of instances where faculty have envisioned such opportunities. Our hope is that those reading these examples will be inspired by the rich diversity of occasions to engage with students in meaningful and authentic work that provides a window onto research, scholarly, and creative activity in English studies.

Seeing and Situating Opportunities

Shane's work with John took place outside the curriculum, but their rapport, as well as respect and trust in one another, were first formed in the classroom. Developing relationships with students through the curriculum may evolve into one-to-one authoring partnerships or to whole-class experiences. We are especially keen on scaling up such experiences when feasible.

As we have mentioned before, undergraduate research is generally the launching pad from which coauthorship arises. Of the more than two dozen professorial faculty in the Department of English, eighty-five percent have mentored students on undergraduate research projects. About sixty-five percent have coauthored, defined broadly, with undergraduates. Where do faculty find these openings for collaboration? Some arise from a stance, attitude, and radar engaged to detect them while others may be student-initiated. A generous marketing and public relations approach also helps. Students and faculty who engage in scholarly and research collaborations are featured online, in the institutional magazine, and in news releases. Awards for outstanding work in mentoring and student research also highlight individuals, and this "leading by example" can bring along faculty to think about how undergrads may be integrated into their own professional work. In other words, a *culture* that values student-faculty collaboration is important. It also helps that students are aware of the possibilities of working with faculty on authentic projects.

In terms of student-initiated coauthorship, Kolbie Astle Blume, a student in the English Education track, enrolled in a course on young adult literature (YAL) and launched a project on teens' digital literacy to fulfill an honors contract. She initially planned to write a guidebook for teachers, summarizing useful applications. The project turned out to be much more than a guidebook; she investigated the history, policy statements, and practice of digital literacy. Kolbie's research paper could have stopped at the level of the course, but Joyce, thinking about Kolbie's future career as a teacher, suggested working through the publication process to get an insider's look at how the profession works. She recommended the National Council of Teachers of English (NCTE) state-affiliate journal as a target for publication (Blume and Kinkead).

Colleague Jessica Rivera-Mueller takes the same attitude of offering professional publication opportunities to students in her English education courses. A consummate teacher-educator, Jessica prepares her students for school-based professional learning communities (PLC) that they will encounter in their careers by engaging them in "PLC facilitation" practice. At the end of the course, she invited students to coauthor a blog with her. As she explains in the blog itself, "Six former students from my English education methods course—Jamie, Stephanie, Morgan, Joshua, Kenzie, and Mackenzie—join me to explain how the project's design choices cultivate a commitment to advocacy in PLCs" (Rivera-Mueller et al.). About one-third of the enrollees opted for this enrichment activity. While Joyce and Kolbie are an example of a one-on-one coauthorship, Jessica garnered those who opted to be involved. Faculty can structure how they wish to engage students in coauthorship: individuals, groups, or whole classes.

Historically, tutors in writing conduct research (Fitzgerald) and have been encouraged to see authentic audiences for their seminar research. Our seminar for writing fellows began encouraging them to seek professional outlets for their papers in the early 1990s. A dozen were published in the Tutor's Column of the *Writing Lab Newsletter*. While these were individually authored, several students coauthored a *WLN* article titled "Situations and Solutions in Writing-across-the-Curriculum Tutoring" (Kinkead et al.). Another project on design and architecture of writing centers, researched by an English major and an interior design student, eventually resulted in a book chapter on these tutoring centers (Hadfield et al.), coauthored by the faculty members in the two departments, who added scholarly context. Writing fellows programs in particular offer strong possibilities for interdisciplinary collaboration and coauthoring.

Individual students working with faculty members often come to these coauthoring experiences because they are high achieving or have a passion for a topic. Scaling up UR experiences to entire classes ensures more students have access to these transformative projects. In this section, we describe various outputs that can arise when classes become CUREs, or course-based undergraduate research experiences (Kinkead et al., "I See Research Questions").

Curating exhibitions for public consumption is an atypical form of dissemination for undergraduate research projects, but as Greer and Grobman have demonstrated, museums, archives, and memorials can be rich sites for student inquiry. (See also Sand et al. for examples of digital exhibits, art museum shows, and library exhibitions.) A focus on public humanities can help create this rich culture that supports coauthoring opportunities for students and faculty. In a course on Shakespeare, taught by colleague Phebe Jensen with collaborator Jennifer Duncan, a librarian, students conducted original research using the resources of the library's special collections, drawing on Early Modern manuscripts to describe the cosmology of the Bard's day, tracing how four elements—blood, black bile, yellow bile, and phlegm—correspond to characters. Understanding medical practices of the era was intrinsically interesting to students and those who came to view the glass-enclosed cases of seventeenth-century medical books. Students were on hand during the public reception to explain how understanding the scientific context increases understanding of his plays.

Do such exhibitions qualify as coauthorship? In developing the report, artifacts, and posters, faculty assist in creating content, collaborating with the students who serve as "first authors." The meaning of coauthoring has become more plastic, embracing collaborators and even audiences (Duranti).

One of our most astute colleagues in creating opportunities for students to engage in public humanities is Paul Crumbley. Drawing on the strengths of the campus special collections, he organized his courses around particular topics to shift the focus from a "largely private form of communication that stays within the confines of the classroom to engagement with a larger public." He noted in his portfolio for a mentor award that these kinds of projects "alter the class dynamic." It "elevates the risk that comes with public accountability that also enhances student motivation." He has organized student-curated exhibitions on Jack London, May Swenson, Emily Dickinson, and Beat Generation writers. For the latter, students met in the Art Book Room of the library and worked closely with special collections as well as the Nora Eccles Harrison Museum of Art. Students organized an exhibit, "Heart Beats," and its opening reception featured Beat poetry reading accompanied by an undergraduate jazz combo. The concept was Professor Crumbley's, with the students individually taking segments of the exhibition and planning the event as cocurators.

These literary-focused cocurated exhibitions demonstrate the power of public humanities and how students can serve as ambassadors, making more transparent scholarship in the field. In a more traditional framework, the department's empirical research methods course for undergraduates begins with an assumption that students will present and/or publish their work, at times leading to coauthorship, particularly on the whole-class project, as the instructor ties together the various contributions into a research article. A special issue of *College English* focusing on UR provided an opportunity for members of the class to conduct a study analyzing the outcomes of an empirically based research methods course on English majors (Stringham et al.). Yet another study asked the question if mnemonic devices in writing persist at the college level. The resulting article on "FANBOYS, POW, & Mount Plot" appeared as a coauthored article in the NCTE state affiliate journal (Kinkead et al.). A cornerback on the Aggie football team, who offered insights on writing and athletes, coauthored an article for a special issue of *Perspectives on Undergraduate Research and Mentoring* (*PURM*) on undergraduate research and student-athletes (Kinkead and Haney). These outputs also demonstrate the variety of publication venues that exist for student work and the radar-like focus of faculty on the alert for just such openings.

Another rich area for study is the institution itself. Institutional ethnography focuses on activities at a particular site (see LaFrance). Students can take an active role in critiquing and improving the institution, resulting in reports that have the power to influence practice and policy. Following are a few examples of how faculty have designed projects to assess and advance campus sites and activities.

Students in Avery Edenfield's technical communication courses worked on a variety of campaigns involving the campus Office of Equity and the Sexual Assault and Anti-Violence Information (SAAVI) Office to prevent sexual misconduct, including efforts to increase participation in Start by Believing Day. New sexual misconduct prevention efforts resulted in four different initiatives by the students: research and creation of a consent/sexual violence prevention zine, audit and overhaul of relevant USU webpages, creation of the It's Enough campaign materials for the annual Start by Believing campaign. In other technical communication courses, students have worked with nonprofits to enhance webpage design.

Analyzing and assessing general education programs can be major initiatives requiring an infusion of time and faculty and staff labor. Two separate groups of students, a few years apart, have done important analyses of the institution's communications intensive (CI) graduation requirement, which is akin to the more common writing intensive (WI) requirement. The first group was the writing fellows while the second were students enrolled in the research methods course. Both times, this was a big job, involving hundreds of syllabi. The instructor structured the complex process, accessing institutional data, going through administrative chain of command, and soliciting syllabi. The students performed the coding and analysis and delivered a report of their findings plus a presentation to the university's General Education Committee, which became an important institutional document providing assessment and recommending future work. (Their processes and methods for the analysis are described in an article in *Across the Disciplines* [Kinkead], providing a model for other writing programs.)

Yet another example of responding to institutional needs came through a faculty-student authored report, "Is the English Department HIP?" It provided an inventory and analysis of current high-impact practices and suggested ways that the department could up its game in improving access to HIPs (which include UR) to enhance undergraduate education (Kuh). Coincidentally, a new strategic plan calls for increased HIP engagement. This is a project that could have been taken on by a faculty committee; however, the report provided by the students offered insights from interviews, surveys, and personal experiences. Although conducted by graduate students, another study, published in *PURM*, provided a portrait of English department mentors (Kinkead et al., "A Portrait"), yet another effort to highlight and value this important work.

Because of the rich undergraduate research environment at USU, students seek faculty mentorship on projects. Some of these students are undergraduate research fellows (URF); others may be funded through university grants, while still others seek independent research study credit. Colleagues Christine Cooper-Rompato and Evelyn Funda and the fellows they worked with wrote about the process of URF-faculty collaboration, not about the projects themselves. Particularly helpful to others is their list of advice. This is yet another hallmark of the capacity of our department faculty to see beyond actual research projects to meta reflection and analysis about the projects themselves.

Research fellow projects also often lead to coauthorship. Natalie Hatch Gregory and Marissa Shirley Allen opted to work on Logan's highly regarded poet, May Swenson, who grew up at the base of Old Main Hill. Although these projects occurred some years apart, both led to increased attention to this writer. Natalie worked on signage that would bring attention to Swenson. The first permanent sign was placed at the childhood home on property owned by the university. The second was more complex, sited at a visitors center at the summit of Logan Canyon, overlooking Bear Lake. Permission to install the sign required work with the Literary Estate, the Cache National Forest ranger, and Utah State Parks. Funding also had to be secured. On a chilly and windy day in 2011, the sign was set in concrete at its 7,500-foot elevation.

Picking up the Swenson thread, Marissa created a tourist brochure for a May Swenson Poetry Path, funded through a scholarship from the Cache Valley Historical Society and available through the local tourist office as well as on campus (Shirley). Marissa presented the project at UCUR and coauthored an article for *Teacher-Librarian* with Joyce, who saw the opportunity to frame this as an example of "literary tourism" (Kinkead and Allen). This is a hallmark of mentoring undergraduate researchers: finding projects that can have multifaceted outcomes and having a sense of the big picture of scholarship that moved a brochure for tourists into a more theoretical essay on literary tourism.

Funded through a university grant, Morgan Sanford Graham (also a URF) traveled to Chile to study the poetry of Neruda. While the project itself did not become a coauthored article, the process of mentoring for the grant was published as an epistolary essay by Morgan and her mentor, Jennifer Sinor (see also Bresee and Kinkead).

A parallel program to URFs is that of our undergraduate teaching fellows (UTF). The program offers meaningful academic employment to students, pairing faculty mentors with high-achieving undergraduate students from multiple disciplines who assist with day-to-day classroom-management, administrative, and teaching tasks. Some faculty members see this as an opportunity to capitalize on the close working relationship and publish scholarly work. Colleague Jessica Rivera-Mueller and UTF Kresten Erickson describe how they designed curriculum collaboratively. Writing about best practices in UTF programs, Joyce worked with a senior UTF, Rebecca Wheatley, who provided on-the-ground insight from peers, bringing student voices to the fore (Kinkead et al., "Best Practices"; see also Kinkead et al., "Cultivating Change"). In each case—URF or UTF—an imperative to offer professional development to the student through coauthorship drives publication.

The Challenges and Rewards of Coauthorship

Shane has already illustrated the conundrum of coauthoring in a discipline in which sole authorship is the gold standard. As Shane put it when we discussed this chapter, "We [in literary studies] don't even collaborate with tenured colleagues, much less undergraduates." By contrast, in many fields of study, particularly social sciences and sciences, contributions from all participants are acknowledged in a lineup that begins with "first author" and proceeds from there. Thus, *authorship* needs to be defined clearly and explicitly for all participants.

Although we applaud the rise of professional journals for undergraduate researchers as sole authors (e.g., Calicchia; Duersch et al.), we also understand that a mentor to a student publishing in an undergraduate research venue, for instance, may be a "ghost" coauthor. For instance, a faculty member who designs whole-class research projects has the idea for the study—a crucial part of authorship—and serves as the principal investigator (PI) for IRB but would be a behind-the-scenes mentor in a submission to *Young Scholars in Writing*, the most prestigious undergraduate research journal in rhetoric and writing studies. In point of fact, in an unusual move for *YSW*, the editors asked Joyce to contribute a preface to the collaborative research essay written by Truman et al. as a result of a first-year honors class on the history of writing. The editors felt that this collaboratively written research essay required context. Mentorship "counting" in annual reviews and merit decisions is very important, but being a coauthor on a publication typically counts more.

In partnerships for coauthorship, either party may drop the ball. A mentor may not establish a set of goals and objectives for the work to be done; a student may go AWOL. For instance, Joyce secured two summer faculty-student grants in which one grantee turned out a terrific website that mapped historical sites in the history of writing (Wyckstra and Kinkead), and the second grantee cashed the stipend but did not complete the project. Fortunately, this is a rare occurrence of a coauthoring project gone wrong, but it reminds us that sometimes missteps happen even in a department that values and structures faculty mentorship. (See Johnson and Rifenburg on difficulties of publishing student authors.) Only recently has our central research office offered professional development workshops on required contracts for UR projects. Embracing written partnership agreements that lay out responsible conduct of research and responsibilities of all parties is important. (Deaver Traywick offers a primer on research integrity practices for English studies; see also

Hosseini and Gordijn for ethics in authorship as well as "Co-Authorship in the Humanities and Social Sciences.")

The overwhelming examples of positive coauthoring experiences keeps us seeking these opportunities. The two of us, as well as several of our colleagues, have found the investment in student research especially rewarding. As our colleague Paul Crumbley puts it, "I gradually began to see how I came to enjoy project-based classes better than more conventional classes until they became the only classes I wanted to teach." Paul also introduced us to the concept of students serving as "ambassadors for the humanities," who demonstrate concretely what scholars and researchers in English studies do.

Throughout this chapter, we have explicated numerous opportunities for faculty-student collaboration. Faculty members have the insights, networks, and knowledge of presentation and publication venues that can lead to dynamic partnerships. They bring students into an exciting disciplinary world by sharing these opportunities. The individual faculty member may make the decision to coauthor with student authors, but opportunities can also arise through student initiative. For both partners in coauthorship, it is these contributing conditions in which we find ourselves—a supportive department, college, and university that value this work—that foster such rich relationships and the potential for lifelong relationships.

Works Cited

Blume, Kolbie Astle, and Joyce Kinkead. "Digital Literacy and Young Adult Literature." *Utah English Journal*, vol. 42, 2014, pp. 37–44.

Bresee, Andrea, and Joyce Kinkead. "The Trajectory of an Undergraduate Researcher." *Pedagogy*, vol. 22, no. 1, 2022, pp. 143–47. https://doi.org/10.1215/15314200-9385539.

Calicchia, Sara. "To 'Play That Funky Music' or Not: How Music Affects the Environmental Self-Regulation of High-Ability Academic Writers." *Young Scholars in Writing*, vol. 11, 2015, pp. 65–72.

Cooper-Rompato, Christine F. Evelyn Funda, Joyce Kinkead, Amanda Marinello, and Scarlet Fronk. "Undergraduate Research Fellows and Faculty Mentors in Literary Studies." *Undergraduate Research in English Studies*, edited by Laurie Grobman and Joyce Kinkead, NCTE, 2010, pp. 143–61.

Duersch, Morgan Drish, Marlee Bennett, Grant Z. Bess, Jocelyn Bitner, Savannah Cook, Jimmy Dotson, Deonna Edgar, Savannah Fleming, Karlie Jordan, Carolyn Lyle, Timothy Pedersen, Justin Peterson, Dawn Rudd, McKenna Simmons, Cali Tovey, and Nisheal Watson. "The Rise and Fall of the Blue Book," *Young Scholars in Writing*, vol. 15, Fall 2018.

Duranti, Alessandro. "The Audience as Co-Author: An Introduction." *Text—Interdisciplinary Journal for the Study of Discourse*, vol. 6, no. 3, 1986, pp. 239–47.

Fitzgerald, Lauren. "Undergraduate Writing Tutors as Researchers: Redrawing Boundaries." *Writing Center Journal*, vol. 33, no. 2, 2014, pp. 15–31.

Graham, Shane, and John Walters, editors. *Langston Hughes and the South African Drum Generation: The Correspondence*. Palgrave Macmillan, 2010.

Greer, Jane, and Laurie Grobman, editors. *Pedagogies of Public Memory: Teaching Writing and Rhetoric at Museums, Memorials, and Archives*. Routledge, 2016.

Grobman, Laurie, and Joyce Kinkead. *Undergraduate Research in English Studies*. NCTE, 2010.

Hadfield, Leslie, Joyce Kinkead, Tom C. Peterson, Stephanie H. Ray, and Sarah S. Preston. "An Ideal Writing Center: Re-Imagining Space and Design." The Center Will Hold: Critical Perspectives on Writing Center Scholarship, edited by Michael Pemberton and Joyce Kinkead. Utah State UP, 2003, pp. 166–76.

Hosseini, Mohammad, and Bert Gordijn. "A Review of the Literature on Ethical Issues Related to Scientific Authorship." *Accountability in Research: Policies and Quality Assurance*, vol. 27, no. 5, 2020, pp. 284–324.

Hughes, Brigitte. "USU Recognized for Best Undergraduate Research Program in Nation." *Utah State Today*. 16 February 2021. https://www.usu.edu/today/story/usu-recognized-for-best-undergraduate-research-program-in-nation.

Johnson, Kristine, and J. Michael Rifenburg. "Guest Editors' Introduction." *Pedagogy*, vol. 22, no. 1, 2022, pp. 1–7. https://read.dukeupress.edu/pedagogy/article/22/1/1/293371/Guest-Editors-Introduction.

Kinkead, Joyce. "Engaging Undergraduate Researchers in the Assessment of Communication across the Curriculum Courses." *Across the Disciplines*, vol. 15, no. 2, 2018, pp. 15–30. https://wac.colostate.edu/docs/atd/articles/kinkead2018.pdf.

Kinkead, Joyce, Nanette Alderman, Brett Baker, Alan Freer, John Hertzke, Sonya Mildon Hill, Jennifer Obray, Tiffany Parker, and Maryann Peterson. "Situations and Solutions in Writing-across-the-Curriculum Tutoring." *Writing Lab Newsletter*, vol. 19, no. 8, 1995, pp. 1–5.

Kinkead, Joyce, and Marissa Shirley Allen. "Literary Landmarks: Honoring Local Writers." *Teacher-Librarian*, vol. 44, no. 5, 2017, pp. 12–14.

Kinkead, Joyce, Sarah Anderson, Alexa Bills, Kaitlyn Conlin, Eve Crawford, Natalie Egglie, Jenae Grant, Lilly Hammer, Andrew Isaacson, Kassandra Jimenez, Ryan Manfield, Brindley Rowley, Samantha Stringham, Megan Waldenberg, Brady Wallis. "FANBOYS, POW, and Mount Plot: Mnemonic Devices Used in Teaching Writing." *Utah English Journal*, 2022, pp. 22–27.

Kinkead, Joyce, Taylor Franson, Zackary Gregory, Lauren McKinnon, Emily Powell, Kylie Smith, R. Elle Smith, and Taylor Wyatt. "A Portrait of English Department Undergraduate Research Mentors Through Faculty Reflection and Student Input." *PURM: Perspectives on Undergraduate Research and Mentoring*, vol. 11, 2023.

Kinkead, Joyce, and Cameron Haney. "Touchdown! A Student-Athlete and Mentor Develop a Playbook for Undergraduate Research." *PURM: Perspectives on Undergraduate Research and Mentoring*, vol. 9, no. 1, 2020, pp. 1–15. https://www.elon.edu/u/academics/undergraduate-research/purm/wp-content/uploads/sites/923/2020/12/Kinkead-Haney.pdf.

Kinkead, Joyce, Andrea Melnick, and Olivia Webb. "Cultivating Change: A Cross-Age Arts, Literacy, and Sustainability Project." *Journal of Sustainability Education*, February 2018. http://www.susted.com/wordpress/content/cultivating-change-a-cross-age-arts-literacy-and-sustainability-project_2018_02/.

Kinkead, Joyce, Jill Singer, and John Draeger. "'I See Research Questions Everywhere': Developing Metacognitive Skills in an English-Major Research Methods Course." *Habits of Mind: Designing Courses for Student Success*, edited by Julia Gossard and Chris Babits, Utah State University Empowering Teaching Excellence, 2023.

Kinkead, Joyce, Frances B. Titchener, and Rebecca Wheatley. "Best Practices in Undergraduate Teaching Assistant Programs." *Journal of Excellence in College Teaching*, vol. 30, no. 3, 2019.

Kuh, George D. *High-Impact Educational Practices: What They Are, Who Has Access to Them, and Why They Matter*. Association of American Colleges and Universities, 2008.

LaFrance, Michelle. *Institutional Ethnography: A Theory of Practice for Writing Studies Researchers*. Utah State UP, 2019.

Rivera-Mueller, Jessica, Jamie Ammirati, Stephanie Ferguson, Morgan Graham, Joshua Killpack, Kenzie Randall, and Mackenzie Wilson. "Framing PLC Conversations as Advocacy: A Project for Teacher Education." *Everyday Advocacy: Shifting the PublicNarrative in Literacy Education*, 4 Apr. 2022. https://www.everydayadvocacy.org/post/framing-plc-conversations-as-advocacy-a-project-for-teacher-education.

Rivera-Mueller, Jessica, and Kresten Erickson. "Designing Curriculum Collaboratively: A Practice for Learning Alongside Undergraduate Teaching Assistants." *Resilient Pedagogy: Practical Teaching Strategies to Overcome Distance, Disruption, and Distraction*, edited by Travis Thurston et al., Utah State U, 2021, pp. 260–71.

Sand, Alexa, Becky Thoms, Erin Davis, Darcy Pumphrey, and Joyce Kinkead. "Curating Exhibitions as Undergraduate Research." *CUR Quarterly*, vol. 37, no. 4, Summer 2017, pp. 12–17.

Shirley, Marissa. *May Swenson Poetry Path*. 2015. Brochure. https://chass.usu.edu/english/swensonpark/files/Poetry-Path-Brochure.pdf.

Sinor, Jennifer, and Morgan Sanford Graham. "Finding the Words: An Epistolary Essay on Mentoring in the Creative Arts." *PURM: Perspectives on Undergraduate Research and Mentoring*, vol. 8, no. 1, 2019. https://eloncdn.blob.core.windows.net/eu3/sites/923/2020/02/Sinor-Graham.pdf.

Stringham, Samantha, Addy Kirkham, Katie Jenkins, Aaron Piscione, Allison McMurray, Kameron Chapman, Kate Chapman, Amanda Horning, Bailee Kent Topalian, Casey Mack Ingram, Arlene Mair, Sabrina Satterthwaite, Maigan Sorensen, Tristan Brockban, and Joyce Kinkead. "Formalized Curiosity: Outcomes of an Empirically-Based Research Methods Course for English Majors." *College English*, vol. 84, no. 6, 2022, pp. 546–69.

Taylor & Francis. "Co-Authorship in the Humanities and Social Sciences: A Global View." Taylor and Francis Group Author Services White Paper, 2017. https://authorservices.taylorandfrancis.com/wp-content/uploads/2017/09/Coauthorship-white-paper.pdf.

Traywick, Deaver. "Preaching What We Practice: RCR Instruction for Undergraduate Researchers in Writing Studies." *Undergraduate Research in English Studies*, edited by Joyce Kinkead and Laurie Grobman, NCTE, 2010, pp. 51–73.

Truman, Avery, Dylan Ash, Mason Bodell, Jane Harvey, Clarissa Lloyd, Ellie Miller, Lauren Myers, Hannah Potter, William Spence, Anna Tuite, Isabelle Vasquez, Nevaeh Villastrigo, and Landon Corbett. "Is the Pen Mightier than the Laptop? Digital Natives and Their Preferred Writing Tools." *Young Scholars in Writing*, vol. 21, 2024, pp. 82–100. https://youngscholarsinwriting.org/index.php/ysiw/article/view/384.

"USU Policy on Tenure and Term Appointments." *Utah State University*. https://www.usu.edu/policies/405/. Accessed February 2023.

Whitt, Margaret, and Matthew Henningsen, "Partners in Scholarship: The Making of an Anthology." *Undergraduate Research in English Studies*, edited by Laurie Grobman and Joyce Kinkead, NCTE, 2010.

Wyckstra, Morgan, and Joyce Kinkead. "The Geography of Writing." 2018. https://geographyofwriting.wordpress.com/.

2
Lingering, Listening, and Cocreating

Undergraduate Writing Center Researchers and the Ethics of Coauthoring

STEVEN J. CORBETT, ANNETTE VARA,
AND KATHERINE VILLARREAL

Increasingly, writing center scholars have written about the importance of peer tutor voices, including undergraduates, as important contributors to writing studies (see, for example, Fallon; Fitzgerald and Ianetta; Bromley et al.; Efthymiou and Fallert; Fitzgerald, "Undergraduate" and "Writing"). But as the editors of this collection detail in the introduction, even in the ever increasingly growing literature on undergraduate research in English studies, relatively little has been written on taking research to the next level of publication and (until this volume) *almost nothing* on coauthoring.

This chapter is coauthored by Steven, a professor, former writing center director, and longtime contributor to writing center scholarship; Katherine (Kat), a former writing center tutor and administrative assistant and published author; and Annette, an undergraduate peer tutor and administrative assistant and burgeoning published author. Steven, Kat, and Annette worked together at the University Writing Center at Texas A&M University, Kingsville (TAMUK) and have copresented at conferences and coauthored pieces for publication since right about the time COVID-19 hit. In this chapter we offer a meta-study that examines the pros and cons of coauthoring in writing center studies—both in terms of researchers making such calls and undergraduate tutors like Kat and Annette attempting to answer these calls. We will begin by framing our chapter in a feminist ethos of research—specifically the concepts of *lingering on relationships, listening,* and *cocreating knowledge*—and connecting it to our focus on undergraduate students as coauthors. We will move on to the heart of our chapter to narrate our experiences working together and with other diverse undergraduates on a variety of presentation and publication projects, comparing our collaborations with others to some of our own successful collaborative—especially coauthoring—attempts.

Overall, we will argue that the very nature of writing center theory and practice allows the *time* and opportunity to listen and linger on our research relationships and to take research projects to the next level of coauthorship for publication whenever possible—projects that can offer lifelong beneficial and memorable experiences for both undergraduates and their mentors-turned-coauthors. Our relationship- and trust-building began when Kat and Steven met in the summer of 2016, continued when Annette joined us at the Writing Center at the onset of COVID-19 in the summer of 2020, and is still going strong today.

The Ethics of Research Reporting and a Feminist Theory of Practice

In exploring our claim about the importance of time, space, and relationship-building in regards to coauthoring in writing center research, we invoke a theory of feminist listening. Like Lauren Rosenberg and Emma Howes in "Listening to Research as a Feminist Ethos of Representation," we believe feminist listening seeks to understand

> how listening can be channeled toward more ethical research practices. We are concerned with our own positions as feminist researchers and with the ways we interact with participants and students; thus, we aim to enact practices that tend to differences among others, while holding ourselves accountable for how our positions orient us as researchers. (77)

We offer Rosenberg and Howes's three principles to guide feminist researchers—lingering on relationships, listening, and cocreating knowledge—as a frame for thinking about coauthoring: (1) *Lingering on relationships* involves slowing down and pausing—writing and reflecting *with* rather than *about* the fellow actors in our pedagogical interactions and research studies whenever possible. (2) *Listening* acts as the all-important bridge between lingering on relationships and cocreating knowledge. Feminist listening entails lingering on the state of mind and emotion of the people we work with, how we design research projects, and what value we assign to how and with whom data is collected and reported. (3) *Cocreating knowledge* involves listening for and seeking out ways of knowing and experiencing beyond our own and, whenever possible, with the people we interact with and our research participants—a process Rosenberg and Howes call "mutual contemplation" (81). We believe the willingness to *listen about listening* in the stories of the diverse students and colleagues we encounter can contribute to an ongoing narrative of feminist transformative teaching, learning, and research reporting.

Scholars in writing studies (Johnson and Rifenburg) and writing center theory and practice (Bromley et al.; Efthymiou and Zea) draw directly from interviews and reflections from undergraduates to add further lessons in the ethics of collaboration and co-inquiry applicable to coauthoring with undergraduates. In "Evaluating the Complexities of Tutor Collaboration in Cross-Institutional Writing Center Research," Pam Bromley, Kara Northway, and Eliana Schonberg report on a study motivated by their belief that there was still too little research on the complex nature of collaborative research between administrators and tutors. Tutor co-researchers were interviewed for their impression of their experiences. The tutors reported benefits from their involvement in the study including increased confidence as researchers exploring complex problems, as well as realizing confidence in the positive effects of their tutoring practices. But Bromley, Northway, and Schonberg also report on some of the complexities of tutor-administrator collaborations. They describe, for example, how tutors wanted varying degrees of involvement in the project, making it hard to assume who wanted to be more or less involved in different aspects of the study. No mention is made of the possibilities of coauthoring with the tutors.

Kristine Johnson and J. Michael Rifenburg, in "Rhetoric and Affect in Undergraduate Research: A Diary Study" extend the benefits of undergraduate research in writing center studies by emphasizing the value of what listening to students telling their research stories and inviting students in as partners in building theories—inspired by their sense of lived experience—can do for their identities and sense of self. The authors maintain that two salient characteristics of undergraduate research emerged from their findings: it promotes deep engagement and facilitates student agency, including affective dimensions of engagement and agency (238–39). Like Bromley, Northway, and Schonenberg, the authors also report and discuss some of the problems with undergraduate research their study revealed, especially the uncertainty, anxiety, and negative emotions undergraduates reported experiencing with the research process. In answer to some of these problems, the authors urge us to listen and linger as we attempt to support undergraduates in their research, encouraging them to voice their experiences, their struggles, and their feelings. The authors claim that it is, in fact, in the crucible of confronting and negotiating these struggles and negative feelings that undergraduate researchers may ultimately discover a deeper sense of purpose and sense of self. But, again, there is no mention of coauthoring.

Andrea Efthymiou and Santiago Zea take Johnson and Rifenburg's call for listening to and lingering on undergraduates voicing their experiences with the research process to the next level of coauthorship, demonstrating what can result from embracing a feminist ethos of collaborative research reporting. In "Doing More with Barely Enough: Narratives of an Undergraduate Tutor Researcher and Mentor," writing center director Efthymiou and undergraduate peer tutor Santiago coauthor the emotional roller coaster ride that was Santiago's involvement with research and conference presentations. While ultimately able to look back on their relationship with a sense of accomplishment and growth, Efthymiou intimates how this "growth comes at a cost" (88). Santiago, through diary entries and reflections, details his emotional struggles as a senior coming to terms with an intensely over-committed academic and work schedule, as he knows his *time* as an undergraduate is running out. He describes incidents while preparing to collaboratively present with fellow students at the 2002 National Conference of Peer Tutors in Omaha, Nebraska, including the anxiety he faced with colleagues trying to bail out of the presentation at the last minute and the enormous emotional energy he had to extend at the conference while also trying to complete his homework and prepare for finals. Efthymiou and Santiago are left reflecting on what might be done to help mitigate such emotionally traumatic experiences in the future. The authors suggest increased resources, money, and programmatic restructuring for more equitable labor possibilities involved with undergraduate research reporting. But, interestingly enough, Efthymiou and Santiago barely mention anything about their coauthoring experience of creating their article. Perhaps, as Santiago suggested, they simply ran out of *time* together.

Writing centers and coauthoring are a natural fit. Writing centers provide the time and space for people to linger on relationships, listen carefully and thoughtfully to each other, and coconstruct knowledge that can then be shared with others through coauthored projects. Undergraduates often find themselves in situations where they can really explore and often realize the potential of their creative and communicative abilities and talents. The flow of the coauthoring process from practice to research to presentation to publication takes time and patience. The writing center *is* that place that promotes and fosters the time and space necessary to linger, listen, and coconstruct knowledge. In this chapter, coauthors Steven and Annette offer first-person accounts of their experiences with coauthoring, reflecting especially on how their experiences lingering on and cultivating their relationship and listening to each other led to the cocreation of knowledge in the form of coauthorship. Demonstrating our feminist notion of listening and coconstructing knowledge, coauthors Steven and Kat offer their dialogic responses *(in parenthetical italics)* to these reflections where they see fit.

Reconsidering Lingering on Relationships, Listening, and Coconstructing Knowledge

STEVEN'S STORY

Where do we—as teachers, directors and mentors—draw (or cross) the line between mentoring student publication and offering students the opportunity (or obstacle) to coauthor? How can we attempt to avoid the sort of emotionally draining and anxiety-producing experiences reported on by Efthymiou and Santiago? While I have been fortunate enough over the years to develop the sorts of relationships with undergraduate students that have led to successful coauthored publications (see, for example, Corbett et al., "Diversity"; Corbett et al., "Small-Group"; Corbett et al., "Peer"; Corbett and Villarreal), I'd like to juxtapose a couple of snapshots of knowledge coconstruction that help illustrate the possibilities, complications, and promise of a feminist ethos of research reporting and coauthorship.

During my time at Southern Connecticut State University (SCSU), I had the opportunity to linger for years on a relationship with an undergraduate tutor, Colleen Sullivan, a student, Nick Guido, and an instructor, Lois Lake Church. Our relationship began during research I was conducting on course-based tutoring in a developmental writing course. Both student participants disclosed neurodiversities (Colleen, dyslexia, and Nick, autism spectrum), and both embraced the idea of telling their stories, as I developed and framed the research gathered on their interactions from interviews and classroom observations. Yet, the most striking thing, in terms of feminist listening, was the way we lingered on our relationship for years. I had met both Colleen and Nick when they were freshman. We all stayed in touch for the rest of their time as undergraduates at SCSU, and even into their time entering the workforce.

Nick, especially, would regularly visit me in my office just to chat. We would talk about how his courses were going as well as such personal things as the female professional wrestler he had a crush on. By the time Colleen and Nick graduated, they both let me know that they had landed successful full-time jobs, Colleen as a registered nurse and Nick as a CPA.

Yet, given that all the circumstances of lingering on relationships, listening, and cocreating knowledge conducive to coauthoring were there, we never made it quite that far. While my research-subjects-turned-collaborators joined me in a campus presentation and we traveled together to present at a regional conference in New York City (Corbett et al., "Reimagining"), as I planned for the subsequent publications, I decided not to invite them in as coauthors. As I describe in the resulting publications, I did take steps to include their points of view, including having them (as well as Lois) read my write-ups, tell me what they thought of them, and subsequently including their impressions in the resulting publications. But I did not take the next step to coauthorship. Looking back, I think I neglected to act on what may have been the ethically right—or better—thing to do. Understandably, it would not have made as much sense to invite them to coauthor the monograph (Corbett, *Beyond*). But the journal articles (Corbett, "Learning," "Toward") could have been coauthored—especially to include their impressions of my write-ups and research reporting of our interactions—like the ones described below. I think I really should have at least asked the instructor of the course, Lois Church, if they would have liked to join me as coauthor. Looking back, I suppose I felt that having included them in conference presentation activities, as well as the relationships I had built especially with Lois and Nick, was somehow enough. But soon I'd get the chance to make amends.

In 2016 I took a position as director of the Quality Enhancement Plan (QEP) and Writing Center at TAMUK. As director of the QEP, I was in charge of our all-important QEP assessment cycle and report (QEPreportSACS(4).docx—Google Docs) that would become part of our overall report for TAMUK's regional accrediting body, the Southern Association of Colleges and Schools (SACS). Immediately, I started organizing conference proposals with my primarily undergraduate staff. One of the tutors who immediately became involved was a freshman named Katherine (Kat) Villarreal. During our many subsequent collaborations together, I realized that Kat would be an ideal person to start considering as a coauthor. She was one of the smartest, most driven, and hardworking undergraduates I'd ever worked with, and she enjoyed coauthoring conference proposals and traveling to and presenting at conferences. I started out just inviting her and others into conference proposals I had already put together in the form of roundtables. All tutors who wanted to attend had to do was read the proposal and think about ways to talk about the topics. But soon Kat began to express her desire to put together conference proposals. So we began to have regular meetings where I would show her some of the tricks of the trade, including where and how to strategically find research articles that would support her topics, how to cite that research so it integrates smoothly with the conference themes, the processes for submitting the proposals, and the multifarious processes for preparing for the conferences she was getting accepted to. Soon she was getting groups of us accepted to present together, conference after conference. *(Kat's response: Once I was shown these tricks, it opened a realm of futures that I never thought could be opened to a minority as well as a woman in academia. With this information, I feel this kind of practice needed to be shared ethically with my peers, who were predominantly Hispanic.)*

So, about three years from the time we started presenting at conferences together, when the time came to answer the CFP for the collection *Emotions and Affect in Writing Centers*, I felt compelled to invite Kat into the project as coauthor. Our successful collaboration resulted in an experience that we both look back on with great pride and sense of accomplishment. The collaborative research relationship we had been developing was definitely taken to the next level. We spent chunks of time meeting, sharing research articles, and discussing theoretical frames. We even codeveloped the basis for the feminist theory of practice employed in this chapter. *(Kat's response: The idea of feminism in writing center scholarship felt sparse, but the works that inspired this allowed me to evolve my own perception of feministic listening as a tutor and future public elementary school educator.)* Although Kat (similar to Santiago above) was one of the busiest people I knew, we were able to schedule time in her hectic schedule that would compensate her for these research activities. She was paid for her time spent reading, discussing, planning, and writing. And we had been collaborating together in the day-to-day activities of the writing center, as well as research reporting, for so long that we grew to understand and appreciate the nuances of listening and responding to each other. In fact, Kat was not initially a coauthor of this chapter. Given my thoughts above on neglecting to invite coauthors, and Kat's substantial presence here, I found this quite ironic. Together, Steven, Annette, and Kat agreed that Kat would be invited into this project as a coauthor via dialogical responses. *(Kat's response: It was an experience to say the least, as collaboration in my career is huge. While sharing one with a cisgender white male was all new to me as I am from Laredo, a largely Hispanic border town, the culture and identities we realized we did share made us both equipped to listen, be patient, and share new perspectives* [see Corbett and Villarreal for more details].)

In the final sentence of their article, Johnson and Rifenburg write: "Let's turn to more stories, told by more undergraduate researchers, as we continue to learn how our students struggle, succeed, and make meaning through undergraduate research" (240). While I thought I might never meet such a talented undergraduate researcher and collaborator as Kat (who was, incidentally, named the 2020 South Central Writing Centers Outstanding Tutor of the Year), I ended up astonished when I hired and began to experience similar interactions with her younger sister and our coauthor, Annette. In the following, Annette details her experiences of our research-reporting and coauthoring relationship.

FOLLOWING IN FOOTSTEPS, WHILE (CO)CREATING MY OWN PATHS: ANNETTE'S STORY

Transitioning from an administrative assistant to a tutor, in my second term, I became immersed in the culture of writing where I realized how writing can help me succeed academically, professionally, and personally. Initially, I was unaware of the impact it would have on me. I was only a witness to my sister Kat's journey but soon saw the opportunities she received involving multiple coauthorships with our Writing Center director, Dr. Corbett. The recent release of their chapter, "Listening about Listening" (Corbett and Villarreal), which centers around the feminist ideals of *lingering on relationships, listening,* and *cocreating knowledge,* helped me realize how these principles apply to the process of coauthorship.

More specifically, in terms of feminist listening, I witnessed how the lingering relationship between Dr. Corbett and Kat resulted in opportunities for coauthorship. *(Kat's response: As a public-school educator navigating a post-COVID classroom, even this observation is noted with my fifth-grade students, who are dealing with gaps from COVID, having learned how to read in kinder and pre-k via zoom, that stunted their emotional growth/ development in reading, writing, and peer-to-peer collaboration.)* For example, with her graduation already near and focusing on her career in teaching, Kat felt I should reach out to Dr. Corbett to join the Writing Center. Instantly, I was welcomed by Dr. Corbett and the staff, who were pleased to have me aboard. Even after she graduated, they would come to know what each other had been up to since then. One could argue it might've been difficult for them to stay in contact given she now focused on her career in teaching. However, the time spent preparing research and now finding out their chapter had officially been published provided all the reason for this lingering. Following that recent release, I was invited to join in coauthoring three other chapters that I felt involved the feminist framework.

When approached by Dr. Corbett to join coauthored projects, I was humbled, since this was going to be a collaborative experience. Though I am a staff member, I knew these opportunities would assist me in learning new ways of writing. Admittedly, thinking of these projects felt intimidating, especially with my sister being an already published author in a coauthored project. *(Kat's response: I will note that Annette is the youngest of six siblings and I am the oldest, so her trepidation does not come unwarranted. However, knowing the pressure of making waves, I was determined to make sure that it could be done, and I look now with immense pride to see* mi gente *get a seat at the table.)* I have second-guessed my ability to do the same. I've struggled with my own insecurities when it comes to writing and didn't know how to feel. *(Steven's response: Coming from Annette, this is almost surprising to hear. Annette has one of the most calm and poised demeanors you are ever going to encounter. She was even named 2023 TAMUK Student Employee of the Year. It just shows that, no matter how secure or talented someone seems, they may struggle with anxiety when writing and coconstructing knowledge.)*

With the everyday pressures that every college student must face, time management was essential to not only completing assignments for other classes but also making sure I made time to develop my thoughts for the coauthored projects. However, I've come to learn about my impact and position at the Writing Center thanks to Dr. Corbett. I've been constantly reminded of my unique experiences as an administrative assistant and tutor. *(Kat's response: Annette acts as the Gen Z representation in this chapter. Our feminist framework is something I wonder if public schools can benefit from when it comes to addressing young writers and future generations' insecurities in writing. It could help prepare them for the challenges and opportunities of higher education, so that perhaps at Annette's age that fear/doubt isn't there but is replaced with a drive to listen and learn more about the unknown of academic writing.)*

In terms of the feminist framework, the involvement of several tutors and our director on coauthored projects, allowed us to linger on our relationships between each other. One such project involved a group of six undergraduates: Katherine Villarreal, Elsa Angelica Alvarez, Alyssa Morales, Larisa Garcia, Casidy Leal, and me (Corbett et al., "Directing"). Once I became more experienced, I began training others including the rest of the tutors mentioned in the project. It didn't take long for us to bond as we grew up in similar areas with similar stories. We would catch up on our personal lives, like what we had been up to that weekend or what trips we planned to go on, and we would even recount any dates we went on. Eventually, we exchanged social media handles to stay updated with each other outside of work.

Once it became official about our plans to also join a conference, some of the less experienced tutors began to ask me what it meant to be part of a publication, though I had not been in a publication myself. This brought up emotions and concerns about what this process would be like, which can be described as the bridge to feminist listening. They explained their concerns about not being familiar with the process, feeling as though they weren't good enough to join.

Following this, we often read each other's responses to share necessary revisions and suggestions. Our overlapping schedules in the writing center helped us work together and even shed light on the other obligations and activities we had outside the center. Similar to Santiago's narrative in "Doing More with Barely Enough," being a college student can be challenging in itself, and making time to invest in our project came as a challenge. While one tutor prepared meetings for their sorority, another would finish their shift and immediately head toward their second job. It was evident we were stressed, but we were able to provide each other with words of encouragement and understanding.

Because of my own concerns, I shared my worries with Kat and wanted to listen to her experiences about being a tutor and now coauthor. I wanted more insight and soon realized how the feminist frame can be applied to coauthorship, as it also had its ups and downs. *(Steven's response: We would also meet for lunches at my house to discuss our projects. Kat's husband, Marshall, who had also been a tutor and administrative assistant and had presented at conferences with us, would also join in on the conversations. This relaxed atmosphere allowed us to open up and discuss ideas and furthered our bonds of friendship and trust.)*

Even though Dr. Corbett tried to schedule her as much as possible for creative activity, Kat was doing extra activities for the center that competed for time with her other activities, including attending conferences, creating presentations, and joining research projects. This to me revealed the nature of what coauthoring can be. While we wanted to further research on writing, finding the motivation to do so was a challenge. Recently, seeing me follow in her footsteps, Kat and I have been able to linger on the intellectual aspects of our relationship. Those wanting to coauthor, like me, know it is something that requires our full attention and commitment. If I am not feeling well mentally, it can be difficult to focus on research.

Additionally, with some conferences being a multiple-day stay, it would require time off from other activities like spending time with family, doing homework, or a second job with higher pay. That being said, I thought it was convenient that I was able to be scheduled for times in which I could research and contribute toward the project while being paid. Furthermore, I was inspired by my sister who worked multiple jobs at one point and still found time to better our writing center. I asked my sister about the significance of committing extra time for the Writing Center. She explained that it was essential to attend conferences as it could help reflect on what can help students succeed, so she was willing to commit her time to these obligations. This stood true for me when I ventured down a similar path to cocreating knowledge.

Upon reading "Contributive Knowledge Making and Critical Language Awareness: A Justice-Oriented Paradigm for Undergraduate Research at a Hispanic-Serving Institution" by Angela Rounsaville, Esther Milu, and Joel Schneier, as a Hispanic woman I connected with the idea of how research conducted in an HSI like ours can serve a great purpose for cocreating knowledge. Attending the 2022 National Conference of Peer Tutors in Writing Conference in Omaha, Nebraska, with fellow Hispanic tutors, I was nervous because I didn't fully know what to expect. Dr. Corbett reminded us of the importance of attending such events and their potential impact on the writing projects, including developing an understanding of how lengthy the publication process can be. During this conference, I realized the various struggles tutors from across the country had. We were able to share our personal experiences and discuss what and how to improve our tutoring and administrative practices. We took notes during our roundtables, as important ideas could be applicable during tutoring sessions as well as our coauthoring projects. The following ideas—involving identity and cultural affiliation and expectations—were discussed at the conference, and they also made their way into our coauthored chapter (Corbett et al., "Directing").

A topic that stirred up a lot of discussion at the conference involved the difference in treatment we received between female and male students. Female students seemed to be outright collaborative during the session by asking questions, making suggestions, and sharing their ideas. On the other hand, male students began the session by explaining their assignment and turning it over to us with the expectation that we would make the corrections for them. *(Kat's response: This observation can also be noted in my own classroom, where I teach English language arts. When it is time for my students to begin their collaborative work, the female students often take these roles and the male students are passive in their learning. So if this form of interaction could be addressed properly now, it could hopefully trickle back up to writing centers and classrooms when they move into college-student and tutor roles.)* During our conference roundtable, we explored the possible impact of our culture in our everyday interactions. In order to combat this trend, we exchanged ideas on how to create more collaborative sessions. *(Steven's response: The conversations surrounding these intersectional ideas on gender-role differences began with all of us brainstorming in preparation for our roundtable. One of our colleagues, Angelica, started talking about this idea, and the rest of our group began to add our own experiences. Then, while at the roundtable, Angelica brought it up again, and it stirred up a lot of conversation from the twenty-five or so diverse attendees, including the perspectives of two tutors from an all-male institution.)*

Pushing further now, as I am encountering feminist theory, reading lots of scholarship about writing and tutoring, and delving deeper into what it means to collaborate and coauthor (including another forthcoming coauthored chapter with Dr. Corbett and Kat), I am imagining even more reasons why our exchanges of ideas are so important.

Fifty, Even a Hundred, Years from Now

Throughout this chapter, we have emphasized the importance of time in lingering on relationships, listening, and coconstructing knowledge. When you factor coauthoring into the equation, and publications result, the span of time and the impact of that coconstructed knowledge can extend in ever-widening ripples ... Fifty, even a hundred, years from now someone might read our little chapter and perhaps cite it and ... We invite you to join us in this lofty goal, and we offer some modest feminist recommendations for coauthoring with undergraduates that might help:

1. Purposefully and strategically plan to *linger on relationships*. A good way to do this is to recruit and hire talented, promising students from the time they first enter college. Steven has especially experienced great success in recruiting strong communicators and writers from his first-year and intermediate writing courses. He has also recruited tutors simply by regularly asking tutors to refer friends and classmates they think would make good peer tutors. These recruitment and hiring methods help build writing centers staffed with people that already know each other.

2. Be sure to *listen* to cautionary tales like Efthymiou and Zea's and try to compensate tutors fairly for their time and efforts in research,

presentation, and publication. The program that Steven, Annette, and Kat worked together in was linked closely to TAMUK's SACs reaccreditation via our successful QEP (QEPreportSACS(4).docx - Google Docs). Efforts can be made to link your writing center to other student support units and communication/writing initiatives on campus. Forging connections with other campus units could potentially lead to more resources and funding.

3. When undergraduates begin to show the talent and promise evinced by students like Kat and Annette, don't hesitate too long in inviting them to *coconstruct knowledge*. Scaffold their experiences, starting with conference attendance and presentations, and working toward coauthoring projects. Then make sure to broadcast loud and clear the stories behind these close collaborative relationships—in publications like this one or the several writing center journals, in university announcements and publications, and in meetings and conversations with colleagues across campus.

4. Plan for and, if it all goes well, make FFLs (friends for life).

Works Cited

Bromley, Pam, Kara Northway, and Eliana Schonberg. "Evaluating the Complexities of Tutor Collaboration in Cross-Institutional Writing Center Research." *SDC: A Journal of Multiliteracy and Innovation*, vol. 20 no. 1, 2016, pp. 10–27. file:///C:/Users/kusjc014/Downloads/BNSSDCFinalArticle%20(1).pdf.

Corbett, Steven J. *Beyond Dichotomy: Synergizing Writing Center and Classroom Pedagogies*. The WAC Clearinghouse and Parlor Press, 2015. http://wac.colostate.edu/books/dichotomy/.

Corbett, Steven J. "Learning Disability and Response-Ability: Reciprocal Caring in Developmental Peer Response Writing Groups and beyond." *Pedagogy: Critical Approaches to Teaching Literature, Language, Composition, and Culture*, vol. 15 no. 3, 2015, pp. 459–75.

Corbett, Steven J. "Toward Inclusive and Multi-Method Writing Assessment for College Students with Learning Disabilities: The (Universal) Story of Max." *WPA: Writing Program Administration*, vol. 40 no. 3, 2017, pp. 23–38.

Corbett, Steven J., Amanda Bender, Emily Simon, and Jackii Ingros. "Peer Pedagogies: Curricular Adventures in Peer-Centered Writing, Speaking, and Learning." *Crowdsourcing with CCDP, Part Two*, blog. Computers and Composition Digital Press/University Press of Colorado and Utah State University Press, 25 Apr. 2020. https://ccdigitalpress.org/blog/crowdsourcing-with-ccdp-part-ii.

Corbett, Steven J., Lois Lake Church, Colleen Sullivan, and Nick Guido. "Reimagining Disability and Response-Ability: Reciprocal Learning and Caring in Course-Based Tutoring." 28th Annual Northeast Writing Centers Association Conference, New York, NY, Apr. 2012.

Corbett, Steven J., Sydney F. Lewis, and Madeleine M. Clifford. "Diversity Matters in Individualized Instruction: The Pros and Cons of Team Teaching and Talkin' that Talk." *Diversity in the Composition Classroom*, edited by Gwendolyn Hale, Mike Mutschelknaus, and Thomas Alan Holmes, Fountainhead Press, 2010, pp. 85–96.

Corbett, Steven J., Stephanie Serenita, Stephanie Gruessner, Heather Brady, Marissa Brown, and Fantasia Gordon. "Small-Group Peer Response and the Role of the Group Facilitator as 'Meta-Tutor.'" *Peer Pressure, Peer Power: Theory and Practice in Peer Review and Response for the Writing Classroom*, edited by Steven J. Corbett, Michelle LaFrance, and Teagan E. Decker, Fountainhead Press, 2014, pp. 185–94.

Corbett, Steven J., Annette Vara, and Katherine Villarreal. "Finish Strong: Directing a Successful Writing-Centered QEP during a Pandemic." *WPAing in a Pandemic and Beyond*, edited by Todd Ruecker and Sheila Carter-Tod, Utah State University Press, 2025, pp. 258–62.

Corbett, Steven J., Annette Vara, Katherine Villarreal, Elsa Alvarez, Alyssa Morales, Larisa Garcia, and Casidy Leal. "Directing a Successful Writing-Centered QEP at an Historically Hispanic Serving Institution: Our (Multi)Culture of Writing." *Writing Center Administrators as Campus Leaders*, edited by Candis Bond, Joy Bracewell, Wonderful Faison, Stacia Moroski-Rigney, and Kem Roper, Utah State University Press, forthcoming.

Corbett, Steven J., and Katherine Villarreal. "Listening about Listening: Narratives of Affect, Diversity, and Feminist Listening in Writing Center Research Reporting." *Emotions and Affect in Writing Centers*, edited by Janine Morris and Kelly A. Concannon, Parlor Press, 2022, pp. 219–36.

Efthymiou, Andrea, and Ryan Fallert. "Redefining Collaboration through the Extended Work of Writing Center Tutors: How Undergraduate Research Expands Opportunities for Collaboration in Higher Education." *College English*, vol. 84, no. 6, 2022, pp. 638–51.

Efthymiou, Andrea Rosso, and Santiago Zea. "Doing More with Barely Enough: Narratives of an Undergraduate Tutor Researcher and Mentor." *Writing Center Journal*, vol. 41, no. 1, 2023, pp. 87–98. https://doi.org/10.7771/2832-9414.1980.

Fallon, Brian J. "Keynote." National Conference on Peer Tutoring in Writing, Miami, FL, 6 Nov. 2011.

Fitzgerald, Lauren. "Undergraduate Writing Tutors as Researchers: Redrawing Boundaries (IWCA 2012 Keynote Address)." *Writing Center Journal*, vol. 33, no. 2, 2013, pp. 17–35.

Fitzgerald, Lauren. "Writing Centers: The Best Place for Undergraduate Research." *Pedagogy*, vol. 22 no. 1, 2022, pp. 27–30.

Fitzgerald, Lauren, and Melissa Ianetta. *The Oxford Guide for Writing Tutors: Practice and Research*. Oxford UP, 2016.

Johnson, Kristine, and J. Michael Rifenburg. "Rhetoric and Affect in Undergraduate Research: A Diary Study." *Across the Disciplines*, vol. 19, no. 3/4, 2022, pp. 225–42. https://wac.colostate.edu/docs/atd/volume19/johnson-rifenburg.pdf.

Rosenberg, Lauren, and Emma Howes. "Listening to Research as a Feminist Ethos of Representation." *Composing Feminist Interventions: Activism, Engagement, Praxis*, edited by Kristine L. Blair and Lee Nickoson. The WAC Clearinghouse and UP of Colorado, 2018, pp. 75–91. https://wac.colostate.edu/docs/books/feminist/chapter4.pdf.

Rounsaville, Angela, Esther Milu, and Joel Schneier. "Contributive Knowledge Making and Critical Language Awareness: A Justice-Oriented Paradigm for Undergraduate Research at a Hispanic-Serving Institution." *College English*, vol. 84 no. 6, 2022, pp. 519–45.

3
Coauthoring the Writing Studies Curriculum

An Ongoing Student-Faculty Partnership

HEATHER THOMSON-BUNN AND MÍA ZENDEJAS

Our collaboration began with an initiative called Faculty-Student Partnerships for Diversifying Courses at Pepperdine University. The goal of our partnership was to revise the Advanced Composition course in the writing and rhetoric major to include more diverse voices and to adopt a wide-reaching approach to diversity (for example, we aimed to increase representation of neurodiversity, body diversity, and religious diversity and to include a broader range of LGBTQ+ perspectives). What we did not realize then was that we were really embarking on two projects: the explicitly defined course revision and an experiment in coauthorship that would challenge institutionally defined power dynamics, as well as our sense of what becomes of student-faculty projects once the initial research is complete. Our work reflects a students as partners (SaP) approach, which "challenges students' as well as faculty's traditional understanding of who is responsible for what happens in the classroom or through the process of teaching and learning" and is grounded in students having "an active role to play in the decisions about what and how to learn" ("Students"). Like the critical pedagogy advocated by Paolo Freire and many scholars in writing studies, SaP "inherently subverts the traditional power hierarchy between learners and teachers" (Mercer-Maptone et al. 14).

https://doi.org/10.7330/9781646427796.c003

Even within this progressive framework, of course, traditional power structures remain, and they are more difficult to subvert than one might hope. This was certainly a challenge that we faced during our collaboration. We also discovered, however, that a continual process of reflection, negotiation, and mutual vulnerability can clear new pathways for the production and circulation of both curriculum and scholarship that is coauthored by students and faculty.

This article is an enactment of that process, a form of resistance to the ways in which student-faculty projects are typically presented. We understand the circulation of "the narratives of discovery themselves" as a way to transform an end product into a "generative event" (Downs et al. 100). We therefore write in a two-voiced, dialogic structure, intended to depict an inclusive and equitable coauthorship. Our approach to composing is also intended to keep our individual voices and experiences present throughout the text, occasionally disrupting the more seamless first-person plural. This is especially significant in relation to Mía's perspective, as student voices are not well represented in SaP scholarship. In their literature review of SaP in higher education, Mercer-Mapstone et al. report "low rates of staff-student coauthorship" and note that the scarcity of student coauthors "obscur[es] the roles of student partners" (18). We would add that it also restores traditional hierarchies, denying student partners the opportunity to shape the public narrative(s) of their own work.

Because the foundation of the research process is inquiry, all participants are *learners*, regardless of expertise. We contend that the circulation of coauthored SaP scholarship should extend this notion, establishing each participant as a *learner-contributor* with authority over the rhetorical shaping of their research—what forms it takes, which audiences it addresses, and what significance it holds.

Who Are "We"?

Because student-faculty partnerships are inevitably shaped by institutional frameworks, subject positions, and power dynamics, we want to begin by introducing ourselves in relation to our research and to one another. Our roles were fluid and dynamic at certain points in the process, and quite rigid at others, due not only to institutional expectations and constraints but to our own failure to anticipate how those expectations and constraints would affect our partnership across various contexts and moments in time.

Mía: I am a Mexican-Puerto Rican, female, first-generation college graduate. I graduated in 2022 with a BA in English writing and rhetoric. As an undergraduate, I worked as a tutor at the Writing Center and served as the editor of Pepperdine's undergraduate literary journal, *Expressionists*. Coauthoring Advanced Composition was the first time I worked within an SaP framework, and the first time I applied my *perspectiva latinoamericana* directly to curriculum. Code-switching—which I have practiced for most of my life but did not understand as a valid linguistic and rhetorical device until I took Heather's Language Theory class—appears often in my writing.

Heather: I am a white, female, tenured professor of English. I direct the first-year writing program at Pepperdine University, where I also teach courses in composition, language theory, rhetorical theory, professional writing, and creative writing. Before revising the Advanced Composition course with Mía during the summer of 2021, I had taught it five times. Mía was enrolled in several of my courses during her undergraduate career. This partnership was the first time that I had formally worked with a student to revise and develop curriculum.

Having known each other as instructor and student for a couple of years before this project began allowed us to start from a place of relative trust. Heather trusted Mía as a dedicated student, a creative thinker, a collaborative worker, and a kind, generous person. And Mía trusted Heather as a professor committed to supporting students, an advocate for linguistic justice, a writer with rhetorical influence, and an individual with an empathetic and graceful nature. Though we would know each other better and from different perspectives by the end of the project, this initial trust was critical to building an SaP project and working as coauthors of the course, of presentations about our work, and of this chapter. We refer to ourselves and each other by first name throughout this essay as a way of emphasizing our pursuit of shared agency and authorship.

The Intersection of DEI Work and Student-Faculty Partnerships

In many ways, SaP and the effort to foster greater diversity, equity, and inclusion (DEI) are a well-suited pair. DEI work involves challenging structures that perpetuate inequity and listening to voices that have historically been silenced. SaP calls for a "shift toward shared and reciprocal teaching and learning," making room for students to have greater say in and responsibility for their own education, and for faculty to listen to voices not typically accepted as part of their curricular development, teaching, or writing (Cook-Sather and Alter 41). *Era importante* to Heather and me that we include not only my student perspective in our SaP research, but also my minority student perspective: a financially independent Latina lacking the socioeconomic privilege of most students at my university.

DEI offers a particularly salient rhetorical space for the "embrace of undergraduates as fellow scholars" (Shanahan xi), especially given that partnering with faculty on research "has a disproportionately positive effect on retention and graduation rates for first-generation students and members of underrepresented groups" (Greer et al. 82). At universities like Pepperdine that have historically had a predominantly white and wealthy student population, such effects are critical.

SaP and DEI can be mutually beneficial when intentionally woven together, and they can also serve to expose each other's weaknesses. For example, I (Mía) consulted the Pepperdine webpage about the Faculty-Student Partnerships for Diversifying Courses initiative, and found that the only names listed were faculty's. My name and those of the fourteen other students involved were absent. We were referenced merely as "15 students"—a label that cast aside our individual identities and contributions. I (Heather) shared Mía's dismay at this erasure, though I also wonder if I would have noticed or reacted so strongly had my own student partner not pointed it out.

I (Mía) wonder what might have changed if SaP scholarship were more common; I wonder if someone would have noticed the erasure of student contributions before the webpage was published. The more that SaP frameworks are implemented, the greater success we will have in "challenging the acceptance that students are passive within curricula processes" (Bovill and Bully 9).

Though we do not assume any malice behind the exclusion of students' names, the absence is striking. Failing to acknowledge student contributors denies them ownership of curricula that they cocreated. Gutman et al. stress that "*ownership* is a linchpin for collaboration," and we would add that ownership is of particular significance in DEI efforts as well (136, emphasis in original). We agree that "[t]oo often in higher education diversity initiatives do not progress past inaugural events, and programming created to counter the exclusion of faculty and students from historically un- and under-represented groups fails to affect actual change" (DelliCarpini et al. 9–10). Actual change seems most likely when ownership is shared and coauthorship is extended through and made visible in the presentation, writing, and publication process. Otherwise, what begins as an opportunity to promote DEI via coauthoring the curriculum can easily revert to faculty-driven projects that neglect one member of the DEI trinity: inclusion.

Power

DEI initiatives must acknowledge and grapple with questions of power, and so must coauthored SaP research projects. We began our work feeling confident in our egalitarian effort. We called each other by first name, texted regularly, and conversed freely. Heather talked about her kids as she would to any colleague, and Mía expressed excitement about a wave she caught surfing as she would to any peer. We brainstormed about the course, both of us raising, questioning, and affirming various ideas.

If you had asked us then, we might have said that we were effectively resisting the convention of faculty-driven research. Heather did not send Mía off in service to *her* project. Instead, we outlined what specific topics of *diversidad* were important to us both. For Mía, intersectionality was a clear choice, as her own intersectional positions (ethnicity, financial status, religion) had shaped her sense of belonging (or not). For Heather, religious diversity had long been a topic of interest. Neither of us remembers who first mentioned neurodiversity, but we were both eager to explore it in the context of a writing course. We pursued ideas regardless of their originator. Generating ideas collaboratively gave us an early sense of this truly being *our* project, which *we* had equal ability and right to shape. It may also have left us a bit too comfortable in our sense of shared power, unprepared for the ways in which that "we" identity would be challenged.

Our work continued smoothly throughout most of the summer—and then came to a more abrupt conclusion than planned when Heather sustained a concussion. We were able to complete the research, create categorized lists of potential texts to assign, and develop assignment prompts, but we did not get to finish the syllabus. Heather went on medical leave. Mía returned to school for the fall semester.

In the spring, Mía stepped into the Advanced Composition classroom and was handed a syllabus that had been completed without her input. The agency that I (Mía) had held so confidently during the summer now slipped through my fingers. I did see many texts that I had championed, and the language that Heather and I had developed was both on the syllabus and in her verbal introduction to the course. But I had not been part of the final decision about what was included and what was not. It felt as though the course no longer bore my signature. Though I was excited for the course, and happy to see our collaboration as its foundation, I wanted to be *parte de todo el proceso* of implementing curricular change. It almost felt like an anticlimactic ending to a movie that leaves the viewer not knowing *cómo exactamente* to pinpoint their *emoción*.

Implementation was more fraught than we had anticipated. This was where I (Heather) struggled most to navigate issues of power. In accordance with the CCCC Position Statement on Undergraduate Research in Writing, I wanted to ensure that the project "fit into student[s'] schedules over a set period of time" and that I was "follow[ing] relevant ethical standards." Mía received a stipend for the summer, and the initiative had "Summer Partnerships" in the title. Once the summer work was complete, was it ethical for me to consult with her? Would she feel free to say no if her academic and work schedules did not allow time for it? I knew how many commitments Mía had, and I knew she sometimes overextended herself. Once we were back to school as professor and student, I worried about putting more on Mía's plate than was ethical. Also—I understand now—I was not thinking of Mía as a coauthor. We had yet to align our work with that specific terminology. It was not until a year later when we began developing a formal presentation that we realized we had already "coauthored" something: the curriculum.

I (Mía) understand now the tension Heather experienced around the issue of compensation, as "[n]on-payment creates challenges for students who cannot afford to undertake unpaid partnership initiatives outside of the curriculum" (Mercer-Mapstone 18). Non-payment potentially undermines the equality called for in coauthorship, especially considering the transactional nature of traditional student-faculty partnerships. I appreciate that Heather was cognizant of my financial circumstances, that she considered my struggle to support myself by working fifty hours a week on top of a full course load.

However, coauthorship under an SaP framework should not be transactional; in fact, the SaP model challenges a number of transactional characteristics of research in higher education, including "[i]ts view of student as client" ("Students"). When a student serves under the traditional research assistant role, they are usually compensated with money or course credit. The "compensation" in coauthorship is acknowledgment. I experienced a slight sense of abandonment with the abrupt end to our coauthorship of the curriculum (and thus to the acknowledgment I was given)—*pero ahora* after engaging in ongoing reflection with Heather, I see how traditional power dynamics created points of conflict and confusion. Some of these points we were aware of and did not address effectively; others we did not see or understand until much later.

As the Advanced Composition course began, we found ourselves more rigidly set in institutionally defined roles: Dr. Thomson-Bunn the professor and Mía the student. The "we" that was so natural in the summer was suddenly not so natural. Heather was concerned that mentioning our work to the class might lead to assumptions of bias or to awkwardness for Mía among her peers. Mía agreed. We thought it would be best for Heather to teach the course like any other single-authored faculty creation.

Though I (Mía) remember a distinct discomfort when I encountered the syllabus on the first day of class like every other student, I also felt proud. I felt a secret excitement to see that many of the course materials I had suggested were there; I felt heard. The feeling of empowerment was so foreign to me as a student that I questioned myself: Was this allowed? I had nurtured diversity practices within the English major curriculum—the very curriculum that was intellectually nurturing me.

As Mía worked to reconcile pride with a loss of agency, I (Heather) wrestled with the notion of responsibility, both *for* and *to*. I was ultimately accountable for the course content and to the students who would enroll in the revised course. These responsibilities obscured some others—most notably, my responsibility to my coauthor. I wish that I had sat down with Mía and talked about this, risked having a conversation that complicated things, and trusted Mía to know and assert her own needs.

Though Heather and I (Mía) had developed a working relationship filled with mutual respect, the notion that the student perspective is less valuable than the faculty member's is a powerful one. SaP is fighting a narrative of education that is deeply ingrained—faculty as leader and student as follower—and SaP does not yet hold a prominent position in writing studies. As a student enrolled in the coauthored course, I often felt as though I was floating in the space between leader and follower, between author and reader. I did not, however, express my reservations about how the syllabus and course were designed until we began working on this chapter. As a student, "it can be difficult to have a realm . . . where you feel incredibly empowered and your voice is valued, and others where it is not" (Cook-Sather and Alter 48). The transition from coauthor to traditional student was uncomfortable, but I felt that I had to accept that discomfort as a return to the way things are "supposed" to be. I also wondered if my desire for acknowledgment stemmed from self-interest.

I also often found myself in limbo when it came to verbal analysis of the course texts. Should I contribute more to class discussions because I had greater familiarity with these texts and knew how they fit into the larger ideas of the course? Or would my contributions put other students at an unfair disadvantage? I played tug of war with the shifting power dynamics, acutely aware of how often I spoke up, hyper-sensitive to denying others an opportunity to speak. In moments of silence, I felt an obligation to propel the discussion forward as though I was a teaching assistant. Our work that "resituate[d] power as shared between students and professors" meant that at times I aligned myself more with Heather than with my peers (Shanahan xii).

In our work, the resituation of power was an iterative process, demanding multiple points of reflection and negotiation. SaP coauthorship blurred the categories of pedagogy and partnership, which meant that as our collaborative work took different forms—the summer research, the course, a symposium presentation at our university, a presentation at a national conference, and this chapter—different power dynamics surfaced and shifted. Writing this piece has given us the opportunity to work through some of those complexities of coauthorship. We have sought to reclaim the more egalitarian terrain that once felt so natural. We determined that Mía would write *with* and not *for* Heather, that Heather would speak *con* and not *para* Mía. This text focuses not on what Mía learned from Heather or on Heather's contribution to the field but on how the *two* of us have navigated this work, and how *we*, as coauthors, have made meaning of it.

Vulnerability

We understand now that many of the disruptions to a fully equal *coautoría* were rooted in obscured power dynamics and might have been resolved with a more conscious and equal distribution of power.

Sharing power, however, often means embracing vulnerability. Student coauthors witness and contribute to a part of faculty life that most students do not see: the unknowns that drive research, the planning and improvisation of teaching, the messiness of drafting, the labor of revision. A coauthor observes how their partner handles obstacles and deadlines. Student coauthors will likely see a more fully human version of a professor than the one teaching class or holding office hours. Even at our small liberal arts institution, where it is quite common for students and faculty to get to know each other, coauthoring curriculum—particularly around issues of DEI—required vulnerability that we were not quite expecting.

For example, when Mía suggested a particular topic to include in our course, I (Heather) disclosed my own history with that issue, and explained how I wanted to proceed carefully with a topic that could be uncomfortable or risky not just for some students but for me as well. Though I had occasionally referenced my experience in class, I had never talked with a student about my own need for protection and boundaries.

Heather's vulnerability made our work more precious to me (Mía); I navigated my research more delicately than I had before. I had known that our work mattered for students who needed to encounter DEI in the classroom (myself included). However, observing the potential effects of our work on a *professor* moved me in a newfound manner. I realized that the intersections of DEI and SaP really do hold the potential to influence students *and* faculty profoundly. I felt empowered by my agency to curate course content that reflected my own background, but I also caught glimpses of a professor with a story to tell. Students often fail to see faculty as more than a mentor or teacher; Heather is a human with meaningful life experiences that shape who she is as a learner—just like me.

I (Heather) chose vulnerability in the instance referenced above. At other points, vulnerability was chosen for me. The concussion that I had sustained severely affected my ability to work, and I had to talk to Mía about my new limitations. I was the one in need of extra time, in need of understanding and grace from someone who was counting on me.

I (Mía) had taken multiple courses with Heather and had done my fair share of asking for deadline extensions. She had witnessed me in vulnerable parts of life that even some of my peers had not: family troubles, heartbreak, financial hardship, and the what-do-I-do-after-graduation crisis. Her empathy allowed me to share when I felt overwhelmed or incapable of my best work. Now she was coming to me, and I could empathize with her. I drew from my own experience with a concussion three years prior to give Heather advice: limiting certain types of stimuli was necessary for proper healing—no texting, no Zoom calls, no binge-watching whatever it is that English professors binge-watch. And little did I know, *I* would get another concussion before our work was done, and the roles would reverse yet again. When I was injured, Heather consoled me, told me to take a break when I needed one, and shared what she'd learned during her recovery. We graduated from concussion novices to concussion experts together.

One way that we were able to embrace all of this vulnerability was by shifting to a "mutual mentoring" perspective. Mentoring is traditionally understood as an experienced faculty member, staff member, or graduate student guiding the work of a less experienced undergraduate, "focusing on each student's learning process" (Shanahan xiii). It seems to us that coauthoring with SaP pushes (or should push) the definitional boundaries of mentorship, moving toward relationships that are "reciprocal and broadly encompassing of the whole person, including emotional and social support" (Moore et al. 31). David Elder and Joonna Smitherman Trapp contend that a good mentor relationship *requires* vulnerability from both parties (11). Though we would not recommend concussions as a vehicle for developing mutual mentorship, in our case these traumas provided practical opportunities for this kind of reciprocity.

Such reciprocity may be particularly significant when undergraduate students are conducting research related to DEI. These students can and should function as mentors to faculty, who may not be aware of some of the issues most important to their students, and who may not have access to the texts and ideas that are shaping students' lives. High-quality, mentored SaP projects flow in both directions, and Mía's mentorship was indeed a significant dimension of our collaboration. Though we decided together how we would approach research and the kinds of texts we were seeking, we each took different paths to finding those texts, and returned with very different collections of sources. When Mía advocated for the inclusion of a particular text, I listened—not simply out of politeness or because she had a keen sense of what her peers would want to read (though that was also true), but because she had knowledge that I did not. The "ethos of students as partners" was critical here; Mía was not my assistant but a coauthor who "shared ownership of the process" (Moore et al. 33). Much of the course material used in the revised Advanced Composition course was a result of Mía's ability to demonstrate how that material suited the course goals.

I (Mía) remember feeling that my perspective as a researcher was not only valued but was shaping a dynamic and more inclusive undergraduate education for my peers and for me. It was an unfamiliar and distinct feeling of agency. Yet this agency should not be so foreign to students. Students *should* be part of shaping undergraduate education. Are not students' voices critical for understanding student needs and interests? Won't these students bring knowledge, experiences, and questions that shape how and what they learn? As Paolo Freire puts it, "Education must begin with the solution of the teacher-student contradiction, by reconciling the poles of contradiction so that both are simultaneously teachers *and* students" (72). This shift in perspective makes room for "students to become co-creators, co-producers and co-designers of their own learning" (Bovill and Bully 1). It is foundational to equitable coauthorship.

Circulation

We agree with Jenny Olin Shanahan that "[s]haring what was learned with an audience for whom it matters is essential to scholarship" (xv). We are fortunate to have seen our work disseminated to multiple audiences, in widening circles. The most immediate audience affected by our work was the students enrolled in the revised Advanced Composition course in the spring of 2022.

Looking back, it might have been interesting to discuss our collaborative process with the whole class. Bringing to light how many of the articles and assignments were products of student research may have inspired Mía's classmates to see themselves as cultivators rather than passive recipients of learning. It might have been an opportunity for more students to develop a broader understanding of SaP and its possibilities.

We did have the chance to present our work to faculty and students across the Pepperdine campus at a symposium celebrating the Student-Faculty Partnerships for Diversifying Courses initiative, hosted by the Center for Teaching Excellence. We then presented our work externally in March of 2022 at the (online) CCCC convention. The theme of that year's conference was "The Promises and Perils of Higher Education: Our Discipline's Commitment to Diversity, Equity, and Linguistic Justice," which seemed especially fitting for our project.

These circulation experiences, in which I (Mía) was valued as an equal participant with Heather, made our coauthorship "a rich intellectual endeavor that is unavailable through traditional classroom experiences" (Greer 1). The hand that I had in this research and have in our continued coauthorship has affirmed my desire to foster diversity in writing studies by becoming an educator myself. Circulating SaP work that troubles the traditional mentor-mentee narrative can ultimately circulate academic confidence, even to *estudiantes* not directly involved. In this way, the "consequential publicness" of coauthorship holds meaning for "an audience beyond the researcher" (Downs et al. 99), and can transform individuals, programs, and even institutions and fields.

Such lofty goals require grounded, intentional engagement with complexity, and the privileging of equity over efficiency. Coauthoring, even between faculty peers, requires rhetorical listening and the negotiation of multiple voices. Faculty-student coauthors must navigate an even finer line so that the more novice writer/scholar does not lose or cede their right to shape the text(s). For example, I (Mía) often compose long analogies; yet, when coauthoring this chapter with Heather, I was self-conscious about this tendency. I considered the potential "professor perspective" that Heather might have when she read my work, particularly in response to the colloquial and disorganized nature *típica de* my first-draft writing.

I (Heather) was also very aware of myself as a reader. I had read Mía's writing as a professor many times, with the goal of providing feedback that would both encourage and challenge her as a writer. That was not my role here. In this rhetorical situation, I was reading as a coauthor, engaging with Mía's ideas; I was also relying on her engagement with mine.

The comment function in Google Docs helped facilitate coauthorship by making rhetorical and physical space to practice dialogue, reflection, and shared power as we wrote and revised. Very few comments were questions about or critiques of the other writer's ideas. Nearly all—from both authors—were requests for feedback or help on our own writing (e.g., *Is this how you remember it, too? Should we connect more specifically to SaP in this paragraph? Not sure if this works better here or in the next section . . . what do you think?*), followed by an exchange of suggestions, follow-up questions, and occasional emojis. When we look back through our comments, we see reflected there our commitment to reciprocity and the "[e]xtension of co-inquiry through to the writing process" (Mercer-Mapstone 14).

In some ways, coauthoring presentations and written texts has been simpler than coauthoring the curriculum. Collaborating on a written text is perhaps the most explicit and traditional understanding of coauthorship, and tools like comment threads allow for continuous exchange and reflection. Coauthoring the curriculum, on the other hand, is relatively new territory, and therefore more challenging to navigate. The curriculum, embedded as it is in institutional structures, requires a more deliberate creation of "a new space where [student and faculty] 'visions' intersect . . . and can either deepen and affirm what they see or imagine changing what happens in the classroom" (Cook-Sather and Alter 41).

Through our imperfect, *complicado*, and rewarding experiences as learner-contributors, we join the larger disciplinary conversations about SaP and coauthorship in writing studies. Our partnership, like others shared in SaP scholarship, illustrates how "[b]ringing into dialogue the disciplinary expertise and pedagogical knowledge of faculty with student expertise and insight as learners can generate more engaging and effective courses, course components, and learning opportunities" (Cook-Sather et al. 29). In this chapter we have highlighted the mutualism that must exist within student-faculty partnerships in order for SaP to stay true to its name and cultivate genuine coauthorship. We encourage more student-faculty partners in writing studies to compose the story of their research, *juntos*.

Works Cited

Bovill, Catherine, and Cathy J. Bulley. "A Model of Active Student Participation in Curriculum Design: Exploring Desirability and Possibility." *Global Theories and Local Practices: Institutional, Disciplinary, and Cultural Variations* (Improving Student Learning Series 18), edited by C. Rust, Oxford, 2011, pp. 176–88.

"CCCC Position Statement on Undergraduate Research in Writing: Principles and Best Practices." NCTE, 2017.

Cook-Sather, Alison, and Zanny Alter. "What Is and What Can Be: How a Liminal Position Can Change Learning and Teaching in Higher Education." *Anthropology and Higher Education Quarterly*, vol. 42, no. 1, 2011, pp. 37–53.

Cook-Sather, Alison, Catherine Bovill, and Peter Felten. *Engaging Students as Partners in Learning and Teaching*. Jossey-Bass, 2014.

DelliCarpini, Dominic, Jenn Fishman, and Jane Greer. "Building Capacity, Cultivating Consequences: Charting the Course of Undergraduate Research in Writing Studies." *The Naylor Report on Undergraduate Research in Writing Studies*, edited by Dominic DelliCarpini, Jenn Fishman, and Jane Greer, Parlor Press, 2020, pp. 3–13.

Downs, Doug, Laurie McMillan, Megan Schoettler, and Patricia Roberts-Miller. "Circulation: Undergraduate Research as Consequential Publicness." *The Naylor Report on Undergraduate Research in Writing Studies*, edited by Dominic DelliCarpini Jenn Fishman, and Jane Greer, Parlor Press, 2020, pp. 94–105.

Elder, David, and Joonna Smitherman Trapp. "Mentor as Method: Faculty Mentor Roles and Undergraduate Scholarship." *Undergraduate Research in English Studies*, edited by Laurie Grobman and Joyce Kinkead, NCTE, 2010, pp. 3–12.

Freire, Paolo. *Pedagogy of the Oppressed*. 30th anniversary ed. Continuum, 2002.

Greer, Jane. "Guest Editor's Introduction." *Young Scholars in Writing*, vol. 7, Spring 2010, pp. 1–5.

Greer, Jane, Laurie Grobman, and Heather Falconer. "Contributing to Knowledge: A Defining Characteristic of Undergraduate Research." *The Naylor Report on Undergraduate Research in Writing Studies*, edited by Dominic DelliCarpini, Jenn Fishman, and Jane Greer, Parlor Press, 2020, pp. 71–87.

Gutman, Ellen E., Erin M. Sergison, Chelsea J. Martin, and Jeffrey L. Bernstein. "Engaging Students as Scholars of Teaching and Learning: The Role of Ownership." *Engaging Student Voices in the Study of Teaching and Learning*, edited by Carmen Werder and Megan M. Otis, Stylus, 2010, pp. 130–45.

Mercer-Mapstone, Lucy, Sam Lucie Dvorakova, Kelly E. Mathews, Sophia Abbot, Breagh Cheng, Peter Felten, Kris Knorr, Elizabeth Marquis, Rafaella Shammas, and Kelly Swaim. "A Systematic Literature Review of Students as Partners in Higher Education." *International Journal for Students as Partners*, vol. 1, no. 1, 2017, pp. 1–23.

Moore, Jessie L., Sophia Abbot, Hannah Bellwoar, and Field Watts. "Mentoring: Partnering with All Undergraduate Researchers in Writing." *The Naylor Report on Undergraduate Research in Writing Studies*, edited by Dominic DelliCarpini, Jenn Fishman, and Jane Greer, Parlor Press, 2020, pp. 29–44.

Shanahan, Jenny Olin. "Foreword: The Transformative Power of Undergraduate Research in Writing Studies." *The Naylor Report on Undergraduate Research in Writing Studies*, edited by Dominic DelliCarpini, Jenn Fishman, and Jane Greer, Parlor Press, 2020, pp. xi–xvii.

"Students as Partners." *Center for Engaged Learning*, centerforengagedlearning.org/studying-engaged-learning/students-as-partners-in-sotl/. Accessed 12 Jun. 2023.

4
Cultivating Boundary Dwellers

Coauthoring Collaborative Relationships with Undergraduates in Community Engagement

TINA LE AND RACHAEL SHAH

When coauthoring with undergraduates in the context of community engagement, the practices that make up the writing process—the ways that we draft a conference presentation about our partnership, brainstorm a grant proposal, edit a website celebrating the partnership—*is* the way we coauthor our community partnership itself. Therefore, these practices make up the way we teach undergraduates how to relate across communities.

While some scholarship examines collaborative writing in community engagement (Nagar), virtually no studies look at the writing process of collaborative authorship teams that include undergraduates, faculty, and community partners. As we have found, undergraduates often play a pivotal role in coauthored community engagement projects, from offering student perspectives on pedagogy in a community-based writing class, to serving as the initial bridge between a faculty member and community in a collaboration, to representing a community that is being written about, to transitioning from undergraduate alum to community partner. Exploring faculty-undergraduate coauthoring in engagement is a rich site for theorizing coauthorship, as when writers work across university-community *and* faculty-undergraduate lines, they navigate stark differences in context, role, and positionality. These differences create challenges, but working at the boundary between academic/

https://doi.org/10.7330/9781646427796.c004

community and undergraduate/faculty knowledge has generative possibilities. The coathorship process can form relationships and set the stage for additional partnership work, as well shape the personal and professional trajectory of the undergraduates. In all these situations, the coauthorship process becomes a critical site for shaping people and partnerships.

We draw upon conversations about boundary zones in community engagement to explore coauthorship. In the cultural historical activity theory (CHAT) framework, a "boundary" is a "sociocultural difference leading to discontinuity in action or interaction" between sites (Akkerman and Bakker 133). Many scholars in community engagement have used CHAT to understand the complexities of working across university-community boundaries. For example, Ross et al. use CHAT to define a "boundary zone" in community engagement as a "transactional space where there is a coming together of individual areas of practice or individual activity systems with the intention of creating a shared area of practice or a joint activity system" (5). Coauthored texts, written in the boundary zone, can serve as "boundary objects" that bridge different activity systems (Akkerman and Bakker). These boundary zones between activity systems can be "'places of challenge, contestation, and playing out of power relations'" (Ross et al. 5). The coauthoring process between faculty, undergraduates, and community partners deserves study because that boundary zone illuminates power dynamics, challenges, and opportunities between activity systems.

This chapter reports on twelve interviews about writing teams of at least one undergraduate, one university faculty or staff member, and one author who holds a deep affiliation with a community group that was central to the collaboration. Sometimes one author held more than one role, such as a former undergraduate who was also a community partner. Most interviewees were recruited through a search for published, coauthored work that featured this kind of authorship team, and some responded to an open call through a community engagement listserv, though some were recommended to us through other contacts. We received IRB approval to host one-hour, semi-structured individual Zoom interviews focused on academic and nonacademic writing projects, such as peer-reviewed articles, reports for nonprofit organizations, conference presentations, advocacy handouts for a city council meeting, and more. Some interviews were conducted by author Rachael Shah as part of a larger book project, and some interviews were co-facilitated with author Tina Le. Questions focused on walking through the writing process, discussing the dynamics among the authorship team, and offering advice for others involved in coauthorship. We transcribed the interview recordings and coded them in qualitative coding software Dedoose, and we coauthored this chapter, mostly while sitting across from one another and working live on Google Docs at a coffee shop.

The two of us are coauthoring as a former undergraduate turned community partner (Tina) and faculty member (Rachael). Rachael is a white, cisgender associate professor of English who studies community-based pedagogy, often publishing with coauthors from various positionalities (nonprofit staff, secondary teachers, local youth, undergraduates, and graduate students). Tina is a working-class, Vietnamese-American, first-generation college student who has worked for various nonprofit community organizations during and after college. Tina was an undergraduate in Rachael's courses, where community partnerships led Tina to become involved with an engagement program Rachael coordinates—first as researcher for her honors thesis, then as coauthor with Rachael for a Conference on College Composition and Communication presentation, next as member of the participatory evaluation team and eventually as community partner when she graduated and became a secondary teacher. She is now a graduate student in writing studies. In addition to reporting on the themes from interviews, we are informed by our own coauthorship experiences. In the process of coauthoring this chapter, we tried out and reflected upon collaborative practices we learned about from our interviewees, and our own reasons for coauthoring echo the arguments that emerged from the data.

The interview data and our own experiences lead us to our argument that success in community-engaged coauthorship between faculty and undergraduates is not necessarily publication or the direct public consequences of the text itself, although those can be part of it. We are redefining success in coauthorship as cultivating healthier collaborative relationships in boundary zones by attending to the writing process. For example, the interactions within the coauthorship process impact how undergraduates understand the ethics of community engagement and can encourage undergraduates toward, or dissuade them from, community engagement in the future as community partners, graduate students, or university faculty/staff.

To make the argument that the value of coauthorship in community engagement is rooted in the collaborative process rather than the textual product, we first discuss coauthored texts as "boundary objects" serving as bridges between sites. Then, we explore the experiences of authors—often undergraduates—who hold a complex role in the boundary zone: "boundary dwellers," our term for writers who are not only interacting across academic-community lines but who identify with both the university and the community involved in the partnership. Boundary dweller experiences foreground complex questions about blending knowledge across contexts, decolonization in community engagement, and the challenges of holding a both-and positionality on a writing team. Finally, we analyze how specific practices can contribute to healthier collaborations with boundary dwellers, as these practices shape partnerships and future trajectories. Thus, we will explore how the coauthoring process between undergraduates, faculty, and community partners can be a space to work for more equitable and transformative community engagement.

Boundary Objects in Coauthorship

Coauthorship across university-community and faculty-undergraduate lines exists in the complex intersection between multiple areas of practice. We suggest these coauthored texts can be understood as "boundary objects," which fulfill "a bridging function" across sites (Akkerman and Bakker 133). Akkerman and Bakker give examples of boundary objects such as a patient record in healthcare, which allows the patient and all medical providers to see a patient's health history, and a student teacher's portfolio, which allows the student teacher, cooperating teacher, and university supervisor to track growth. While these examples are not always publicly consequential, we can apply the same idea of "a bridging function" to collaboratively authored texts, and we are particularly interested in how different forms of knowledge are bridged through exchange or synthesis.

Several boundary object texts in our data functioned as exchange bridges, most commonly helping collaborators better understand each other's experience of their community partnership. One example arises from an interview with community partner Keira Wolfe, who coauthored an academic article with a faculty member and undergraduates about a pedagogical project that published oral histories from Keira's community. Keira noted that the publication itself did not impact her life, as an academic text like this "is not something that would even appear on the radar of people [in her professional world]," but when asked to identify positive aspects of the experience, she offered, "It's rewarding just to read how the students responded and to grasp what an effect this project had on them." The value of the text, for Keira as a community partner, rested more on its bridging function of exchange than on its published status.

Other coauthored boundary objects moved beyond exchanging insights to synthesizing them. We draw an example from interviewee Emily Crawley, a community organizer who coauthored an academic article with students and a faculty member about their reproductive justice work. Emily described the synthesis process, as they created new insight by combining their perspectives: the students spoke from their experiences as the ones who had initiated the partnership, she pulled in her community organizing frameworks to describe what the group had been doing, and the faculty member "would say 'well X, Y Z scholars actually explain what that is.'" In the blend of these perspectives, the writing team was able to build "a name and a structure" for their work, which was valuable "because we were just *doing* it." When asked about the value of this kind of collaborative authorship, Emily emphasized the opportunity to "make sense"—to *create meaning*–about community-based work, illustrating the potential of boundary objects to synthesize insights in powerful ways.

However, it is important to highlight that the bridging function of boundary objects can be fraught and even not fully possible. This messiness was evident in an interview with Madison Anderson, a BIPOC undergraduate alumna who coauthored an article with white scholars and a community partner. The team was striving for exchange and synthesis in long Zoom conversations about their perspectives and a collaborative Google Doc, but they ran into, as Madison put it, "deep-seated ideological differences." The team encountered disagreements about the nature of racism, as authors would question each other's addition—or omission—of the term. As Madison noted, these different perspectives were linked to stark differences in life experience, which is not easily packaged for exchange or synthesis. In other words, building boundary objects through coauthorship is no simple task. Richa Nagar, writing about collaborative authorship in community-based research and activism, suggests, "These are journeys enabled by trust with the ever-present possibility of distrust and epistemic violence . . . journeys that insist on crossing borders even as each person on the journey learns of borders that they cannot cross" (5–6). Marking the borders that coauthors cannot fully cross—as well as the boundaries that coauthors straddle—becomes critical to understanding coauthorship in community engagement. Anticipating or acknowledging these dynamics allows us to coauthor with the recognition that the process will not be clear-cut, and that there is value in dwelling in this complexity.

Undergraduates as Boundary Dwellers in Coauthorship

As engagement scholars have theorized, "boundary spanners" play a critical role in community engagement by negotiating power dynamics, representing multiple interests, sharing cultural knowledge, and establishing relationships

(Ross et al.; Weerts and Sandmann). Weerts and Sandmann, drawing on earlier work by Scott, define "boundary spanning" as the "bridge between an organization and its exchange partners" (634). They focus on university employees who form bridges with community partners, and who might not already have their feet in both academic and community worlds. They propose a boundary-spanning model with a "social closeness" continuum, which has a "community focused" end and an "institutionally focused" end; a boundary spanner's placement on that continuum depends on how much they are "integrated with the community or institution" (650).

While the model of boundary spanner has been very helpful, it does not center people who hold multiple roles simultaneously. We wonder about the people who are socially close to *both* a community and university. An example of this both-and position is evident in Blancato et al.'s study of the experiences of university instructors teaching community-engaged writing courses centering Black literacies. They find that the instructors who brokered relationships between their students and Black communities did so through "their personal and professional lives coming together" and their "situatedness within Black community spaces" (33). These boundary workers do not occupy just one point on Weerts and Sandmann's model; their positionalities as university instructors *and* community members lead to multiple roles at the same time.

To describe this position of identifying across the university and communities in a partnership, we use the term *boundary dwellers*. Boundary dwellers do not just interact across different areas of practice like boundary spanners do; they deeply identify with more than one of the communities in the collaboration—they dwell or *live* in the boundary. Boundary dwellers are important to understanding community-engaged coauthorship with undergraduates, because as we discovered in our interviews, undergraduates often played the role of boundary dwellers.

To help conceptualize boundary dwellers in coauthorship and the ways that "boundary dwelling" disrupts singular or separate definitions of community or academia, we draw from the interviewee Andromeda Shum. Andromeda became involved in a community partnership as an undergraduate in an Asian American studies course that partnered with a nonprofit devoted to mentoring Asian American Pacific Islander (AAPI) youth. After graduation, she became a staff member at that nonprofit, supporting the ongoing partnership. During that time, the faculty member invited her and other alumni to coauthor an article about the class. At the time of our interview, Andromeda was a graduate student. Andromeda talked about how she went through "different parts of my life as we were writing," which allowed her to contribute in different ways. From her academic perspective, she added to the theoretical framework. From her undergraduate perspective, she analyzed the impact of pedagogical practices. From her work as nonprofit staff, she explained the grant and program objectives that shaped the organization's involvement. From her experience as a member of the AAPI community, she wrote from "a certain level of understanding that we have just based on our own personal experience as being part of the community," even as she emphasized the *vast* diversity of that community. She saw the article and the partnership itself from all of these vantage points simultaneously.

Andromeda dwelled in the boundary rather than crossing it, and she reminds us of the multiple dimensions of "community" in community partnerships. She noted, for example, the presence of an undergraduate on the writing team who was formerly a youth mentored through the partnership, bringing experiential knowledge of community program participants instead of only nonprofit staff. Community is not monolithic or exclusive of academia, and to Andromeda, these multiple perspectives led to deeper understandings. Breaking apart the "university-community" dichotomy, Andromeda argued, "Just because I'm a student and I'm in an academic setting doesn't mean I'm no longer a part of this community. Like my community's my community, no matter where I go. And I'm a part of different communities." Andromeda's story illuminates that it is the blurriness in defining academia and community that can lead to generative ideas in the boundary zone.

One contribution boundary dwellers can make to authorship teams is to forward decolonizing efforts. Speaking as a boundary dweller, an Indigenous researcher who identifies with researched Indigenous communities, Linda Tuhiwai Smith invites others like her to use this position to resist colonial practices: "To resist is to retrench in the margins, retrieve what we were and remake ourselves" (4). Given their belonging in communities being written about, boundary dwellers can mitigate bias and push back against stereotypical or flat representations of communities, contributing toward this resistance. Interviewee Joua Lee, a health disparities researcher, offers an example. She held deep affiliations with a community being researched, and she collaborated on a team of academics, community researchers, and undergraduates on a report that turned into an academic piece. She explained that she was able to "catch the nuance" when gathering data and feedback from community members in their native language, integrate their voices "throughout the whole process," and help "community members and researchers understand each other" to ensure that her community is represented appropriately—an important safeguard given the ways that minoritized communities are often stigmatized for their health. We suggest these interventions were important for the undergraduates to witness as they learned the ethics of engaged research.

Boundary dwellers can help coauthored texts to be not only more ethical but more rhetorically effective. Interviewee Archer Thompson illustrates this point, as an undergraduate who coauthored reports with a staff member for his university's student voting campaign. Also having worked for his state's election commission off campus, Archer leveraged the expertise of his various identities to craft more effective texts. Archer explained the importance of his undergraduate identity, asserting that when universities only employ staff to work on voting registration, "those programs typically aren't as successful." Archer gathered input for his voting report from other undergraduates in spaces they were naturally in together: "When I was going out to meetings with other student leaders for things that weren't necessarily related to the report, I would always have a copy with me ... I would just ask them if there's anything that they saw that they wanted to have added to it." Archer's student experience also provided him a kairotic interpretation of factors impacting student voting, from how many students voted in the 2020 election but only filled out one box, to how undergraduates missed a year of social experiences. His student understanding impacted "how I co-wrote the report ... how we planned things ... how we did our actual work as an organization."

In addition to being an undergraduate, Archer's work at his state's election commission informed his coauthored texts. At the election commission office, he learned to vet public statements, given the need to avoid saying anything that could appear politically motivated. He brought this rhetorical awareness to the campus voting report, helping his coauthors be selective about "what should we be publicly stating, and what should we be putting in this report? What are the unintended effects of including something?" Because he worked with voter registration stipulations at the election commission, he was able to guide his campus voting organization on maximizing impact while staying within legal guidelines, constantly asking, "Is there anything that specifically says in [state] law that we can't do this?" During our Zoom interview, he proudly held up a hefty book of voting statutes he had received as a gift at the election commission and discussed how he referenced these statutes in the coauthored report, using his boundary-dweller positionality to blend knowledge from the campus and external site in the text.

While boundary dwellers reveal the benefits of identifying with multiple groups across university-community lines, it can be difficult to hold a multifaceted positionality. Archer described boundary dwelling as "a strange experience because you gotta keep track of your hats." Each "hat" comes with "traditions," "norms," and "confidentiality agreements" to honor. Sometimes these conflict: "I have to be conscious when I'm at the [campus] office that I can't talk about this, and I have to be conscious at the [community organization] office . . . I kept on getting into these things where these boundaries overlapped." For example, at the election commission, Archer was privy to confidential information about pending legislation on voting that would impact his campus role, and he had to steer the student voting group in light of these legislative changes without disclosing that information. As another example of boundary-dwelling conflicts, we return to Emily Crawley, the academic article coauthor who worked for a reproductive justice organization. Emily described how she had to be careful about what she wrote because "I had longer-standing relationships with folks at other organizations or non-profits . . . and I knew I would continue to work with them in the future," which required thoughtful attention to how these people were represented. As someone officially affiliated with the organization, Emily noted, "If you work in that field [of reproductive justice], anything that you write or you put out into the world, you can assume ends up in the inbox of the opposition . . . I had some concerns about how much do I write, what kind of detail do I use?" Emily, along with the undergraduate coauthors who were interning with her organization, had to face the people and the political risks involved with the community organization in an immediate way. Being a boundary dweller entails being deeply beholden to relationships, responsibilities, and political dynamics outside of academia, and these ties to the community that is being represented in the piece can make coauthorship fraught.

A related challenge boundary dwellers face is that their multifaceted identity is not always accepted. Health disparities researcher Joua, introduced earlier, explained about her coauthoring process: "Folks in academia, depending on what is convenient for them, it seems like they would associate me with one more than the other [community member or academic], whereas I see myself as really a mixture of both." Similar to Joua, voting report author Archer experienced being pigeonholed into his identity as an undergraduate, rather than also his role as staff at the election commission office or leader of a voting organization. Some people in election offices assumed his writing was for a class: "You either get welcomed, or you get that like, 'Oh, that's wonderful, we're glad to see you doing this research project. It's great to see young people getting involved.' You get actually welcomed, or you get condescended." It was difficult for Archer's identity as a political leader to be honored because of the power dynamics, which he described as "a 19 year old playing in the field of a 63 year old election official, where I'm punching above my weight class." As a boundary dweller, Archer had to establish his role as more expansive than just a student, from contributing to high-level conversations about voting in the state to editing grammar issues in his university staff coauthor's sections of the draft.

It can be especially difficult to negotiate boundary dwellers' roles in light of differences in power and reward structures across contexts. While faculty may have dedicated research time and merit reviews that reward publications, offsetting the additional time needed to coauthor, the stakes may be different for undergraduate boundary dwellers, even while they may feel obligated to agree when they are invited to coauthor with faculty. Offering an example is interviewee Brian Johnson, a staff member at a university engagement office, who described initiating a coauthored article with a faculty member and a former undergraduate who worked full-time at a nonprofit. Brian reflected, "She was the student body president at the same time that she was working for me [in the engagement office], so I both advised and supervised her during her senior year. So we are very close, and in retrospect, I would be concerned that those power dynamics would coerce her to participate in the project more than I think I understood at the time." These dynamics may be important given that, as he acknowledged, this coauthor was incredibly busy at her nonprofit and may not receive professional rewards for publishing. Boundary dwellers often pursue coauthorship while wearing "hats" other than academic researcher. Undergraduates' boundary dweller positionalities often supported boundary-spanning efforts and held great epistemological promise, but this position was also challenging to hold, calling for careful attention to the coauthoring process.

Coauthoring Processes in the Boundary Zone

Attending to the coauthoring *process* with undergraduates can help teams move toward decolonizing community engagement and creating a pipeline of boundary dwellers and spanners committed to community engagement. In this section, we showcase examples of practices in our interviewees' writing processes, which we hope helps readers look for opportunities in their own coauthorship experiences.

Relationality is one key aspect of coauthorship across difference. Madison Anderson, the BIPOC undergraduate who struggled to write an academic article with white scholars, pointed to the lack of personal relationships as a factor that contributed to challenges. Undergraduate interviewee Elizabeth O'Connor similarly highlighted the significance of relationship-building as she described coauthoring an academic article with a faculty member and a community partner: "We would talk for solid 20 to 30 minute periods of time at the beginning of every meeting just checking in and talking to each other about our lives." As she identified, this relational practice mitigated the sense of power imbalances between herself as an undergrad and her faculty and nonprofit coauthors. In fact, when asked what she learned from her coauthorship experience, she turned not to academic skills but instead shared that she "learned a lot from [her coauthors] about the relationality of community partnerships and coauthoring," which she said continues to shape her community engagement. Given the complex power dynamics from which boundary dwellers write, relational practices help build interpersonal connections needed for healthy collaborations. When these relational practices are in place, undergraduates like Elizabeth notice, and they carry these practices forward into future work.

A second aspect of the writing process that interviewees discussed was how different kinds of expertise were honored. Reproductive rights organizer Emily, introduced earlier, described how the epistemic dynamics that are critical to community organizing also appear in coauthorship. When she was organizing stakeholders to testify at a city council meeting, she recruited voices from different positionalities and drew arrows on the proposed ordinance to pinpoint where different people's expertise was critical. She offered encouragement like, "I have a lawyer from the National Institute of Reproductive Health here [to testify as well], but you live here, and you've lived here for 30 years, and you know this community." Emily noted that the faculty coauthor played a similar role in the article coauthorship, highlighting the expertise of the undergraduates and community partner and suggesting how their insights could be detailed in the article. As Emily suggested, balancing the epistemological hierarchies in coauthorship and in larger coalitional work "is the hardest part, because people stay quiet if they don't feel good."

Ensuring that different forms of expertise are valued informs authorship tasks. Returning to our discussion of how boundary objects can bridge through exchange or synthesis, we first address epistemological dynamics focused on *exchange*, when each participant is honored for their individual insights, and discuss how these dynamics may impact choices about writing structure. For example, community partner interviewee Justice Blazer noted that having her own section in an academic article coauthored with faculty and undergraduates was one way to mirror her contributions to the larger partnership. She explained that she initiated the partnership—a collaboration between university students and older residents to compose narratives about a racial event in the city—so it was appropriate that she have a direct voice in telling the story, with her name credited as author. A Black woman herself, Justice reflected, "It makes me think about that movie *Hidden Figures* about the Black women, and they were that important and no one ever said anything. I kind of feel that sometimes. I just wanted to have some ownership of what I kind of got going." Given that certain forms of expertise are often silenced or hidden, writing processes can contribute toward more equitable dynamics in community engagement—even as the need for ownership must be balanced with time constraints, different reward structures, and concerns about labor. The fact that Justice had her own section was important modeling for the undergraduates on the authorship team about how to engage community knowledge.

While Justice's story illustrates how boundary objects that bridge through exchange are important in certain situations, coauthoring can also provide opportunities for synthesis. College faculty may be less familiar with approaches for *how to* write toward collaborative synthesis, as the process is less clear-cut than assigning sections of a draft, so we highlight examples:

- **SKETCHNOTES:** Undergraduate interviewee Danielle described a process her writing group termed "sketchnotes," which involved the authors prompting each other with questions and then one author writing down words that captured the discussion in real time. Then, the group would color-code these words to combine them into themes for the article. The group was "coding our conversations" to facilitate synthesis.
- **CO-INTERVIEWS:** Danielle's writing team recorded conversational interviews with each other, as some authors were also boundary dwellers who had first-hand experience with the article topic. This practice allowed the oral blending of author insights to shape the piece.
- **WRITTEN REFLECTIONS AS BASIS FOR DISCUSSION:** Andromeda, the alumna who coauthored the article about the AAPI mentoring partnership, described how her writing team wrote reflections based on prompts determined by the faculty member or the group. Brainstorming for the article began with reading these reflections, moving the group from individual to collective insights.

- **VISUAL MODELS:** Andromeda's group worked together to design a figure—a collection of words, circles, and arrows—that encapsulated their argument. Andromeda started sketching this image during one of the discussions, and the faculty member refined it with feedback.

The undergraduates on authorship teams that featured synthesis—and notably, all of these teams included boundary dwellers—had the powerful experience of seeing their insights transformed across university-community and faculty-undergraduate lines into something new. While not an exhaustive list, each of these practices can facilitate the combination of different types of knowledge into collective insights. Decisions about which synthesis practices to use or create (along with the question about whether exchange or synthesis bridging is the goal) can be negotiated by authorship teams, as these decisions are contextual. These decisions are critical to shaping an authorship team and a community partnership—in addition to shaping the undergraduates who learn from this process.

Developing Boundary Spanners Through Coauthorship

Coauthorship in community engagement calls for shifting our attention from the text itself to its "bridging function," as it brings together different knowledges across boundaries. The value of coauthorship may sometimes lie in how this bridge is built, as coauthorship can become an opportunity to strengthen relationships, come to new understandings about a partnership, lay the groundwork for future collaborations, and—especially important for undergraduates—cultivate boundary dwellers holding deep affiliations with both academia and communities who can host engagement collaborations. Faculty interviewee Nathaniel Carda, who regularly coauthors academic and public texts on citizen science, emphasized the need to change academia by building a "pipeline" of community-engaged scholars that starts with undergraduates, helping students heal the "disconnect between . . . what they can do in 'the Academy' versus what they actually care about outside." By inviting undergraduates into the boundary through coauthorship, these emerging scholars can build a scholarly identity centered on the boundary.

Through their "bridging function," coauthored texts can serve to bridge these lines in both directions. For example, undergraduates who have deep connections to community groups can strengthen their academic identities. Alumna Andromeda Shum followed this path, as the invitation from her former professor to collaborate while she was a nonprofit worker at the AAPI organization served as a "gateway" into academia. She was "terrified" of grad school, but the collaboration helped her understand that her community experience could "translate into the academic world and vice versa." Andromeda gained this understanding through the coauthorship process, as the article synthesized her experiential and academic insights, helping her reimagine the nature of knowledge at the intersection of academia and community.

The bridging function works in the other direction, too: undergraduates at home in academic spaces can build community affiliations. Undergraduate interviewee Danielle began her coauthored article about a specific group of protesters with no on-the-ground experience protesting. Yet throughout the writing process, "I felt like I was missing out on something that I cared about, and I was like, all these people, I get why they're doing it, why have I not been here the whole time?" Since the article, she has participated in multiple protests on this issue. Coauthoring an academic article with two boundary dwellers in that activist community helped Danielle step into this boundary dweller positionality herself—and, as she noted, this experience was a deciding factor in whether to apply to graduate school. In short, Andromeda and Danielle composed their boundary dweller positionality through coauthorship. As a boundary object, a coauthored text in community engagement can pull people from different areas into a space defined by the boundary, and this text can help them imagine future opportunities at this boundary.

It is in this bridging potential that we—Tina and Rachael—see noteworthy value in coauthorship. This book chapter contributes to our ongoing identity development as engaged scholars. Tina experienced this coauthorship process as a boundary dweller: this chapter began when Tina was a community partner, and we submit it as she is a graduate student. Rachael began this chapter as the first dive into her new research on collaborative writing post-tenure, and this experience has been formative in developing concepts that will be featured in that project. Coauthoring has illuminated practices to add to our toolbox for community collaborations. For example, we used our Google Doc for metaconversations, corresponding in different font colors—in what we once joked was an instant-messenger style—to synthesize our unformed thoughts, learning about how to have messy metadialogue about a piece. We have also used some of the open-ended writing strategies we learned from these interviews, such as Sketchnotes, in our other collaborations. The way we honored messiness in our drafting shows the potential of using boundary objects to synthesize knowledge across role, context, and positionality. Some people might focus on this chapter in its final form, but what matters most to us is the process of its creation. As we have argued and experienced, success in coauthoring expands beyond publication to the cultivation of healthier collaborations.

Works Cited

Akkerman, Sanne F., and Arthur Bakker. "Boundary Crossing and Boundary Objects." *Review of Educational Research*, vol. 81, no. 2, June 2011, pp. 132–69. https://doi.org/10.3102/0034654311404435.

Blancato, Michael, Gavin P. Johnson, Beverly J. Moss, and Sara Wilder. "Brokering Community-Engaged Writing Pedagogies: Instructors Imagining and Negotiating Race, Space, and Literacy." *Literacy in Composition Studies*, vol. 9, no. 1, 2022, pp. 23–46.

Nagar, Richa. *Muddying the Waters: Coauthoring Feminisms Across Scholarship and Activism*. U of Illinois P, 2014.

Ross, Laurie, Katie Byrne, and Jennifer Safford. "Navigating the Boundaries of Youth Violence Prevention and Reduction: Reflections on Power in Community Engaged Scholarship." *Gateways: International Journal of Community Research and Engagement*, vol. 14, no. 2, 2021, pp. 1–12.

Smith, Linda Tuhiwai. *Decolonizing Methodologies: Research and Indigenous Peoples*. 3rd ed., Bloomsbury Academic, 2022.

Weerts, David J., and Lorilee Sandmann. "Community Engagement and Boundary-Spanning Roles at Research Universities." *The Journal of Higher Education*, vol. 81, no. 6, 2010, pp. 632–57.

SECTION II

Models and Methods of Coauthoring

5
Nested Coauthorship

A Framework for Building Productive Undergraduate Research Experiences

TERESA CONTINO, ISABELLA GOMEZ,
LEAH SENATRO, AND AMY LUECK

Picture a nest tucked high in the branches of an apple tree. Twigs and grasses jut out unevenly in places, leading out and away in different directions, but still collectively curve together to form a rounded shape that will, however provisionally, protect an egg.

A bird's nest is built over time with woven layers of diverse materials, suggesting the long process of nest-building as much as the nest itself. Constructed of materials found in the area, it is an adaptable, creative, and even makeshift structure and process, but also one full of intent. Its purpose is to provide a space of safety, nurturing, and growth, as well as connection and relationship.

We have much to learn from nests.

Our chapter uses the image of the nest to describe our experiences of coauthoring. Taking our cue from the birds who innovated the practice, our nested coauthoring practice seeks to describe a durative process built collaboratively from diverse experiences and resources, sometimes as an ad hoc structure, to support the growth of ideas and relationships. If the tree in our metaphor represents the university campus where we met, the nest represents the infrastructure we have created as coauthors. In this chapter, we describe the process of building the nest, and theorize the nest itself as a metaphor for coauthoring. In so doing, we not only theorize what nested coauthored projects are and can be, but also enact such authorship practices by building out yet another layer of engagement in our own nest. As coauthors, we are building that layer in this very moment, as we type. As you read.

We use this space to show the ways that nested mentorship relationships and coauthorship experiences can maximize what is already considered, in relation to undergraduate research, a high-impact practice, and create "consequential publicness" (Downs et al.) for writers. For coauthors, writing that enacts consequential publicness helps knowledge work reach "interested publics," which could include campus community members as well as online or local community groups beyond academia (Downs et al. 94–95). By embracing writing as a public act that is "thoroughly hermeneutic, and always situated" as well as irreducible (Olson 5), we value the varied, and often serendipitous, paths that create such projects and opportunities on college campuses.

Our approach to this topic is three-pronged. First, we use meta-cognitive reflection to visualize and narrativize our individual experiences, showcasing the ways that our relationships have built out from curricular and extracurricular opportunities. From our written reflections, we visualize nested diagrams that showcase the ways that our coauthorship experiences were defined by their status as meta-cognitive moments. Thus, we also showcase the intrinsic value that meta-cognitive work during coauthorship proved to have for each student beyond the scope of the original learning experience, facilitating coauthorship opportunities.

Second, we build a theoretical definition of nested coauthorship from the material in our reflections. By beginning first with our personal experience, rather than a theoretical framework, we emphasize the value of situated knowledge and also acknowledge our own positionality as scholars at a particular institution with particular privileges and opportunities. Though such opportunities may vary across institutions, we feel that telling our stories and identifying both consistencies and inconsistencies between them will help more clearly articulate what worked for us, and what may work for others. By beginning with our personal stories, we are employing a feminist epistemology (Royster and Kirsch) that values our experiences as scholars at different positions in the academic community. Additionally, such a move revalues student knowledge within the academic community as sophisticated and publishable (Waite). When we value such knowledge, we work to reproduce it—making way for experiences of "consequential publicness" (Downs et al.). While our nest-making and relationship-building has created a feminist infrastructure that privileges individual perspective and story, such a practice is not limited to gender or feminine expression, just as both sexes of birds often create nests.

Third, because it is our hope that we can encourage student-faculty collaboration on undergraduate research as a "high-impact practice" (American Association of Colleges & Universities) fostering "legitimate peripheral participation" for students with a range of academic and professional interests and goals (Lave and Wenger), we offer pragmatic approaches for individual instructors, departments, and undergraduate research programs to foster such "nested" relationships and maximize the benefits of "mutual mentorship" (DelliCarpini; FitzGerald; Moore et al. 30–31) by imagining classroom work as "unfinished" and overlapping and embracing iterative projects.

Articulating nested coauthorship and the varied connectivity, engagement, and scholarship such relationships can foster is significant for undergraduate research because it promotes mentorship and situates academic knowledge in the minds of both students and faculty members, drawing on meta-cognitive/reflective values to envision and enact a collaborative pedagogy that emphasizes the iterative and situated process of writing. Mentorship is pedagogical, but, with nested coauthorship, authorship is also revealed to be pedagogical. We argue that pedagogical, consequential, and engaging authorial relationships are best understood as a process that can empower students and faculty members to create new, publishable knowledge at the university level, enacting consequential publicness and revaluing student knowledge and scholarship.

Studying Our Own Nests: Methods and Methodology

We begin here by describing our own nests. On the one hand, we conceptualize the nest as a spatial metaphor—describing the relationship between multiple discrete experiences, accumulating like layers of sediment, from the inside outward in concentric circles as we confronted new pedagogical and intellectual experiences together. On the other hand, a temporal metaphor of nesting emphasizes the process of nest-building as relationship-building in ways critical to our approach. Understanding nested coauthoring as more of a process than an outcome, we each composed a brief reflection narrating and contextualizing our coauthoring experiences. We began with the following questions, which all four coauthors answered:

- What engagements/experiences led up to your opportunity to coauthor together? That is, what is your account of how we came to develop an

idea worth writing about together? Were there structures that seemed to facilitate getting to that point (courses, specific assignments, fellowships, disciplinary questions, etc.)? What were the barriers?
- What motivated you to take on that opportunity? What did you expect to get out of it?
- What *did* you get out of it? How have you seen value from the experience in how you think/write elsewhere in your life, or in terms of how that experience has "counted" for you professionally (on a resume, etc).?

These reflections are represented below as a polyvocal weave of narratives meant to convey the layered entanglements that led to coauthorship. Drawing on mobility studies scholars who understand spatio-temporal movement as central to conceptualizing literacy practices (Nordquist), we have come to recognize that durative, processual, embodied process as key to what we seek to describe. We also draw on Indigenous scholars to see the centrality of story and relationality modeled by the nest itself (Riley-Mukavetz; King; Wilson). These scholars help to illuminate the importance of our own relationships to one another and to conditions around us as crucial intellectual resources in all research, including coauthorship. Further, they emphasize the importance of story as a method for representing those relationships and conditions. We represent this storied, relational aspect of our methodology by relying on narrative reflection as data to capture the story of nesting over time. From there, we analyze themes that emerged from these stories, and close with recommendations for others considering coauthoring.

Stories of Nesting: Woven Narrative Strands

In what follows, we share our own experiences of nested coauthorship, from which we derive our key insights about the durative, iterative nature of this process. While there are complex and multiple threads of connection between us, the overall structure of activities and relationships is usefully represented by identifying the major project on which each student was most recently working with Amy, the faculty mentor: Leah and Amy currently have an article forthcoming in *Composition Studies* about undergraduate research that reflects on their experience as a mentorship pair during Leah's senior year at Santa Clara University. Teresa and Amy published an article in *Kairos* about their experience creating a born-digital an(ti)thology project in a course on women writers. Isabella worked on a year-long internship to develop a youth cultural camp for members of her tribe and wrote an article about the experience that was published in *College Composition and Communication*. While Amy previously had relationships with each student, Leah, Teresa, and Isabella did not meet until they began coauthoring this chapter.

Before sharing the narratives that led to these publication opportunities, we begin here with visualizations of these experiences that provide a bird's-eye view of Leah's, Teresa's, and Isabella's nested mentoring experiences. These represent experiences of being mentored by Amy across a range of experiences, leading to a coauthored publication and then, ultimately, to being mentored by one another in the present work. The innermost part of the circle represents each student's initial research interests—the burrow of the nest. The surrounding words indicate students' changing roles as their research expands outward into various contexts. To showcase the process-based road to authorship, the visualization does not have firm boundaries. Instead, each extraneous layer builds upon one another circularly without a defined hierarchical ranking of each stage or role. Though separated visually, each student's individual nest shares twigs and overlaps with each other's nest in this project as we continue to learn about one another's research and coauthoring experiences.

As these visualizations illustrate, nested coauthorship does not *have* to begin or end in the classroom. While Leah's (figure 5.1) and Teresa's (figure 5.2) experiences share much in common in being grounded in an initial curricular experience, our fourth coauthor—Isabella—joined us as a collaborator not through the classroom but through community collaboration (figure 5.3). Though Isabella was not an undergraduate student at the time of drafting this chapter, she was an aspiring one with important connections and contributions to make to academic writing at the university level, and deep connections to Santa Clara University's campus through her tribal identity as Muwekma Ohlone, tracing her ancestry to this land and the Spanish mission that came to occupy it (muwekma.org). Including Isabella's experiences of coauthorship in our analysis challenges our perspective of "undergraduate research" in a generative way, extending the boundaries beyond "undergraduates" and exemplifying additional ways in which our resulting publications can enact "consequential publicness" on and off our campuses.

Additionally, incorporating community branches—like Isabella's—into our nest of coauthorship enacts an opportunity for, to borrow Aja Martinez's term, a counterstory narrative that may challenge, support, or complicate

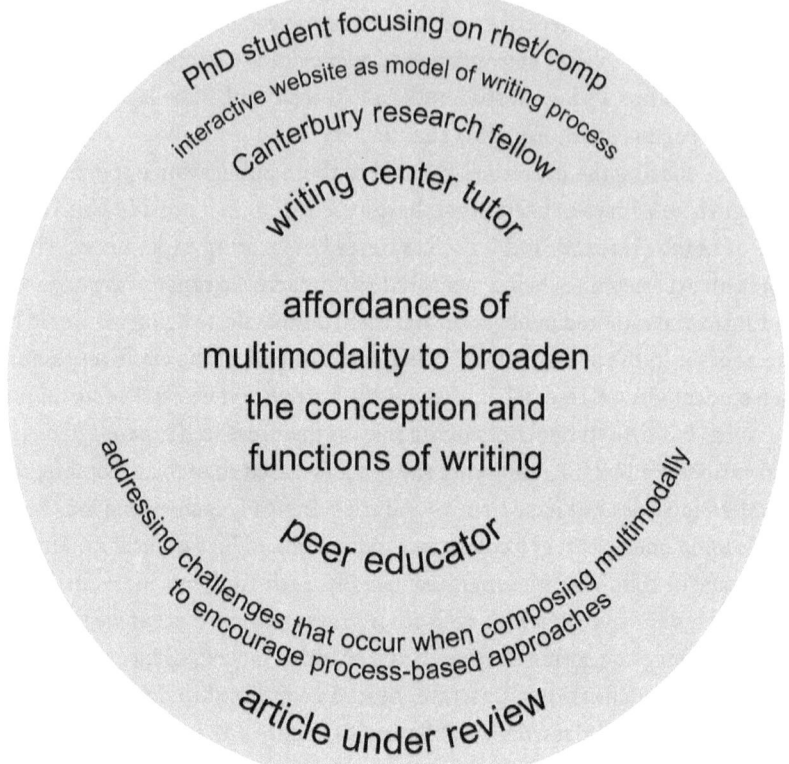

FIGURE 5.1. Leah

the academy's narratives surrounding authorship and writing. Such stories complicate the university campus's role in community writing projects and elucidate historical relationships between the community and the campus, challenging the typical knowledge domains.[1]

Across these examples, intellectual relationships were extended outside of the classroom to provide moments of reflection, metacognition, and portfolio-building. As students step into the roles of teacher assistants, mentees, research assistants, conference presenters, and coauthors, they determine their personal and disciplinary interests, which shift according to the project's goals and audiences, and they create knowledge that can be shared via coauthoring. Below, our polyvocal reflection illustrates our individual—and collective—experiences stepping into these roles together. In what follows, we use our stories to build another version of this nest together.

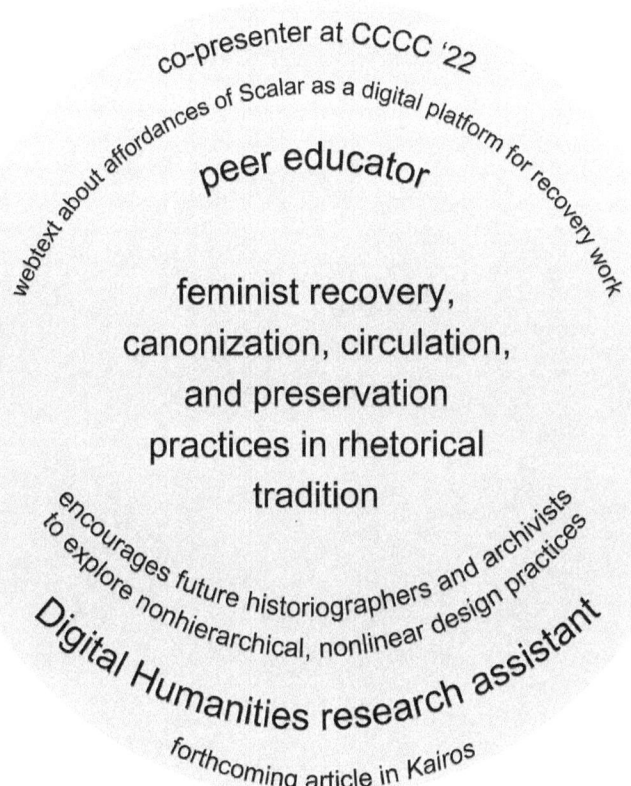

FIGURE 5.2. Teresa

Isabella

When I think of Santa Clara University's campus, I think about my mom and aunt's dedication to preserving our Tribal cultural legacy. I have frequently attended ethnohistory lectures at Santa Clara University where my aunt and mom have spoken. After the lecture, I'd stand hugging my mom's arm, listening in on her conversations with the people who came up to her, either congratulating her or asking her more detailed questions about the presentation. This campus context is where I met and started working with Amy.

Leah

I first met Amy, and the field of writing studies, in English 16, Introduction to Writing Studies, as a sophomore in college. In a lot of ways, the course structure itself facilitated a strong student-teacher relationship. Weekly exploratory writing assignments asked us to reflect on our own relationships to writing, which facilitated connections with other students and with

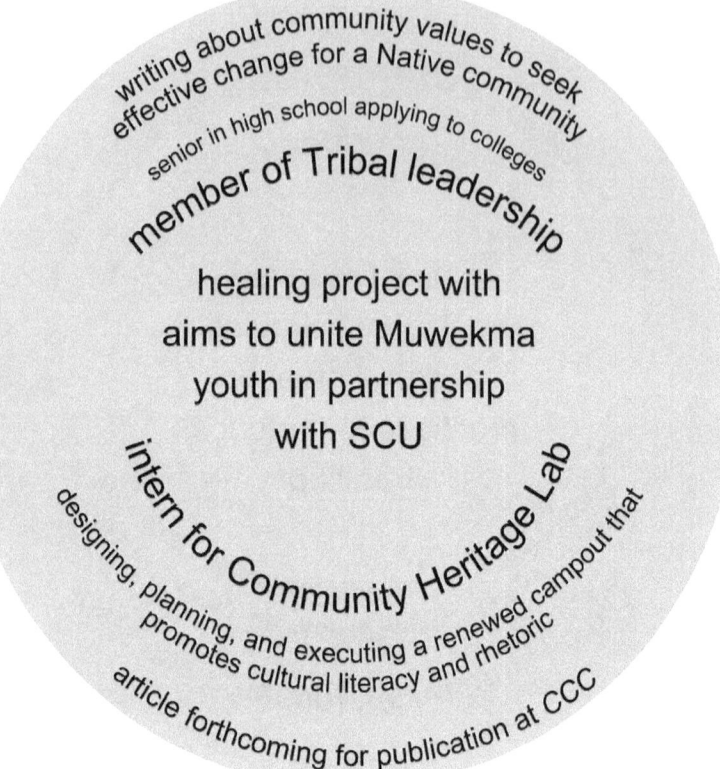

FIGURE 5.3. Isabella

Amy. After writing, talking, and thinking about writing for a quarter, I was excited to do more work in the field.

Teresa
As an English major, I felt drawn to my first-year writing course series with Amy, which relied on collaborative exercises and close reading to explore the meaning of writing and rhetorical knowledge. Toward the end of the first course in the series, we created e-portfolios that represented data of our cognitive habits as readers and writers. I began to appreciate the reflective power of writing and the possibilities of technical communication through website construction. Amy promoted self-reflection so we, as first-year students, felt confident to not give up on the immersive and sometimes messy process of research.

Isabella
I met Amy through my Tribe, the Muwekma Ohlone Tribe of the San Francisco Bay Area.[2] Amy worked with my mom and other leaders of my Tribe on a community-engaged project at the university, and expressed interest in working with youth. We had a Zoom meeting and I answered questions about my professional goals, personal strengths, growth areas, and goals related to Muwekma Ohlone youth. I elaborated on my desire for fellow youth to be able to do more activities with each other. I mentioned how our Tribe used to have cultural campouts, which became our first project.

AMY: My first time coauthoring with undergraduate students was a direct response to a problem I faced in my pedagogy. A student's interest in researching the history of the Tribes indigenous to our campus lands revealed the limitations of both the archival research assignment I had designed for my first-year writing course and my institution's archives. I didn't have a great solution for the student at the time, but I invited her and a friend to join me after the course ended to think more about the issue she had raised, which became a conference presentation and eventual publication (Lueck, Law, and Zhang). This is how other coauthoring experiences have begun as well: with unfinished business that students and I want to keep thinking through and working on together. And that project led me to conversations with campus and Ohlone collaborators that led to other community-based projects and ultimately to my meeting Isabella.

Leah
While I was preparing to be a writing center tutor, Amy asked if I would be interested in being a Peer Educator for English 16. I was so excited to return to my favorite course! While Amy was a mentor to me as the instructor when I took the class, her mentorship became more involved as our relationship grew and she advised me not only on the content of the course, but also on pedagogical approaches that I could transfer to the writing center. Amy was also very generous with her time and was open to my thoughts and ideas about the course, which gave me confidence to help support my peers.

Teresa
I became Amy's peer educator for the first-year writing class, where I was able to reencounter the class lessons on writing as a social, iterative process that requires metacognition, concentration, and time. I worked with students one-on-one to brainstorm essays and research proposals. Additionally, my work with Amy has blended into intellectual engagement with other classes.

LEAH: Amy helped me learn what it means to be a teacher, a researcher, and a writer in the field of rhetoric and composition. Each opportunity I had to work with her as an undergraduate helped provide a nested curriculum to my coursework that helped me learn what it means to work in academia and in the field of rhetoric and composition.

Amy

Isabella and I decided to revive her Tribe's cultural campout together as part of her internship. Our work for the campout involved grant writing, program development, project management, and work with other genres that enabled Isabella to see how her advocacy work for her Tribe transforms across contexts. When we decided to then reflect on this process for a special issue of *College Composition and Communication*, that provided another layer of metacognitive engagement and learning for us both, as well as a new context and genre to explore in her Tribal advocacy work.

> ISABELLA: This exact concept of twisting affliction from history into sprouting forms of healing is what I ultimately knew would be worth engaging my time in.

Leah

I took the ideas I developed as a student and peer educator in English 16 and applied to the Canterbury Fellowship, a research fellowship available for senior English majors, with Amy as my formal mentor. Around the same time, Amy invited me to copyedit her book manuscript. After Amy's mentorship and guidance around teaching, I received guidance about writing from her *while* also reading her writing and learning about her research as a scholar.

> TERESA: The co-nested student-professor experiences themselves are examples of how writing is a reflective and metacognitive process through conversation. From these experiences, Amy helped me to grow an applied understanding of composition and rhetoric.

Teresa

I enrolled in Amy's class Women Writers and Writing, which examined the preservation and circulation processes of underrepresented voices in the Santa Clara Archives. Soon after the course, Amy asked if I would like to help in the creation of a web text titled "Composing Collaborative Feminist Recovery Projects with Scalar," which was published in *Kairos: A Journal of Rhetoric, Technology, and Pedagogy*. Our project outlines the feminist goals and processes of creating an online anthology of recovered women's writing and guides future historiographers to organize archival work with nonlinear free-form design practices.

> LEAH: A key component to our relationship as student-teacher, mentor-mentee, and coauthors has been the link between the content and form of what we are doing. Just like our relationship began in a class

designed to talk about writing, we have pursued similar ideas in different forms ever since.

Isabella
Writing about the cultural campout allowed me to address the different viewpoints I hold in regards to both the intricacy of my people and culture and the aspects of our peoples' plight in the past and present. Morphing both the educational aspect of writing and the cultural viewpoints from my Tribe is what ultimately makes this project fulfilling. The cultural rhetorics within our project do not neglect the different ways we are able to maintain culture for our youth. Instead, they highlight the importance of maintaining cultural legacy so that it never becomes dormant.

> AMY: Through her internship relationship, Isabella and I engage in the professional practice of research, planning and composing documentation for the campout in a mutually educating way, with Isabella providing the expertise as both a youth and member of Muwekma, and myself providing the professional and bureaucratic experience to translate our vision for funders and the university.

Teresa
Our project outlines the feminist goals and processes of creating an online anthology of recovered women's writing and guides future historiographers to organize archival work with nonlinear free-form design practices. Amy guided us in developing the project according to its changing modality, audiences, and goals, as it emerged from the classroom into the atmosphere of publication. Included in the process of revision with the reviewers, I felt empowered as a student-author to follow my interdisciplinary interests in composition, technology, and rhetoric.

Isabella
Because of our focus to twist justice back into the hands of our people, members of my Tribe sometimes don't have time to focus on other matters. This is why I view this community-engaged project with fondness and appreciation. Because being able to help my community with a Native lens of merit is something with immense value.

Teresa
Amy and I virtually copresented our work at the Conference on College Composition and Communication, again shifting our tone and presentation to cater to the pedagogical interests of the audience. As I continue to draft our web text, I am regularly referring back to readings, discussion posts, and notes from Women Writers and Writing. My work from the course lives on in the context of the current project.

AMY: Coauthorship allows me to engage students in a meaningful reflective practice, acknowledging the labor and expertise they contribute to these processes through their feedback and empowering them to further theorize their experiences in conversation with me, if they choose. But it does not happen all at once. It happens over time and in stages of reflection and relationship-building that we are conceptualizing as nested coauthorship, with the nesting indicating layers of engagement and shared reflection that accumulate around an initial course or research experience, leading eventually to coauthorship and publication. only through this durative process, which is often obscured or entirely invisible in the final product.

Leah
After graduating, Amy and I transformed our experience working on the Canterbury Fellowship into an article on undergraduate research, which is currently under review. Now, my mentor is also my coauthor. Amy introduced me to the publication process while going through the process herself. She provided me with genre models for query letters and abstracts, and she helped me learn what counts as a publishable piece of writing. I learned how to do the work, by doing the work alongside Amy.

TERESA: The layered research experiences of coauthoring have provided me with opportunities to enrich my learning of the course material: collaboration inherent in the writing process, digital archive work in contemporary contexts, flexibility as a key habit of mind, and the significance of metacognition for revision. Thus, coauthoring has materialized the course curriculum into ongoing disciplinary acts, empowering my role as a student to embody a capable writer and researcher.

Isabella
Working with a university shifted my views about different ways professionalism can unfold when seeking effective change for a Native community. I have learned how to leverage my writing by incorporating culture and experiences, with the end product being the ability to highlight community values. One way I have done this is by beginning our *College Composition and Communication* article with our Tribal land acknowledgement. By acknowledging the land that my people have tended to and built memories on since time immemorial, I acknowledge how this same land should be a space where my people are able to thrive in any manner, especially in higher education.

Analysis: Parts and Patterns

Both Leah and Teresa tell a somewhat familiar story for academic mentorship on a university campus—each student first met Amy in a classroom setting that helped them initiate their research. After that course ended, the range of interactions that constituted their nested coauthoring experiences invited them to engage in academic conversations beyond the syllabus with different social norms and expectations. In Isabella's experience, her engagement was always outside the classroom and public facing, but what makes her relationship with Amy reflective of nested mentorship are the ways in which she similarly used metacognition and reflection to build on an initial point of contact and extend her thinking through academic inquiry and coauthorship. Reciprocal and repeated growth emerges as a pattern in all three of these experiences.

The concept of nested coauthorship helps illuminate the mechanisms by which one might build from students' initial research interests, scaffold further reading and writing opportunities, and keep the scholarly dialogue going while also providing professionalization opportunities. Amy invited each student into the process of research and provided support for them to pursue their curiosities in community with her. Coauthoring between students and professors enables each person to engage in reflection with thoughtful dialogue and listening, revisit past intellectual labor, and expand their knowledge. Placed in unfamiliar contexts, each student stepped into the role of a coauthor, challenged and encouraged to cultivate their unconscious competence for writing through mutual mentorship. And the resulting publications can benefit both the students and the faculty member, who is advancing her own research program through these projects as well.

Cultivating a wide set of knowledges and writing practices through this process serves a critical function in a range of disciplines and contexts (Estrem 56). For example, as Teresa learned about the goals and challenges of feminist anthologization practices, she also practiced building a website on Scalar with Amy. Coauthoring solidifies various course curricula into a series of ongoing disciplinary acts, empowering students to embody capable writers, researchers, and activists. Discourse in one context fosters deeper understanding in a seemingly different context through generative, iterative processes. Thus, similar to disciplinary boundaries that "can sometimes be quite fluid" and how writing itself is a "way of enacting disciplinarity," discourse communities and contexts are fluid too (Lerner 41). Moving across contexts together, student and faculty coauthors are afforded an opportunity to reflect on these boundaries and their crossing.

Similarly, Isabella was able to see her tribal activism take new forms through academic coauthorship and collaboration that encouraged professionalization. Her experience coauthoring a grant for the campout with Amy enabled her to examine structures of power and use writing to engage with them. She also designed the camp content, facilitated the program, and shared the camp with various administrative audiences. The coauthored academic article that followed provided the opportunity to reflect on the complexity of these rhetorical processes she had engaged.

Now, as we reflect on past projects by virtue of our current project—this chapter—we are adding a new layer of meta-cognitive reflection and relationship to our nesting practice. The nest we are constructing together here uses and reconfigures the twigs and sticks of each of our individual nests to build something new—not just a new publication, but a new series of relationships and knowledge practices. This durative, collaborative, and impactful process has helped us develop as writers and scholars and has also given us a way to tell our stories of pedagogy, learning, and growth.

Conclusion: A How-To for Building Nests

Reflecting back yet again on the experiences we've had together in order to infer disciplinary insights has built out yet another layer to our nests that supports a rich learning community. We encourage other faculty, students, and community participants—or, more simply, all writers—with university ties to embrace nested opportunities for mentorship and coauthorship by:

1. thinking about ways to continue "unfinished business" after a class or community-engaged project concludes;
2. embracing mentor-student relationship overlap across contexts and projects as a way to fuel writing relationships and ideas; and
3. actively engaging in reflective practices throughout writing, not only as a way to build intellectual relationships or produce writing projects, but as a way to theoretically inform such work.

Looking for the overlap between the classroom, external research projects, and relationships, we can see the underlying nest that can foster collaborative writing and coauthoring opportunities.

Additionally, while the writing and publication processes were of intrinsic value professionally and academically to Isabella, Leah, and Teresa, it is worth noting that the students were also compensated monetarily or in the form of academic credit for their work through Santa Clara University, and we want to suggest that funding be considered as the foundational branch that supports the nested relationships that lead to coauthoring. We understand that this is not always possible and still believe in the value of coauthorship as an extension of undergraduate research as being incredibly beneficial to students. At the same time, we also argue that it is crucial to try to support student work materially and suggest that the concept of nested coauthoring can help faculty identify funding possibilities by reimagining the position of student researcher (for which many faculty have access to funding support either through internal or external grant awards) as a coauthor producing research alongside the faculty member. If we see mentored research as something we are building together, like a nest, we can rethink what a student researcher does and how we can include—and creatively compensate—their work, recognizing the ways students' work of reading, learning, and reflecting on a shared project also benefits the faculty's research profile, and supporting it accordingly.

In this way and others, embracing nested coauthorship is a strategy for supporting undergraduate research and bringing the voices of students—those our institutions are made to serve—into the scholarly conversation of their disciplines. Such coauthorships can foster meaningful relationships and rich writing and research projects rooted not just in the classroom but in the community. While we articulate our experiences working with academic publications and a community internship/outreach program, nested projects also help us to recognize the value of relationships and engagement with the general public and with activist projects that contribute to and connect universities with local communities as well. Nested relationships can provide support—with regards to both budgets and research materials—to make public projects happen.

We hope our nest provides a model for others interested in building community with young writers. These nests might begin in a classroom, or at a community event, it might include a fellowship or funded research project, or even an internship. Our hope is that illuminating these practices of nest-making helps to support diverse voices, communal methods of knowledge-making and -sharing, and supportive writerly relationships that help us all to build and transform not only future nests but also the very trees that hold them.

Notes

1. While Isabella's involvement most definitely challenged such boundaries conceptually, it also contributed to material pathways by which she could more directly challenge these boundaries when she enrolled in Santa Clara University as an undergraduate student in the fall of 2023 and entered the campus space on her homelands prepared to speak back to it and transform it.
2. Learn more about the Muwekma Ohlone and how to support their efforts to achieve reaffirmation of their federal recognized status at Muwekma.org.

Works Cited

American Academy of Colleges & Universities. "High-Impact Practices." *AAC&U*, https://www.aacu.org/trending-topics/high-impact.

Contino, Teresa, Nathan Barnes, and Amy Lueck. "Composing Collaborative Feminist Recovery Projects with Scalar." *Kairos: A Journal of Rhetoric, Technology, and Pedagogy*, vol. 28, no. 2, 2024.

DelliCarpini, Dominic. "Serendipity and Bureaucratization: Loosening the Gordian Knot." *The Naylor Report*, edited by Dominic DelliCarpini et al., Parlor Press, 2020, pp. 154–57.

Downs, Dough, Laurie McMillan, Megan Schoettler, and Patricia Roberts-Miller. "Circulation: Undergraduate Research as Consequential Publicness." *The Naylor Report*, edited by Dominic DelliCarpini et al. Parlor Press, 2020, pp. 94–105.

Estrem, Heidi. "Disciplinary and Professional Identites Are Constructed through Writing." *Naming What We Know: Threshold Concepts of Writing Studies*, edited by Linda Adler-Kassner, UP of Colorado, 2015, pp. 55–57.

FitzGerald, William. "Curriculum; Or If You Build It, They Will Do It." *The Naylor Report*, edited by Dominic DelliCarpini et al., Parlor Press, 2020, pp. 138–53.

Gomez, Isabella, and Amy Lueck. "To Embrace Tension or Recoil Away from It: Navigating Complex Collaborations in Cultural Rhetorics Work." *College Composition and Communication*, vol. 75, no. 1, 2023, pp. 75–96.

King, Thomas. *The Truth About Stories: A Native Narrative*. U of Minnesota P, 2005.

Lave, Jean, and Etienne Wenger. *Situated Learning: Legitimate Peripheral Participation*. Cambridge UP, 1991.

Lerner, Neal. "Writing is a Way of Enacting Disciplinarity." *Naming What We Know: Threshold Concepts of Writing Studies*, edited by Linda Adler-Kassner. UP of Colorado, 2015, pp. 40–41.

Lueck, Amy, Beverlyn Law, and Isabella Zhang. "Inclusivity in the Archives: Expanding Undergraduate Pedagogies for Diversity and Inclusion." *Diversity, Equity, and Inclusivity in Contemporary Higher Education*, edited by Rhonda Jeffries, IGI Global, 2019, pp. 1–12. https://doi.org/10.4018/978-1-5225-5724-1.ch001.

Martinez, Aja Y. *Counterstory: The Rhetoric and Writing of Critical Race Theory*. National Council of Teachers of English, 2020.

Moore, Jessie L., with Sophia Abbot, Hannah Bellwoar, and Field Watts. "Mentoring: Partnering with All Undergraduate Researchers in Writing." *The Naylor Report*, edited by Dominic DelliCarpini et al., Parlor Press, 2020, pp. 29–44.

Olson, Gary A. "Toward a Post-Process Composition: Abandoning the Rhetoric of Assertion." *Post-Process Theory: Beyond the Writing-Process Paradigm*, edited by Thomas Kent, Southern Illinois UP, 1999, pp. 1–6.

Riley-Mukavetz, Andrea. "Developing a Relational Scholarly Practice: Snakes, Dreams, and Grandmothers." *College Composition and Communication*, vol. 71, no. 4, 2020, pp. 545–65.

Royster, Jacqueline Jones, and Gesa E. Kirsch. *Feminist Rhetorical Practices: New Horizons for Rhetoric, Composition, and Literacy Studies*. Southern Illinois UP, 2012.

Senatro, Leah, and Amy Lueck. "Storying Undergraduate Research as a Pedagogical and Research Practice." *Composition Studies*, vol. 54, no. 2 (forthcoming 2026).

Waite, Stacey. *Teaching Queer*. University of Pittsburgh Press, 2017.

Wilson, Shawn. *Research Is Ceremony*. Fernwood Publishing, 2008.

6
Feminist Pedagogy and Coauthorship

Decentering Meaning-Making and Valuing Students' Authentic Voices

LETIZIA GUGLIELMO

Drawing on my coauthoring experiences with undergraduate students guided by feminist pedagogy, in this chapter, I explore feminist pedagogy's ability to disrupt and distribute expertise and to foreground coconstructed knowledge and collaborative meaning-making foundational to student-faculty publishing collaborations. Through these examples, I argue for and illustrate the importance of reflective practice and meta-analysis in the writing process. I also explore the significance of discussion and dialogue in coauthoring, deliberately integrated and extended as part of course designs and made more meaningful and generative given the affordances of virtual learning environments. As a theoretical framework for coauthoring with undergraduate students, feminist pedagogy, grounded in shared and decentered teaching and collective meaning-making (Chick and Hassel; Crabtree et al.; Ochoa and Pershing; Rinehart; Ryan), has the potential to facilitate more equitable, inclusive, and diverse opportunities for writing and research, particularly when intentionally guiding course designs and the writing and research processes of student and faculty coauthors. In the sections that follow, through a macro-level reflection of my coauthoring experiences with undergraduate students, I offer strategies for developing collaborative projects that grow out of a variety of

https://doi.org/10.7330/9781646427796.c006

courses, including online asynchronous courses, and lead to student-faculty coauthorship.

Essential to this process, I argue, are opportunities for ongoing reflection and dialogue shaping both student engagement with course content and subsequent publications, as well as opportunities to disrupt traditional notions of academic publishing with personal narratives foregrounding student voices. As bell hooks explains,

> All efforts at self-transformation challenge us to engage in ongoing, critical self-examination and reflection about feminist practice, and about how we live in the world. This individual commitment, when coupled with engagement in collective discussion, provides a space for critical feedback which strengthens our efforts to change and make ourselves anew. (24–25)

These reflective illustrations of personal learning frame student collaborators as whole knowers contributing to the knowledge of the field, fully surfacing students' perspectives that may be obscured in third-person accounts, and disrupting expectations of who can contribute and where and how they do so. I explore how these individual narratives coupled with collective theorizing foreground and value positionality and lived experience in ways that can disrupt traditional academic genres and highlight students' authentic voices and expertise. Finally, I invite readers to consider what it means to make student voices part of the knowledge of the field when student-faculty coauthoring becomes an outcome of our work with undergraduates.

Foundations of Feminist Pedagogy

A significant body of work informs my engagement with feminist pedagogy and how these pedagogical moves have shaped my approach to student-faculty coauthorship. Feminist pedagogy, according to Crabtree, Sapp, and Licona, "is an *ideology* of teaching inasmuch as it is a framework for developing particular *strategies* and *methods* of teaching in the service of particular *objectives* for learning outcomes and social change" (emphasis in original, 4). "Feminist pedagogy," the authors explain, "seeks not only to enhance students' conceptual learning, but to promote consciousness-raising, personal growth, and social responsibility" (9). Although much of my teaching and scholarship exist at the intersection of writing and rhetoric and gender and women's studies, it's worth clarifying here that feminist pedagogy is not about simply teaching a course on women or in women's studies, and it does not require that courses supported by feminist pedagogies focus exclusively on the work or experiences of women. Instead, feminist pedagogy is grounded in and guided by engagement, shaping the classroom into a space for reflective and collective learning, supporting activism, and fostering change (Shrewsbury 6).

Across disciplines, teacher-scholars continue to theorize feminist pedagogy to expand its scope and its student-centered goals. With connections to the collective engagement of consciousness-raising groups of the women's liberation movement, these liberatory, decentered, and activist tenets shape teaching and learning environments into spaces where students *and* instructors play active roles as co-teachers, engage reflectively with each other and with course content, identify opportunities to blend theory and practice, and apply feminist rhetorical strategies like intervention, interruption, and counterstory to highlight and amplify marginalized voices and perspectives (Crabtree et al.; Chick and Hassel; Ewell; Guglielmo "Classroom"; Guglielmo and Stipe; Hocks; hooks; Martinez; Micciche; Reynolds; Rinehart; Ryan). Significantly,

> feminist pedagogy emphasizes the epistemological validity of personal experience, often connected to notions of voice and authority. Through a critique of the ways traditional scientific and academic inquiry have ignored or negated the lived experiences of women, feminist pedagogy acknowledges personal, communal, and subjective ways of knowing as valid forms of inquiry and knowledge production. (Crabtree et al. 7)

This perspective on inquiry and knowledge becomes central to the sections that follow and to the approach to student-faculty coauthorship that I advocate in this chapter.

Within the context of mentoring undergraduates in academic publication and coauthorship, feminist pedagogical strategies like these have the potential to increase student engagement, self-efficacy, self-confidence, and activism, "provid[ing] a space and structure for students to articulate their own activist and theoretical positions by thinking critically about their experiences" (Tice 124). Notably, decentered collaborative groups that include students and faculty facilitate peer relationships and peer mentoring and foster integrative learning across disciplines and creative responses to complex problems (Palmer et al.; Mumford et al. 28). These coauthoring collaborations can reshape disciplinary knowledge and discourse through a diversity of voices and perspectives and support meaning-making outcomes that are flexible and adaptable for work both inside and outside of the classroom across a variety of courses, from first-year to upper-level.

Supporting student-faculty collaborations through feminist pedagogy and mentoring also creates space for conversation, for cocreating knowledge, and for expanding what "counts" as research, including how foregrounding lived experience increases the diversity and inclusivity of research and writing processes and the significance of that work for audiences. Most notably, "feminist groups like these can build solidarity, enhance [participants'] understandings of each other, and develop a support system that furthers student resiliency and agency . . . creat[ing] conditions for student success, as students know they have an advocate who wants them to flourish as scholar-activists" (Fahs and Swank 254). Beyond theoretical grounding and broad descriptions, what do these feminist pedagogical moves look like in practice, both in the classroom and in student-faculty coauthoring? In the sections that follow, I provide a meta-analysis of two of my own coauthoring experiences with students, explain their outgrowth from and connection to my teaching, illustrate the role of feminist pedagogical strategies in supporting the coauthorships, and share best practices for future engagement in this work. Although the published coauthored pieces include student voices, with reflection growing out of those individual collaborations, in the sections that follow, my larger purpose is to provide a broader view of the pedagogical process supporting the coauthoring experiences in order to guide readers in shaping future coauthoring with undergraduates.

Feminist Pedagogies and Coauthoring in Practice

Because much of my teaching occurs in asynchronous online learning environments and it is out of those courses that many of my collaborations with students have grown, the descriptions that follow lean heavily on feminist pedagogies within online contexts. However, these pedagogical moves can be adapted for the face-to-face classroom as well, as online learning technologies are quite often part of teaching and learning across modalities. As a foundational pedagogical value, I consistently affirm and reinforce that knowledge is coconstructed in the digital spaces of my online courses, ensuring that "students [are] encouraged to make their own meanings and connections" (Chick and Hassel 202) as agentic co-teachers within the space and with opportunities to draw from personal experience and expertise. As I explore elsewhere, these pedagogical moves can lead to deeper engagement with course content, reinforce that students are co-teachers in the course, and invite students to ask questions that foster analysis, critical thinking, and revisiting and building on previous knowledge, including knowledge shared by peers (Guglielmo, "Feminist"). They also create spaces that invite students to enter as equal contributors, with opportunities to speak from where they are and draw from personal experience. Pedagogical strategies like these applied consistently over the course of a semester and through online discussions may create foundations for student-faculty writing collaborations and coauthorship, most significantly in facilitating collaborative meaning-making and coconstructed knowledge. Two notable elements of this work include reflection questions that extend teaching and learning strategies from courses and conversations from those reflections that continue to foster knowledge-building as content that follows will illustrate.

Before moving into those illustrations, I want to clarify that both publishing projects I will draw from perform and begin to theorize the kind of reflective practice and meta-analysis that is essential to successful student-faculty coauthorship. Although the essays themselves are not focused on the topic of coauthorship, readers can learn more about how faculty-student collaborations come about from those pieces, especially the process of facilitating high-impact learning practices and classroom-based feminist pedagogical strategies (Guglielmo et al., "Facilitating"; Guglielmo et al., "Feminist"). Given the interdisciplinary nature of my teaching and scholarship, I am often both theorizing and performing writing and rhetorical strategies simultaneously, as are my coauthors in both pieces. In the remainder of this chapter, however, I aim to theorize the process of coauthorship with undergraduate students, with particular attention to the ways that feminist pedagogy creates a foundation and framework for that process. Two significant facets of that work include the role dialogue and meta-analysis play in that process and how coauthorship can be facilitated and enhanced in virtual environments.

Exploring intersections of feminist rhetorical theories and practices with writing across the curriculum (WAC), specifically writing to learn (WTL) and writing to engage (WTE) activities, the first coauthoring project grew out of an interdisciplinary course on feminist rhetorics that I taught in 2021, both cross-leveled (undergraduate/graduate) and cross-listed with three prefixes. Broadly and deliberately interdisciplinary, the course enrolled students across seven departments and multiple programs. Having designed the course as an online asynchronous section supported by feminist pedagogical strategies, I invited students to engage in collaborative meaning-making and shared expertise and to find their own ways into course content through their individual interests and experience (Guglielmo et al., "Feminist," 29–30). As I explore elsewhere, discussion boards—whether in online asynchronous courses or as an element of face-to-face courses—can become a central site for enacting a feminist pedagogy (Guglielmo, "Feminist"). Within online asynchronous courses in particular, feminist pedagogy can support collaborative meaning-making and reinforce students' contributions as knowers as part of course designs, and these pedagogical moves can be fostered both through the design of online discussion activities and in an instructor's engagement with that content.

To ensure that discussions are not only complex but also meaningful and not a source of busywork for students, discussion activities should provide multiple ways in for students, with multiple and varied prompts, with opportunities for reflection on content and on learning, and with opportunities to make connections to and build upon both peers' contributions and previous discussions. As my coauthors and I illustrate, the discussion board can provide an opportunity for students to hear and listen to the perspectives of their peers rather than holding their own ideas and perspectives as primary, with "internal dialogue" or "self-rhetoric" as essential to that process of meaning-making: "Our dialogue, both internal and external, allowed knowledge to be co-created just as much as it was individually created" (Guglielmo et al., "Feminist," 33, 35–36). In this way, online engagement becomes a form of coauthoring course content and can facilitate ongoing opportunities for coauthoring among students and faculty in publications beyond the course, including in publications not limited to exploring teaching and learning.

As part of the WTL and WTE activities that we describe in the article, writing assignments created space for students "to connect on a personal level, to find meaning beyond the specifics of the assignment itself, and to imagine future selves or future writing identities connected to their goals and interests" (Eodice et al.). As the semester was drawing to a close, I read a call for submissions from the *WAC Journal*, the leading peer-reviewed journal on writing across the curriculum, for articles that blended feminist rhetorics with WAC. In the midst of teaching a broadly interdisciplinary writing-intensive course on this topic, I was deep in collaborative thinking about how we can engage and apply feminist rhetorics in spaces outside of a course on the topic, spaces that allow us to underscore foundations of feminist rhetorical theories and practices as part of writing, research, and critical-thinking processes. With new knowledge gleaned from our engagement with feminist rhetorics, students had already demonstrated much of what this work might look like through their final projects and contributions to online discussions.

Following submission of course grades, I reached out to a small group of students with a diversity of disciplinary backgrounds and varied approaches to the final project. These students had remained engaged in online discussion activities throughout the semester and had applied and theorized feminist rhetorical theories across disciplines and outside of classroom spaces in ways that productively and creatively extended our collective meaning-making. This coauthored project certainly was not a planned assignment in the course or a course outcome, but it naturally grew out of the shared inquiry and collaborative meaning-making of our course grounded in feminist pedagogy. The project allowed us to extend the work of the course—the exploration of theory and practice, the refection and discussion, the application of collective meaning-making outside of the classroom space—into a project growing out of content generated during the course.

Given how we had used discussion board activities throughout the semester and how feminist pedagogical strategies shaped teaching, learning, and engagement, I invited students to draw on content from online discussion activities, longer writing assignments, and major projects in generating content for our manuscript drafts. This approach—replicable in courses across disciplines—created space for us to say something new about feminist rhetorics in ways that contributed to and advanced ongoing scholarly conversations in the discipline (Guglielmo et al., "Feminist," 25). Furthermore, because our course was a writing-intensive course, the project also invited us as collaborators and coauthors to extend course reflection activities toward a meta-analysis of teaching and learning strategies and not content alone. Faculty interested in similar coauthoring opportunities might identify a current CFP around which a project could be developed or identify a target publication venue or conference for future submission. These venues might already invite submissions from undergraduates or focus on undergraduate work, but that is certainly not a requirement and was not the case for this publication. Although projects like these may contribute to and advance ongoing scholarly conversations in the discipline, they also may have wider application for teaching and learning outside of the discipline, as our piece does, creating multiple lenses through which to imagine undergraduate-faculty coauthoring experiences.

Because of the timing of the project (work primarily over the summer) and the tight deadline for submissions, a number of students were not available to contribute. The project began initially with four of us and ultimately became three when another collaborator was unable to move forward. Our writing process began

> with both individual reflections on our course experience and the final project, and pre-writing via email developed by guiding questions. In online virtual meetings, we identified points of connection in this initial self-reflection and writing and began to articulate how feminist rhetorical theories and practices had allowed us to make meaning and connections with disciplinary expertise and to envision the applications of these practices in a variety of rhetorical spaces. (Guglielmo et al., "Feminist," 24)

Following the initial drafting and sharing of reflections with all team members via email, I scheduled our first virtual meeting to discuss project goals and key ideas and common themes among the initial reflections. This decentered and distributed process allowed all team members to cocreate this set of ideas and themes and prompted collective meaning-making among the group that extended the decentered teaching and learning of the course. Again, this is the kind of work that can be replicated in and applied to other courses across disciplines as a foundation for undergraduate-faculty coauthoring. Collaborators might ask, for example, What were the recurring questions explored in this course? What were the key problems being explored or solved? What new ground were students invited to chart? What interventions or interruptions were students making as they contributed to collective meaning-making? How can this work be shared publicly? As these questions illustrate, topics for undergraduate-faculty coauthoring need not be limited to the process of teaching and learning alone.

With feminist pedagogical strategies as a foundation for the course and with reflection as a recurring activity, engaging in the meta-analysis that guided development of the article did not feel like a heavy lift. Students had already become practiced in many of the WTL activities that would guide our coauthoring experience, and their engagement with course texts on feminist rhetorical practices, both through online discussion activities and final projects, allowed them to approach the writing and revision process with content knowledge that underscored our work. Returning to the reflective questions included in the course continued to be generative to dialogue and meaning-making throughout the coauthoring process (see Guglielmo et al., "Feminist," 29–30). Furthermore, extending the framework of that writing and reflective process from the course, including the reinforcement of student contributions as meaningful and expertise as distributed, also supported our work. As my coauthor Dominique so aptly explains,

> Feminist rhetoric reworked my concept of writing from an isolated act of typing onto a white void into a community undertaking. You don't write for yourself or for your papers to die in a hole, but to connect with scholars of the past, present, and future. You write to join the conversation. . . . When we understand writing in general as a communal effort, we start to consider what has been said in the conversation and what we can bring to it. (Guglielmo et al., "Feminist," 34)

To capture our authentic voices and experiences, the final publication includes both collective and individual theorizing and reflection, a move that I find to be essential to meaningful coauthored pieces. We approach this process of narrative self-reflection with multiple aims: "narratives explain to ourselves and to others what we have learned . . . and . . . how we are constructing our own subjectivities (as points of view), the subjectivities of others (as characters in our own narratives), and the cultural spaces that we all share (as settings)" (Ratcliffe 506). These narratives foreground distributed expertise in ways that value students as whole knowers and their knowledge and experience as essential to advancing scholarly conversations across disciplines.

The second project, a coauthored chapter in an edited collection, grows out of similar reflection on and meta-analysis of a group of high-impact practices (HIPs; undergraduate research, internships, directed studies) with four undergraduate students. While the details of the specific HIPs and the corresponding projects are outside the scope of this chapter, including the logistics of designing and supporting undergraduate research and internship projects, I do want to share here how a commitment to making this collaborative work public was a grounding outcome for each of the projects, including publication of the students' work. Although readers can learn more about the individual projects that led to the coauthored piece in the published chapter, including how to identify institutional resources for supporting HIPs with undergraduate students (Guglielmo et al., "Facilitating"), here I want to highlight how dialogue and collaborative meaning-making served as a foundational feminist pedagogical strategy for the projects that again contributed to and facilitated the coauthoring experience. Although this project does not grow out of a single course, the collective HIPs still involve teaching, learning, and mentoring grounded by feminist pedagogical tenets. A commitment to students publicly sharing their work in these projects included preparation for conference presentations, which required both conversations that continued to foster knowledge-building and reflection questions that guided our ongoing collaboration and coauthoring. In other words, similar to the WTE and WTL activities that supported classroom practice in the previous example, this reflective practice and dialogue was embedded in the undergraduate research and internship experiences from the beginning. Preparing for collaborative conference presentations, panels, and roundtable discussions invited reflection that laid the groundwork for later extended reflection and dialogue that informed our coauthored chapter.

Continuing to imagine possibilities for sharing this work publicly, especially through the kind of meta-analysis of the process that I described with the feminist rhetorics project above, I invited four students to coauthor a chapter for an edited collection on feminist collaborations for which I had received a CFP. I envisioned reflecting on the experience and impact of our feminist collaborations, specifically those grounded in HIPs. Again, preparation for conference presentations, on-campus research symposia, and events within our Gender and Women's Studies (GWST) program, including sharing insights about the GWST program with prospective students, had already required my coauthors to engage in reflection on and discussion of the content of their projects, questions audiences might ask, and what they wanted to share about their experiences, including how these experiences shaped their activism and change agency. Notably, the students had also adapted content for different audiences in moving between these public venues, which made them comfortable and confident with the content and able to take a wider lens or view on the writing and research process (Guglielmo et al., "Facilitating").

Similar in many ways to the process my coauthors and I followed for the feminist rhetorics and WAC project, I initiated the coauthoring on this project with individual reflections on the undergraduate research and internship experiences and pre-writing via email developed by guiding reflection questions grounded in current scholarship. I asked my coauthors to begin making connections between their reflections and larger scholarly conversations—connections between theory and practice—and I then edited the responses for length and blended the individual narratives into the text I had begun drafting. Although we did not meet initially and worked exclusively via email given a tight deadline for initial drafts and my unexpected move into a department chair position during what would have been our initial drafting stage, the project deadline was further disrupted by COVID-19 and other personal and professional developments the project editors navigated. A nearly three-year timeline between initial draft and feedback from both external reviewers and project editors certainly is not unheard of, and fortunately, for many reasons, we had the opportunity to revisit this work from completely new perspectives over three years later. When we reconvened, a lot had changed: all of my coauthors had graduated, many had begun or completed graduate work, and all had moved into new and exciting professional work. After our first attempt, continuing to revise the original narratives didn't feel authentic. One of my coauthors explained, "[T]hat's not how I write anymore." This experience of coauthorship-interrupted allowed us to reconnect and completely reframe what we shared in the chapter given both the distance from the original reflections, the broader expertise we had to share, and the new ways we each were thinking about authentic collaboration and coauthorship. It also demonstrated that although we each evolve as scholars and as writers throughout our careers, including as we take on new projects and explore new scholarly threads, this process may be even more visible or felt for our undergraduate student collaborators as they build knowledge and expertise and apply theory and practice beyond their undergraduate experiences.

I scheduled an initial meeting to discuss editor feedback, the project goals, and our initial thoughts upon revisiting the original chapter draft, including individual narratives. In online virtual meetings, we engaged in open conversation, discussing how we might reimagine (and rewrite) those earlier reflections, and we identified points of connection that we had not had the opportunity to articulate fully in the initial version of the chapter. I repurposed from the feminist rhetorics and WAC project the strategy of online virtual meetings framed by an initial set of reflection and discussion questions, yet for this project, I also recorded and transcribed those conversations as a deliberate part of the writing and revision process. This format had a practical element given that not all coauthors now lived in the same place and not all could be present for each virtual conversation; however, we soon realized that having a member of the group work from the transcript of the conversation alone provided a different reading and synthesizing of our collective meaning-making that became essential to subsequent conversations and to the writing and revision process.

Furthermore, these transcribed conversations created a space for what Licona and Chávez describe as "relational literacies": "Understood as practices, relational literacies imply the labor of making meaning, of shared knowledges, or of producing and developing new knowledges together. In other words, relational literacies are understandings and knowings in the world that are never produced singularly or in isolation but rather depend on interaction" (96). The benefit of this revisiting is that the text was made richer by the wealth of experience and expertise each of us brought to the task, and we quickly realized that the original format no longer achieved our collective goals. Rather than framing content in a collective voice followed by individual narratives, I suggested that representing our collective meaning-making as a dialogue among the four of us could more authentically capture the feminist collaboration we were theorizing in the text, "personal, communal, and subjective ways of knowing as valid forms of inquiry and knowledge production" (Crabtree et al. 7). The dialogue goes one step further in illustrating and performing the collective meaning-making process essential to coauthorship without obscuring individual positionality and lived experience, a rhetorical choice that I realized was necessary given our evolving roles as coauthors.

What was missing in the original draft that the revised version captured was the generative conversation, the way we took up, engaged with, and extended ideas and continued to make meaning together through meta-analysis that went beyond the content of the individual projects and our individual reflections. Given the topic of the chapter and the larger edited collection—feminist collaborations—the dialogue both theorizes and performs feminist collaboration for readers. However, this disruption of traditional academic genres also creates space for more authentic student voices, for richer conversation, and for reflection and analysis with the potential to significantly shape work in our field and across disciplines. As part of the writing and revision process, this dialogue also extended the mutual mentoring of the original projects, "allow[ing] [coauthors] to recognize various strengths [they] each brought to the projects, strengths [they] recognized in [their] peers but perhaps had not recognized in [themselves]" (Guglielmo et al., "Facilitating," 17–18). Finally, the conversation also gave us room to see in practice and to imagine possibilities for the kind of collective meaning-making and distributed expertise that can grow out of coauthoring projects grounded in feminist theory and pedagogy as my coauthor Andrea articulates: "So much continues to come out of these conversations. Maybe I could not articulate it myself, but there was always someone who could, and then we bounce ideas off each other. These feminist collaborations allowed me to be seen and validated and know that our voices matter" (Guglielmo et al., "Facilitating," 214).

Conclusion

As previous sections of this chapter illustrate, feminist pedagogical strategies, when providing a framework for student-faculty coauthorship, reinforce expertise as decentered and distributed, support knowledge-construction as social and communal, and create and hold space for lived experience and reflection. Gleaned from my experience coauthoring with undergraduate students, including projects discussed in previous sections of this chapter, these outcomes can be productively fostered within online learning environments and through digital technologies whose affordances amplify and make visible students' authentic voices and collaborative knowledge-construction. Finally, when guided by reflection, dialogue, and meta-analysis, student-faculty coauthorship can grow out of coursework with the potential to shape scholarly conversations on theory and practice across disciplines, conversations that may not be limited to course design or to students' learning experiences alone and, as noted earlier in this chapter, that "provide a space and structure for students to articulate their own activist and theoretical positions" (Tice 124).

Extending the scholarly threads within this piece and building on the scholarship of teaching and learning (SoTL), future work on student-faculty coauthorship might continue to explore how dialogues with students and extended personal narratives provide richer, more complete insights into student learning experiences and personal growth (see Delpish et al.; Moore et al.), and how extended student voices in our scholarship allow us to disrupt or reimagine expertise, including who can and should contribute to knowledge-making in the field. We also might continue to theorize how the label or identifier "student" may be imperfect given how long undergraduate student-faculty collaborations may last and what that means for the additional insight, life experience, and expertise coauthors bring to these projects and how that knowledge and positionality informs the work. Finally, I invite readers to consider the multiple ways that feminist pedagogical strategies and meta-analysis provide frameworks for future work with undergraduate students to address persistent questions across disciplines and engage students as change agents.

Works Cited

Chick, Nancy, and Holly Hassel. "'Don't Hate Me Because I'm Virtual': Feminist Pedagogy in the Online Classroom." *Feminist Teacher*, vol. 19, no. 3, 2009, pp. 195–215.

Crabtree, Robbin D., David Alan Sapp, and Adela C. Licona. *Feminist Pedagogy: Looking Back to Move Forward*. The Johns Hopkins UP, 2009.

Delpish, Ayesha, Alexa Darby, Ashley Holmes, Mary Knight-McKenna, Richard Mihans, Catherine King, and Peter Felten. "Equalizing Voices: Student-Faculty Partnership in Course Design." *Engaging Student Voices in the Study of Teaching and Learning*, edited by Carmen Werder and Megan M. Otis, Routledge, 2010, pp. 96–110.

Eodice, Michele, Anne Ellen Geller, and Neal Lerner. "What Meaningful Writing Means for Students." *Peer Review*, vol. 19, no. 1, 2017.

Ewell, Barbara C. "Feminist Pedagogy in Cyberspace: Learning to Teach (a Little) Differently." *Works and Days*, vol. 16, nos. 1–2, 1998, pp. 99–114.

Fahs, Breanne, and Eric Swank. "Redefining the Work of Feminist Praxis: Making Space for a (Rebellious) Undergraduate Feminist Research Group." *Equity & Excellence in Education*, vol. 53, nos. 1–2, 2020, pp. 244–58.

Guglielmo, Letizia. "Classroom Interventions: Feminist Pedagogy and Interruption." *Who Speaks for Writing: Stewardship in Writing Studies in the 21st Century*, edited by Jennifer Rich and Ethna D. Lay, Peter Lang, 2012, pp. 102–11.

Guglielmo, Letizia. "Feminist Pedagogy and Collaborative Meaning Making." *Feminist Pedagogy for Teaching Online*, edited by Jacquelyne Thoni Howard, Enilda Romero-Hall, Clare Daniel, Niya Bond, and Liv Newman, Athabasca UP, 2025, pp. 19–36.

Guglielmo, Letizia, Jordyn Alderman, Jeremy Hall, Brayden Milam, and Andrea Putala. "Facilitating Feminist Collaborations in Undergraduate Education: Models for Undergraduate Research and Internships in Gender and Women's Studies." *Pedagogies of Interconnectedness: Feminist-Queer Collaborative Transformation*, edited by Isis Nusair and Barbara L. Shaw, U of Illinois P, 2025, pp. 203–217.

Guglielmo, Letizia, Judson T. Kidd, and Dominique McPhearson. "Feminist Rhetorics in Writing Across the Curriculum: Supporting Students as Agents of Change." *WAC Journal*, vol. 32, 2021, pp. 23–41.

Guglielmo, Letizia, and Meghan Stipe. "U.S. Women's Suffrage as a Strategy for Counterstory and Coalition: Creating Shared Rhetorical Space Through Library-Campus Partnerships." *Peitho*, vol. 25, no. 4, 2023.

Hocks, Mary E. "Feminist Interventions in Electronic Environments." *Computers and Composition*, vol. 16, no. 1, 1990, pp. 107–19.

hooks, bell. *Talking Back: Thinking Feminist, Thinking Black*. Sheba, 1989.

Licona, Adela C., and Karma R. Chávez. "Relational Literacies and their Coalitional Possibilities." *Peitho*, vol. 18, no. 1, 2015, pp. 96–107.

Martinez, Aja Y. *Counterstory: The Rhetoric and Writing of Critical Race Theory*. NCTE, 2020.

Micciche, Laura R. "Feminist Pedagogies." *A Guide to Composition Pedagogies*, 2nd ed., edited by Gary Tate et al., Oxford UP, 2014, pp. 128–45.

Moore, Jessie L., Lindsey Altvater, Jillian Mattera, and Emily Regan. "Been There, Done That, Still Doing It: Involving Students in Redesigning a Service-Learning Course." *Engaging Student Voices in the Study of Teaching and Learning*, edited by Carmen Werder and Megan M. Otis, Routledge, 2010, pp. 115–28.

Mumford, Karen, Stephen Hill, and Laurel Kieffer. "Utilizing Undergraduate Research to Enhance Integrative Learning." *Council on Undergraduate Research Quarterly*, vol. 37, no. 4, 2017, pp. 28–32.

Ochoa, Alisha, and Linda Pershing. "Team Teaching with Undergraduate Students: Feminist Pedagogy in a Peer Education Project." *Feminist Teacher*, vol. 22, no. 1, 2013, pp. 23–42.

Palmer, Ruth J., Andrea N. Hunt, Michael R. Neal, and Brad Wuetherick. "The Influence of Mentored Undergraduate Research on Students' Identity Development." *Scholarship and Practice of Undergraduate Research*, vol. 2, no. 2, 2018, pp. 4–14.

Ratcliffe, Krista. "Afterword." *Composing Feminist Interventions: Activism, Engagement, Praxis*, edited by Kristine L. Blair and Lee Nickoson, The WAC Clearinghouse; UP of Colorado, 2018, pp. 505–10. https://doi.org/10.37514/PER-B.2018.0056.

Reynolds, Nedra. "Interrupting Our Way to Agency: Feminist Cultural Studies and Composition." *Feminism and Composition Studies: In Other Words*, edited by Susan C. Jarratt and Lynn Worsham, MLA, 1998, pp. 58–73.

Rinehart, Jane A. "Collaborative Learning, Subversive Teaching, and Activism." *Teaching Feminist Activism: Strategies from the Field*, edited by Nancy Naples and Karen Bojar, Routledge, 2002, pp. 22–35.

Ryan, Jennifer D. "Writing the World: The Role of Advocacy in Implementing a Feminist Pedagogy." *Feminist Teacher*, vol. 17, no. 1, 2006, pp. 15–35.

Shrewsbury, Carolyn M. "What is Feminist Pedagogy?" *Women's Studies Quarterly*, vol. 15, no. 3/4, Fall–Winter 1987, pp. 6–14.

Tice, Karen. "Feminist Theory/Practice Pedagogies in a Shifting Political Climate." *Feminist Teacher*, vol. 14, no 2, 2002, pp. 123–33.

7
Collaborative Coauthorship among Graduate and Undergraduate Students

A Horizontal, Mutual Mentorship Model for Writing Projects

JENNIFER BURKE REIFMAN, MIK PENARROYO-SMITH,
MIKENNA MODESTO, AND LOREN TORRES

Our research team formed in the winter of 2021 as part of an emerging program in our institution's assessment office. Born from the Center of Educational Effectiveness at our institution of UC Davis, undergraduate researchers were invited to become actively involved in research around assessment practices on campus under the tutelage of an advanced graduate student. In this vein, the assessment coordinator of the program compiled a team of graduate students (Jennifer and, later, Mikenna) and undergraduate students (Loren and Mik, as well as several graduated members: Laura, Mahalia, and Leah) to conduct research. The original design of the program was primarily focused on undergraduate students becoming active in research endeavors in a traditional top-down research team format; however, over time our research cohort known as student assessment researchers (StARs) began developing a less hierarchical team structure. Our coauthoring team of graduate and undergraduate students curated our writing practices based on the realization that fuller representation of student voice meant breaking down notions of "expertise" in the practice of coauthoring.

In dismantling a perceived authority in our writing group, we have been a successful writing team and have published three peer-reviewed manuscripts: our first in *Intersection: A Journal at the Intersection of Assessment and Learning*, describing our unique student-centered methodology; our second in *The Learning Assistance Review*, detailing findings from the project; and our most recent in *Peitho*, positing that legitimacy exists as a construct or a barrier of academia that serves to keep diverse student voices on the sidelines. We have also utilized this co-mentorship model for several conference papers related to the StARs Project such as Writing Research Across Borders (WRAB), American Educational Research Association (AERA), the Assessment Institute in Indianapolis, and Association for the Assessment of Higher Learning Education (AAHLE), among others. In each of our writing situations, our team forgoes a traditional "lead," a strategy that is aided by our positions as students. Without naming a lead, the writing experience can act as a venue where we can mentor one another in our perspectives, positionalities, and writing strategies, which, we argue, helps form our individual and collective academic identities. This has allowed us to write for many audiences and purposes in a short amount of time and is a testament to the success and feasibility of our coauthoring model, which will be described at length in the sections to follow.

In this chapter, we describe the ways in which we attempt to deemphasize perceptions of who is capable and who is not in a writing partnership via a horizontal, mutual mentorship model. We then describe how our coauthorship process lends to the coconstruction of our writerly and academic identities that are integral to our developing scholarly positionalities.

Authored by the research team, which consists of two graduate students and two undergraduate students who represent several marginalized identities, this chapter brings attention to the way that positionality can shape partnerships in academia and forwards how positionality can be reimagined, particularly as we collectively work toward common goals, write for public audiences, and deepen our understandings of the complexities of multiple genres. Our efforts diverge from traditional top-down mentoring where there is an appointed expert or leader who is bestowing their knowledge and expertise on the less experienced individual. Instead, we embrace a horizontal, mutual mentorship model where expertise is distributed among members and where writing happens in deep collaboration. In this model of coauthorship, each writer mentors one another through engaging in our personal approaches to writing, perspectives on the work, and positionalities, which allows for the development of writerly and academic identity. By detailing this practice, we then offer a set of practices that can be used to inform collaborative coauthorship processes, particularly when working with graduate and undergraduate emerging scholars alike.

Literature Review

Coauthoring is typically used as a direct form of mentorship and as a means of facilitating identity formation in academia. Many times, writing groups are formed to supplement mentorship (Cassese and Holman), and coauthoring endeavors become ad hoc mentorship moments (Lorenzetti et al.). Mentoring is an essential component of graduate education (Enos). For graduate students, faculty advisors are typically tasked with demystifying academic writing genres and coaching students toward publication for success in the field (Micciche and Carr); these acts are seen as an essential part of mentoring graduate students. Similarly, mentoring undergraduate students in writing for publication and academic audiences has been associated with increased feelings of belonging for undergraduate students (Overman) and is often seen as a high-impact learning experience for those involved (Kuh), demonstrating the value of including undergraduates in this practice. However, while research clearly indicates that both undergraduate and graduate students benefit from mentorship through collaborative writing projects, we have found little discussion of how mentorship can be reimagined among graduate students and undergraduate students in writing projects. Further, we push to extend the conversation on what mentorship can offer emerging scholars, particularly when we begin to dismantle notions of expertise and perceived power in these roles. We see partnerships between undergraduate and graduate students as especially productive for this reason, as both positionalities are in the process of forming and learning, making power differences easier to disrupt.

Research suggests that in a variety of contexts mentoring can reduce anxiety and stress (Gyllensten and Palmer; Grant et al.) and increase self-efficacy (Evers et al.; Leonard-Cross), well-being, goal attainment, and resilience (Grant et al.). However, despite its many psychological benefits, critical work on mentorship notes how it "too often becomes deprioritized, professionalized, and reinscribes power hierarchies" (Singh and Mathews 1703). In this vein, Heilbrun describes the tradition of mentorship in academia as one in which only white men could exemplify the ideals of an intellectual (1), and Enos further posits that men are "still more networked" (Enos 162) and "probably better mentored than women" (Enos 163). As Enos contends, the mentoring relationship is then very much a system of power. In this paradigm, the role of a mentor is reserved for a select few, which in turn limits those who benefit from mentoring relationships.

In response to this, co-mentorship models have been leveraged to develop a more intentional relationship where teaching and learning are reciprocated

(Mullen). This is a frequently sought-after form of mentorship, often duplicated in peer tutoring models in writing centers. However, co-mentorship assumes an equal playing field and ignores potential power differences; given this, we employ a horizontal mentorship model (VanHaitsma and Ceraso), where we actively disrupt the perceived hierarchical relationships of our positions during the research and writing process (Ardent). Mutual mentorship in academia "calls for collaboration reciprocity, and connection" (Glenn 151) and necessitates the legitimizing of experiences across collaborators and the investment of affective labor (Okawa). We adopted this form of mentoring model in order to value the perspective of each author and better meet our goals of highlighting undergraduate perspectives in research, but it has come to fruition most of all in our writing practices.

Throughout our mutual mentorship process, we recognize each writer, despite past experiences, perceived expertise, or current role, as both novice and trained, both growing student and experienced human, and both beginning scholar and emerging expert. As we individually open ourselves to acting as writers who both know important, helpful strategies and as writers who are learning and developing, we can value each other's voices and approaches to writing in valuable and affirming ways. In this, we can foster growth and formative construction of our personal and academic identities, as well as successful collaborative writing projects.

Our Process

When we originally drafted this, the StARs team consisted of Jennifer, a fifth-year PhD candidate in writing studies; Mikenna, a second-year PhD student in writing studies; Mik, a recent UC Davis graduate in sociology; and Loren, a fourth-year undergraduate sociology and anthropology major. As historicized in our introduction, our team is designed to intentionally capture student voices and their experiences with assessment. In this vein, Jennifer, along with Mikenna, have trained Mik and Loren to develop student-based inquiries. As a team, we have worked together to cocreate research questions, collect data in both surveys and interviews, analyze data through specific frameworks, and then coauthor together to disseminate findings across publications and presentations. While the development of our methodological approach has been impactful (see figure 7.1; also see Burke Reifman et al., "Students," for a discussion of this process), it is through the writing process that our work as co-investigators and emerging academics has solidified. That is, through our

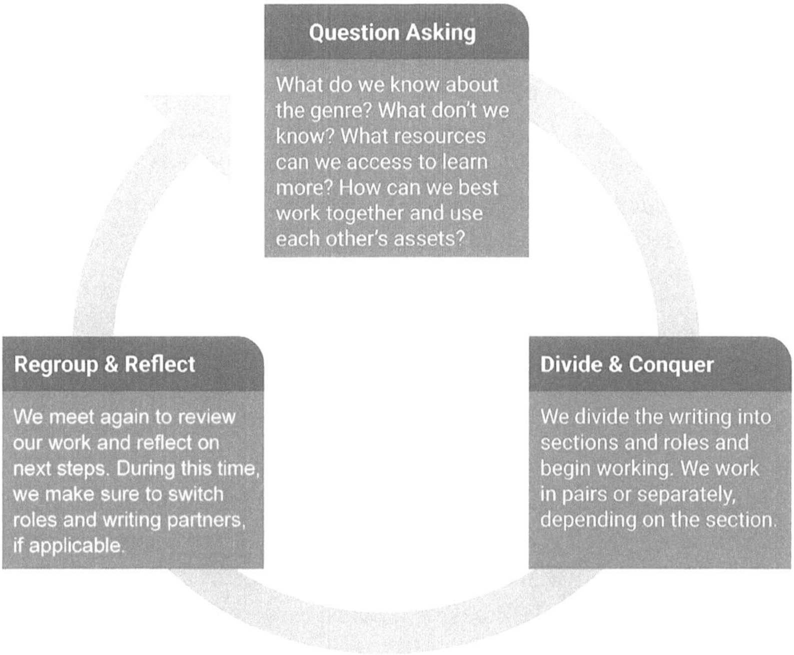

Question Asking

What do we know about the genre? What don't we know? What resources can we access to learn more? How can we best work together and use each other's assets?

Regroup & Reflect

We meet again to review our work and reflect on next steps. During this time, we make sure to switch roles and writing partners, if applicable.

Divide & Conquer

We divide the writing into sections and roles and begin working. We work in pairs or separately, depending on the section.

FIGURE 7.1. Our coauthoring process

coauthoring exchanges, all parties can mentor one another in their perspectives, positionalities, and writing strategies, which, we argue, lends to both writerly and academic identity formation.

As the graduate students on the project, Jennifer and Mikenna have been producing their own writing for a broad academic audience for the last four to five years. As the team members who are seen as having more expertise and experience, they enter the conversation with their undergraduate partners around writing enthusiastically and without judgment, leveraging their more than fifteen years of combined experience as writing teachers, but intentionally removing the built-in power difference of the classroom. As recent initiates into formal academic writing conventions, they bring fresh experiences of learning about and detangling these genres and are able to speak to the difficulties and process of learning. With this in mind, they often begin a writing project with a discussion of what they have learned about the genre so far as graduate students and how they have learned it, remaining honest and transparent about our confusion or struggles. In this way, they do not instruct students or act as pedagogues but rather converse with the undergraduate partners about their learning practices, acknowledging the gatekeeping aspects of this kind of writing and working alongside them to think through difficult questions around genres. As graduate students who do indeed hold more experience in these genres, Jennifer and Mikenna implore the undergraduate members to consider their own learning and out-of-school experiences with writing and the ways in which they have already engaged in some of the more gate-kept academic genres in classes, jobs, or personal projects. In turn, the undergraduate authors push their graduate-student partners to reconsider how academic writing is described, reified in its mysticism, and gate-kept. For example, it was important for Jennifer and Mikenna to remember that an IMRaD paper, or a paper formatted with demarcated introduction, methods, results, and discussion sections, was not immediately apparent as a structure to our undergraduate partners and that this format still needed explanation and conversation.

As the undergraduates on the project, Mik and Loren have felt they have limited experience working in academic writing genres. Most of their experience has largely occurred within the traditional classroom. As the undergraduate partners, Mik and Loren look to their graduate partners as a source of support and reassurance with the understanding that their graduate student partners are there to help them navigate their own personal journeys with academic writing. Mik and Loren believe that our team's detachment from built-in power differences provides them with a unique sense of autonomy as they are encouraged to approach the task in a way that suits their own personal needs and serves to deconstruct difficult writing concepts. This is particularly notable during the beginning stages of writing projects, when undergraduate writers are offered the opportunity to tackle the writing task head on after having an open discussion on what may seem confusing to them as learners. Through these conversations, the undergraduate writers can recognize the connections, or lack thereof, between their personal learning experiences and how the team attempts writing tasks. In turn, the undergraduate writers acknowledge that their graduate partners are better equipped to identify ways in which we can improve our academic writing practices, as they are more often armed with the language to describe the writing process. From the undergraduate perspective, this feedback and meta-conversation on writing is bolstered by the graduate student's willingness to be transparent with their own experiences as more experienced students of these gate-kept genres. For example, the graduate partners would often narrate their writing process as a means for providing conversation about strategy in approaching writing and as ways to make the process more apparent.

Practically, the team meets once a week to discuss our ongoing projects. Often, the coauthorship process begins with a team member bringing a CFP of interest to one of these meetings. Together, the four of us will look at the call, consider whether we think it will be a good fit for our work, and gauge whether we all have the capacity to take on a new project. This is an important step for our team, particularly as our identities as students demand a lot of time and attention: Mik has just graduated with a bachelor's degree, Loren is an upper-division undergraduate student completing their coursework, Mikenna is working toward advancing to candidacy, and Jennifer is dissertating. If we're all in agreement that undertaking a new project sounds feasible and is of interest, we'll begin brainstorming during our initial meeting, collaboratively taking notes on a shared Google Document. After this initial discussion and brainstorming session, one or two of our team members will take a "first pass" at fleshing out the writing project at hand, after which we engage in an iterative revision process.

For example, when writing this chapter, Jennifer and Mikenna took the first pass on our team's response to the call for proposals (CFPs). After constructing a first draft, we all met virtually to discuss the expectations and general details about the chapter's purpose. Unlike conference proposals, Mik and Loren had limited experience with writing a chapter of an edited collection. After several minutes of back-and-forth deliberation wherein Mik and Loren asked how to effectively respond to CFPs, they were asked to add and clarify throughout. In particular, Mik and Loren were encouraged to add and expand upon specific details in the proposal that would highlight their personal contributions as undergraduate coauthors. To better support the undergraduates, Jennifer and Mikenna provided Mik and Loren with examples of previously submitted CFPs to further clarify the writing expectations for an edited collection call. For the two undergraduate researchers, access to examples of similar work is crucial to identify and meet expectations for genres they are unfamiliar with.

After being invited to submit a full chapter, Mik and Loren then took the first pass at generating a full-detail outline for our chapter. Due to the unfamiliar nature of this narrative-driven piece, Mik and Loren struggled with laying the framework for the chapter for fear of being incorrect or deviating from its core purpose. After composing an initial outline, Mik and Loren presented their work to Jennifer and Mikenna, which facilitated another open discussion within the cohort. This allowed Jennifer and Mikenna to see the overall vision Mik and Loren had for the chapter and helped the team articulate what is most valuable in our coauthoring process. We did this by performing a short exercise in which each member wrote one sentence that summarized the main argument we wished to communicate to our audience. Jennifer and Mikenna then returned to the outline and began developing areas of the manuscript that necessitated some additional contextualization, such as the historical background of our team, as well as the field-specific literature on our topic. At this point, the team worked in pairs, but at other times we will change partners or tackle sections alone, each of us asking questions about our processes and seeking feedback from one another. Specifically, throughout this process, we use Google Docs to leave questions and notes for one another, strategizing what might be the most effective approaches to communicating our ideas and asking for feedback in the moment. For example, while drafting this chapter, we had questions as a team about voice and how to collectively write this piece. Mik rightly asked, "Should I write about my experience in the third or first person?" and in response, we engaged in a conversation via comments to weigh the options between possible pronoun usage where the team went back and forth between the pros and cons of each option. In order to sound cohesive, we landed on the collective "we" and moved forward.

Our process for coauthoring empirical manuscripts takes a bit of a different shape, as each team member's comfort levels with different portions of an academic article shift depending on the topic and approach. In each case, we begin our coauthoring process the same way, by asking ourselves as a team what we are trying to accomplish with this piece of writing and what we already know about developing writing in that genre. We seek out model texts, which sometimes come from our own past writing or from the journal in which we are aiming to publish. Then, depending on comfort, we divide the tasks. In one of our most recent manuscripts, which was recently published in *The Learning Assistance Review* (Burke Reifman et al.), Loren and Mik were instrumental at the beginning of the description of our findings and in drafting our discussion. Because the inquiry was focused on undergraduate perceptions of learning, they were able to capture the essence of what interview participants were saying and contextualize these excerpts with great ease and nuance. Then, Loren and Mikenna began working on the literature review, each contributing pieces to help further explain the data. Mik and Jennifer worked on developing the discussion and the whole team added to the introduction. As the manuscript took shape, we then traded who would read through and revise, devising a new purpose for each reader until we felt the paper was ready to send. We revisited this process when we were asked to revise for publication.

Building New Relationships to Mentorship and Writing

The team's intentional shift in how we think of positionality and mentoring allowed for a horizontal, mutual mentorship structure that values each member's perspectives and reshapes how we think about the writing process, changing our identities as writers and authors. For Mik, working as a student researcher offered the unique opportunity to approach writing without the additional stressor of being graded. They found that traditionally graded writing projects had instilled a sense of "right" versus "wrong," which proved difficult to push back on when they were being asked to write for academic genres of writing. They felt that writing only for assessment had hindered their willingness to take on new writing expectations in fear of being reprimanded for approaching it incorrectly. However, horizontal mentorship has given Mik the reassurance that they are allowed to explore new ways of writing, thereby increasing their personal development with writing strategies.

Like Mik, Loren feels they have been able to grow their writing skills under the impactful mentorship of the graduate students. Specifically, Loren feels like the writing tasks that they engage in serve a different purpose than regular writing assignments for class. The two realms of academic writing are distinct in this sense, as Loren feels like their writing with the team allows them to form an independent academic identity—they are writing for a purpose as opposed to appeasing a grading scale. Additionally, having graduate students who also share a passion for the subject allowed Loren to change their perception of writing. Loren has been able to gain mentors who they trust to guide and challenge their academic writing capabilities. In fact, Jennifer and Mikenna often reemphasize that writing can always be reorganized, if need be, to encourage both undergraduates to continue writing in ways that come the most naturally to them.

Jennifer's first peer-reviewed publication was coauthored with the undergraduate students from this team, and, as it did for Mik, this process changed her sense of what it means to be a writer in academic spaces. While much of the writing graduate students do is meant to have utility beyond the classroom, the coauthoring from this team and the team's ability to think about research and writing in new ways has given both Jennifer and Mikenna new perspectives on their ability to write for a broad academic audience and the power of academic writing projects. The intentional shift away from the novice versus expert paradigm has given this project new freedoms in what the team feels it can and should contribute to academic conversations.

Loren and Jennifer both identify as first-generation students and have found great frustration throughout their varied experiences as students in the ways that academic writing is often obscured and made inaccessible. Through their experiences on this team, Jennifer has found immense gratification in working alongside undergraduate students to demystify academic writing and acknowledge the inherent gatekeeping of these genres. The open approach to coauthoring alongside undergraduate students has demonstrated the necessity of not just explicit instruction on writing for undergraduates but also the importance of immersive experiences in the act of composing.

Demystifying Academic Writing and Shifting Dispositions

Another clear benefit of our model for this team is the way that hands-on work with academic writing has demystified previously obscured aspects of academic writing for all members of the team and led to changes in disposition around writing for the team members. Prior to joining the team, Loren felt they did not have much experience writing for publication or writing about research, despite being in their third year at a major research institution. To Loren, writing in higher academia meant encountering near-indecipherable research articles, each with its own jargon that would take hours to dissect for class. After joining the team, Loren was asked to complete some writing that they initially felt hesitant and unsure about, learning to break down research articles, synthesize sources, and support claims with more nuance and confidence. With the guidance and support of the team, they felt comfortable taking what felt like risks in writing and making explicit claims about research. Now, a year after joining the StARs team, Loren feels more confident in their academic writing capabilities than ever before and finds the practice of writing for an academic audience satisfying as an undergraduate student—a stark difference from how Loren felt prior to joining the team. Likewise, Mik previously had no clear pathway to leveraging themself as a legitimate researcher or coauthor of an academic paper outside of class. Like Loren, being a part of the StARs team has helped Mik feel much more capable in their ability to read, write, and deconstruct enigmatic texts within the academic genre.

For one, we have all learned to push against the myth that polished drafts happen overnight. Throughout our experiences with collaborative writing and subsequent peer review, we have all seen how writing products can be shaped and reshaped through intensive and pointed revision. In actively coauthoring and moving through the publishing process, the team as a whole has more expertise and awareness of how academic writing is disseminated.

Additionally, we were able to work together to narrate our processes and build metacognition about our writing processes. To do this, we encouraged the exploration of ideas through memoing and other low-stakes writing practices that allowed personal experiences to be connected to research. In negotiating our coauthoring process, each of us also had to point to our specific weaknesses and strengths in the writing process; through writing together in multiple iterations, we knew how to lean into each other's strengths and support each other in the moments we were developing.

We also developed specific knowledge about academic writing genres through leveraging mentor texts and iterative feedback among ourselves to make previously buried expectations of academic writing apparent. For example, both Loren and Mik became well-versed in the IMRaD article format but also learned that academic writing comes in a variety of structures and employs different rhetorical choices depending on the purpose and audience. Particularly, in writing this chapter, we had to leave the traditional IMRaD format for a more narrative-informed argument. In addition, Loren and Mik have become much more adept at communicating via iterative feedback throughout the writing process. Although short feedback exercises are common in undergraduate-level coursework, the feedback given for this type of academic writing has given them more awareness of the audience and varying genres, while providing them with a formative understanding of how to compose constructive and helpful feedback in other writing situations. If Loren and Mik had been told that they weren't prepared for the active work of writing in these projects, they may have never had the opportunity to learn by trial and error about how to effectively report research, describe findings, and speak to their experiences.

Coauthoring as Identity Affirmation

Finally, while our approach to mentoring and coauthoring has opened us to new paradigms and ways of seeing writing and served to demystify academic genres, we have also found that each team member has personally developed because of our team model. Mik, as a second-year transfer student, has found the experience of working alongside fellow undergraduate and graduate students integral to the ongoing development of their academic personality.

Through working as a StAR, Mik has felt more aware of their strengths and weaknesses as a writer within an academic environment, especially as it exists outside of the traditional hierarchical contexts of the classroom. In their time on the team, they went from doubting their ability to feeling strongly that they could pursue postgraduate studies with the newfound confidence spurred by their coauthors' constant affirmations. Before coming to their current institution, Mik approached all forms of writing in a transactional manner simply to receive a grade in exchange. This transactional writing approach worked for most of their writing assignments, but not without consequence. Mik's former approach to writing was devoid of any enthusiasm for their projects; the writing process was viewed as a negative chore that needed to be completed. However, once Mik joined the StARs program, their outlook on writing shifted to a more positive collaborative attitude. Likewise, Loren has been increasingly interested in the prospect of entering graduate school and is progressively confident with the idea of applying and being a graduate student.

For Loren, envisioning graduate school as a viable path came from the confidence of writing for a presentation and presenting in front of and speaking to academic professionals, where they felt seen as a legitimate contributor. Meeting and interacting with professionals in higher education was, at first, incredibly daunting as they felt out of their element. Through writing with the StARs, both Mik and Loren continue to fight against ingrained feelings of inferiority when faced with an audience that carries prestigious titles alongside years of experience. However, they have discovered that professional audiences are less intimidating than they had initially perceived. In particular, the work we have done to coauthor and present at conferences to academic professionals has boosted the StARs' confidence and reaffirmed their sense of accomplishment. Overall, Mik and Loren have been empowered by their realization that even those who appear to be much more knowledgeable and experienced are still benefiting from their insights and perspectives as undergraduates.

For all members of the group, it was particularly helpful to be open and frank about struggles with academic writing. Honest, vulnerable conversations around difficulties with writing were largely uncommon for all members of the team, which often left us feeling isolated and alone in any difficulty. Each member of the group, despite their positioning and experience, had their own feelings of isolation and imposter syndrome to contend with around writing that has been eased through the transparency of our conversations and the support we offer one another. Despite all of us feeling like strangers in a strange land, faking it till we make it, our conversations around overcoming academic writing genres helped ease internalized feelings of inadequacy in higher education, which improved our outlook on writing and our identities as writers.

Through a process that does not position one person as more knowledgeable, correct, or more of an expert than another, we have forged a coauthoring experience that allows us to take risks and through this we have been rewarded. For example, submitting to an edited collection and multiple peer-reviewed journals required a level of risk-taking where, as a group, we needed to be prepared for rejection of our hard work. Additionally, we have engaged in several grant-writing projects to continue the funding for our team, which if unsuccessful would have meant the end of our paid labor. Each grant proposal has felt precarious and uneasy, but our shared labor in the writing process has allowed us to secure funding across academic years.

To this end, as we collaborate and come together through our coauthoring, we honor the ways in which our positionalities and prior writerly experiences inform our unique writing processes. In doing so, we facilitate a more equitable dynamic that holds space for one another. We understand that there will always be an inherent gap of power between undergraduate and graduate student collaborators due to differing degrees of experience. This gap, however, can be bridged through the development of reciprocal trust. Jennifer and Mikenna *trust* in Mik and Loren's ability to provide significant insights into the writing process, and Mik and Loren *trust* in Jennifer and Mikenna's gentle guidance. In this sense, Mik and Loren are inspired to take more risks in their writing yet remain reassured that Jennifer and Mikenna will provide constructive feedback that does not harm their willingness to engage in writing projects.

Ultimately, the team believes that to demystify gate-kept genres in academia we must be willing to promote accessibility and diversity of thought through the development of reciprocal trust, rooted in nonhierarchical, mutual mentorship.

Conclusions and Recommendations

At UC Davis, an R1 research institution, research opportunities are not hard to find. However, these research opportunities are usually geared toward a certain type of student, particularly ones who were able to access the resources needed to tailor their schooling and extracurriculars for research positions. These students are often not people of color, first-generation, or queer-identifying, like many of the members of our team. Having the StARs program act as an open space for all students helps break down barriers that keep underrepresented students out of higher academia, that keep undergraduate students in general from participating in academic conversations, and that keep graduate students siloed in their work. The StARs program allows Jennifer, Loren, Mik, and Mikenna to navigate genres of academic writing together that have been traditionally gate-kept. The StARs team is incredibly unique in what it offers to both graduate and undergraduate students. Often, research projects and initiatives that utilize data from students do not include students as coauthors and meaning-makers of research. We have found that having undergraduate students present in the data collection, the analysis, and the written dissemination of this work is vital for giving undergraduate researchers an empowering facet of independence and for teaching graduate students about mentorship.

In closing, we offer our horizontal, mutual mentorship model through which graduate students can approach coauthoring alongside undergraduates. Specifically, we forward an iterative coauthoring process; grounded in questioning assumptions about genres, resources, and team members' assets; committed to the equitable division of labor; and deeply reflective. Further, our mentorship model affords us the ability to forge meaningful, mutually beneficial relationships that work to build new paradigms, demystify academic genres, and affirm our identities through our coauthoring processes. Graduate students who are actively seeking both mentorship and authorship roles can act as formative guides and cocreators with undergraduates in ways that allow for power to be distributed and dispersed equitably. As the StARs team has demonstrated, a well-synthesized composition that values every writer's voice does not require a framework dependent on traditional power structures. We hope that the insights into our writing process provided here inform future coauthoring efforts among graduate and undergraduate students and provide a framework with which graduate advisors can encourage their own mentees to approach coauthoring with the undergraduate students on their campuses.

Works Cited

Ardent, Hannah. *The Human Condition*. U of Chicago P, 1958.

Burke Reifman, Jennifer, Mik P. Penarroyo, and Loren Torres. "Because We Already Are Legitimate: Feminist Coalition Building among Graduate and Undergraduate Students to Counter Patriarchal, White, Heteronormative 'Expertise.'" *Peitho: Journal of the Coalition of Feminist Scholars in the History of Rhetoric & Composition*, vol. 28, no. 1, 2023.

Burke Reifman, Jennifer, Mikenna Sims, Mik Penarroyo, and Loren Torrres. "Investigating Student Confusion and Self-Efficacy with SLOs to Support Student Learning." *The Learning Assistance Review* (TLAR), vol. 28, no. 1, 2023.

Burke Reifman, Jennifer, Mahalia White, and Leah Kalish. "Students as Researchers and Participants: A Model of Iterative Member-Checking for Inclusive, Equity-Centered Assessment Research." *Intersection: A Journal at the Intersection of Assessment and Learning*, vol. 3, no. 1, 2022.

Cassese, Erin C., and Mirya R. Holman. "Writing Groups as Models for Peer Mentorship among Female Faculty in Political Science." *PS: Political Science & Politics*, vol. 51, no. 2, 2018, pp. 401–5. https://doi.org/10.1017/S1049096517002049.

Enos, Theresa J. "Mentoring—And (Wo)Mentoring—in Composition Studies." *Renewing Rhetoric's Relation to Composition*, edited by Shane Borrowman et al., Routledge, 2009, pp. 171–79, https://doi.org/10.4324/9780203869222-18.

Evers, Will J. G., André Brouwers, and Welko Tomic. "A Quasi-Experimental Study on Management Coaching Effectiveness." *Consulting Psychology Journal: Practice and Research*, vol. 58, no. 3, 2006, pp. 174.

Glenn, Cheryl. "Mentoring." *Rhetorical Feminism and This Thing Called Hope*, Southern Illinois UP, 2018, pp. 149–73.

Grant, Anthony M., Linley Curtayne, and Geraldine Burton. "Executive Coaching Enhances Goal Attainment, Resilience and Workplace Well-Being: A Randomised Controlled Study." *Journal of Positive Psychology*, vol. 4, no. 5, 2009, pp. 396–407.

Gyllensten, Kristina, and Stephen Palmer. "Can Coaching Reduce Workplace Stress? A Quasi-Experimental Study." *International Journal of Evidence Based Coaching and Mentoring*, vol. 3, no. 2, 2005, 75–85.

Heilbrun, Carolyn. *When Men Were the Only Models We Had*. U of Pennsylvania P, 2002.

Kuh, George D. *High-Impact Educational Practices: What They Are, Who Has Access to Them, and Why They Matter*. Association of American Colleges and Universities, 2008.

Leonard-Cross, Elouise. "Developmental Coaching: Business Benefit–Fact or Fad? An Evaluative Study to Explore the Impact of Coaching in the Workplace." *International Coaching Psychology Review*, vol. 5, no. 1, 2010, pp. 36–47.

Lorenzetti, Diane L., Leah Shipton, Lorelli Nowell, Michele Jacobsen, Liza Lorenzetti, Tracey Clancy, and Elizabeth Oddone Paolucci. "A Systematic Review of Graduate Student Peer Mentorship in Academia." *Mentoring & Tutoring: Partnership in Learning*, vol. 27, no. 5, 2019, pp. 549–76. https://doi.org/10.1080/13611267.2019.1686694.

Micciche, Laura R., and Allison D. Carr. "Toward Graduate-Level Writing Instruction." *College Composition and Communication*, vol. 62, no. 3, 2011, pp. 477–501. http://www.jstor.org/stable/27917909.

Mullen, Carol A. "Constructing Co-Mentoring Partnerships: Walkways We Must Travel." *Theory into Practice*, vol. 39, no. 1, 2000, pp. 4–11. http://www.jstor.org/stable/1477435.

Okawa, Gail Y. "Diving for Pearls: Mentoring as Cultural and Activist Practice among Academics of Color." *College Composition and Communication*, vol. 53, no. 3, 2002, pp. 507–32.

Overman, Amy A. "Strategies for Group-Level Mentoring of Undergraduates: Creating a Laboratory Environment That Supports Publications and Funding." *Frontiers in Psychology*, vol. 10, 2019, p. 323. https://doi.org/10.3389/fpsyg.2019.00323.

Singh, Taveeshi, and Tayler J. Mathews. "Facilitating Queer of Color Feminist Co-Mentorship: Reflections on an Online Archive of Scholar-Activism." *Gender, Place & Culture*, vol. 26, no. 12, 2019, pp. 1701–20. https://doi.org/10.1080/0966369X.2019.1636768.

VanHaitsma, Pamela, and Steph Ceraso. "'Making It' in the Academy through Horizontal Mentoring." *Peitho: Journal of the Coalition of Feminist Scholars in the History of Rhetoric & Composition*, vol. 19, no. 2, 2017, pp. 210–33.

8
Archives as Sites of Collaboration

"Side-by-Side" Coauthoring

LYNÉE LEWIS GAILLET

In the Foreword to Tarez Graban and Wendy Hayden's *Teaching through the Archives: Text, Collaboration, and Activism*, Ryan Skinnell views the "archives as sites of *epistemic possibility* [original emphasis]," casting the archive itself as "collaborator, not master" (xiii) in the drama that plays out in primary investigation. In explaining the recent "archival turn," Skinnell recounts ways in which scholars now approach collections not with reverence but to "imagine what we (and our students) can be, what knowledges we can make in" it, and "what we can change beyond the archive(s)" (xiii). He reminds archival researchers that we "give as many gifts as we receive" (xiii) and that current approaches to this research method open spaces that provide "new orientations to the archive" (xv). Graban and Hayden's beautiful project demonstrates ways that the field of rhetoric and composition offers possibilities that differ from other disciplines through a "focus on theories of teaching"—in this case, a willingness to teach with archives and train students not only to become historians of rhetoric but also to develop sociocultural literacies, understand histories of social justice advocacy, maintain community archives, and study professional, familial, and cultural materials (5). Contributors to the collection focus on students' collaborations with librarians, archivists, community members, and the archival materials themselves, paying particular attention

https://doi.org/10.7330/9781646427796.c008

to avenues for undergraduate research and opportunities for forming community partnerships.

The following discussion expands upon this existing scholarship, suggesting that in addition to fruitful collaborations with texts and stakeholders, students who coauthor with teachers, peers, and special collection specialists also discover a gateway to academic publishing. I label this practice "side-by-side" coauthoring, which serves to introduce students to new research strategies, the possibilities inherent within digital archival inquiry, and ways to create new knowledge through primary research investigation. In side-by-side partnerships focused on archival research, senior coauthors may take on more nuanced roles than those typically associated with coauthoring, as illustrated in the examples below.

Defining Side-by-Side Coauthoring via Lunsford and Ede

My experiences working side by side with students resonate with longtime coauthors Andrea Lunsford and Lisa Ede's prescient list of questions concerning collaboration, published forty years ago in "Why Write . . . Together?" Lunsford and Ede hoped that future scholars would take up these issues, and the renowned collaborators returned to this list repeatedly in their subsequent joint scholarship (overtly in "Collaborative Authorship and the Teaching of Writing," 1992). I rely upon Lunsford and Ede's salient queries to illustrate my conception of side-by-side archival coauthoring. Their work reflects the need for ongoing examination of inherent possibilities within cooperative research and writing, suggesting new applications of the influential pairs' enduring praxis. While the famous collaborators don't focus specifically on writing with students, their 1983 work emphatically asked readers to consider student collaborations: "And perhaps most importantly, do we have ways to teach students to adjust readily to co- or group-writing tasks?" (156). Four decades later, I expand and reshape their questions in this examination of the potential of researching alongside students and providing unique pathways for student publishing, which locates possible roles the teacher might play in coauthoring. Illustrations from side-by-side coauthoring experiences provide a retrospective look at Lunsford and Ede's visionary coauthoring queries, with an archival gaze. Therefore, this chapter is single authored, crafted from my decades of experience as a pedagogical guide for teachers; the illustrations throughout, however, represent coauthoring projects including multiple partners.

As the present collection illustrates, the humanities still wrestle with concepts of student-teacher collaboration, ethics of work division and attribution, and, yes, nomenclature. Lunsford and Ede's first predictive query asks, "What specific features distinguish the processes of co- or group-authoring from those of single authorship? . . . Can these features of process be linked to any features of the resulting products? In short, how can we best define coauthorship?" ("Why Write," 155). In side-by-side views of undergraduate writing partnerships, the teacher may serve simultaneously as editor, facilitator, coach, and coauthor. The three illustrations below tease out nuances of writing with students, using the archives as a location for this work and redefining the significance of coauthoring for teachers as well as students. While many studies of undergraduate research focus on the value for students, working in the archives can pave the way for reciprocal learning through collaboration that benefits teachers as well. For example, by adopting the metaphor of "accompaniment" as a concept for engaging in multidirectional conversation (Brereton and Gannett 120), student-teacher coauthors share new interpretations that resist entrenched scholarly practices and disrupt apprenticeship models of mentoring sometimes associated with teacher-student coauthoring. As intersectional and intergenerational collaborators have recently noted, coauthoring and coediting provide a key for moving beyond our present contentious cultural moment; their claim holds especially true for archival research as student-teacher partners learn from one another as they negotiate representations, recoveries, layered histories, and community ground-up archives.

This chapter's examples of coauthoring through archival investigation touch on these and other issues by exploring (1) ways to unsettle archival histories, particularly given the expanded access to digital archives; (2) opportunities for coauthoring and possible hurdles when coauthors include students; and (3) potential avenues for coauthoring within textbooks. Each illustration explores how side-by-side collaboration can encourage undergraduates to take possession of intellectual ethos and view coursework as potentially public-facing scholarship; how teachers can extend archival publishing opportunities to undergraduates via redesigned curriculum; and the tangible, intergenerational benefits for experienced scholars who coauthor with undergraduate students. But first . . .

Why Archives and Coauthoring?

By routinely incorporating archival and primary investigation into classes throughout the vertical curriculum (wherein one course's research strategies and subject-matter content prepares students for subsequent study), teachers can engage students in topical community investigation that naturally appeals to a wider readership than classmates and instructors in isolated courses. For decades, I have assigned primary research activities in every class, from first-year writing courses through advanced doctoral seminars, and each semester students disseminate their findings at conferences, as contributors to coauthored articles and chapters, in bibliographies and reference materials, as interviewers and collectors of oral histories, and as part of community records and finding aids. Initially, students may feel overwhelmed by the demands of primary investigation, especially when their past academic experiences focused almost exclusively on secondary research. However, engaging in side-by-side researching and subsequent coauthoring with teachers and librarians that archival research often invites can ameliorate frustrating inequities that undergraduates often associate with coauthoring or group projects. Once students understand that nuanced and layered collaboration can yield publications and opportunities for disseminating their ideas, they become more willing and even eager to coauthor.

Current pedagogical scholarship touts the benefits of teaching with archives (Bahde et al.; Comer et al.; Daniel-Wariya and Lewis; Enoch and VanHaitsma; Gaillet and Eble; Gaillet and Rose; Graban and Hayden; Hayden, "And Gladly" and "Gifts"; Greer and Grobman, etc.), but archival research also goes hand-in-glove with faculty-student coauthoring. Conducting archival investigation while simultaneously learning about the rhetorical conventions of academic publishing may seem overwhelming for emerging researchers, but I've found the opposite to be true. In fact, identifying goals related to publishing or other means of dissemination can assist students in developing beneficial research strategies, particularly in archival investigation where students often select research topics based on their personal interests, community and familial memberships, and cultural events. In this work, usually targeted to specific audiences, the student serves as the subject matter expert (sometimes adding to existing collections by conducting interviews, adding ephemera and artifacts to local holdings, or assembling materials from distinct collections into tailored digital portfolios or commonplace books). Teachers, then, may serve dual functions as they model academic and workplace writing practices, take the lead on archival method/ologies, and pave the way for circulation of students' original work via coauthoring, side by side. This nature of shared expertise resonates with Lunsford and Ede, as they ask, "What epistemological implications does co-authorship hold for traditional notions of creativity and originality?" They answer, "[O]ur own strong sense that two may create ideas that neither would have reached alone argues for the value of dialectic as invention" ("Why Write," 156). I agree, particularly in archival investigation where partners may co-research ground-up materials from communities to which the teacher does not belong.

This kind of coauthoring, according to Kami Day and Michele Eodice, is best described as *(First Person)*[2] collaboration wherein coauthoring shouldn't be about dividing and conquering a project but instead writing together in ways that yield a rich product that neither partner could produce independently. Day and Eodice explain that through interviews with successful authoring teams (including Lunsford and Ede), they learned from "stories of how [the partners] came to work together; how they negotiate their different ways of learning, knowing, and writing; how they merge their voices; how they have come to value their relationships with each other over the products of their collaboration" (5–6). They further explain, "Successful coauthoring, as we've learned from our own experience and from the coauthors we studied, goes well beyond what we have formally believed constitutes collaborative writing into an ineffable realm that involves relationships based on trust, respect, and care" (5). This relationship-building, reliance upon each other's expertise and positionality, and interest in learning from the act of collaboration undergirds teacher-student coauthoring with archives as well. Additionally, students and teachers must find ways to suspend (or at least balance) traditional notions of teacher-student authority. Although Day and Eodice's study doesn't focus on students, they do cite Kathleen Yancey's prophetic words from 1998, noting that she

> provides a useful parallel in her description of a particular moment in the history of composition studies. She points out that "[in crediting students with knowledge of what was going on inside their heads and in awarding it authority, early composition researchers] did something very valuable and very smart. These students are the ones who have allowed the rest of us, the teachers, to investigate, to understand, *to theorize our classroom practice.*" . . . Likewise, the stories we have collected allow "the rest of us"—from writing teachers to authorship theorists—"to investigate, to understand, to theorize" what it means to write together. (Day and Eodice 6)

Jumping ahead twenty-five years from Yancy's pedagogical assessment, archival scholar-teachers now understand that student authors bring their own community knowledge and fresh perspectives to bear in coauthoring with teachers. Partnerships among senior writers (teachers and librarians) and emergent scholars (students) help us all learn to bridge sociocultural and ageist divides—when coauthors engage in rhetorical listening and writing. This conception of side-by-side coauthoring intricately blends two-way learning and a reliance upon partners to achieve rich, unique, and multi-layered publications. However, coauthoring with students also comes with a set of caveats, expectations, outcomes, and consequences, discussed within the following illustrations.

Examples of Side-by-Side Coauthoring

ILLUSTRATION #1: UNSETTLING ARCHIVAL HISTORIES

Amy Lueck and Nadia Nasr ask what epistemic and orientation possibilities the archives provide for disrupting and unsettling holdings, for normalizing discomfort, for grappling "with cultural difference in archives as a learning outcome for our courses" (297). Coauthoring with students provides one avenue for addressing their challenge while also adding student research experiences and new voices to public scholarship. For example, several of my students recently investigated ways in which even deliberately feminist/inclusive archival projects can be unsettled to include overlooked voices and factions. In fall 2022 I taught the national #SuffrageSyllabus, "which explores the tangled history of gender and United States citizenship created by scholars, Harvard College students, and Schlesinger Library staff as part of the Long 19th Amendment Project." Speaking from distinct sociocultural positions and identities, undergraduates who enrolled in the split-level course identified gaps in examinations of one hundred years of suffrage and women's activism. Addressing "the current political, environmental, social, and historical moment, when questions of public memory, public commemoration, and archival work have taken on a new urgency," students diligently worked to add overlooked religious women, ethnic minorities, and migrant women into the existing national suffrage syllabus (Kirsch et al. 1). Their impressive course research led to a cowriting opportunity, currently in progress and accepted for publication in a forthcoming edited collection.

Using the #SuffrageSyllabus as a guide, students; fellow archival teacher Jessica Rose; Morna Gerard, a colleague in special collections at the Georgia

State University (GSU) library; and I are designing a similar archival course grounded in digitized images found in our library's extensive collection of ephemera. In "Collective Invention: Learning through Women's Activism and Material Culture," we first discuss the course design, rationale for creating an archival course grounded in local/digitized materials for national adoption, and underlying pedagogical theories; then we provide a fully accessible syllabus that any teacher can adopt. The students, who have experience researching GSU's archival holdings and national online records, are cocreating the curriculum/units for the syllabus. This project relies upon specific expertise of coauthors: the pedagogical and archival research skills of Jess and Lynée; Morna's knowledge of the collection she helped build and her collating/digitizing prowess; and the students' innate understandings of the stakeholders and community members represented by the archives (along with a firsthand recognition of the needs of students enrolled in this kind of course design). In Day and Eodice's terms, none of the coauthors could produce this chapter individually, and intergenerational mentoring/coauthoring enriches the project by providing broader and more inclusive perspectives.

This project also addresses another of Lunsford and Ede's coauthoring questions, albeit in ways they might not have imagined in 1983. They ask, "How does technology affect the processes of coauthoring?" and specifically mention the affordances provided by "the telephone, xerox, and self-correcting typewriter" (156). While this point seems superseded given advances in technology, their question explicitly applies to this coauthoring example and other archival investigations post-COVID-19. As we learned in the pandemic, archival researchers and writers must now depend upon digitized finding aids and materials. Given recent experiences moving archival research online (see illustration #2), we now have increased awareness of the possibilities and limitations associated with online digital research, information that changes how we examine archives, design courses, and coauthor. The Schlesinger Library's #SuffrageSyllabus, students' ability to examine digitized materials from across the country, and the in-progress coauthored chapter grounded in acts of digitizing and sharing GSU materials absolutely would not exist without these advances in technology. In archival research, the widespread digitization of materials represents a sea change in terms of democratic access to primary materials, including the process of finding materials through digitized finding aids; convenience of learning from/with nonlocal special collection librarians and collators; and opportunities to study materials housed across collections and then expand/unsettle existing holdings. As David S. Ferriero, archivist of the United States from 2009 to 2022 explains, "In the 21st century, access means digital access. For many, if a record isn't online, it simply doesn't exist" (n.p.). This increased accessibility and unprecedented convenience in conducting archival research also applies to capabilities and potential for coauthoring, especially since coauthors no longer need to travel extensively to research materials.

Teachers and students writing side by side assist one another in exploring community archives and access to those materials (physical and digital) by providing backstory and contextualization of content for one another in some instances. In other cases, we add to existing holdings as we rely upon our membership status and research capabilities to conduct oral histories and interviews. And we often collaboratively test our assumptions and interpretations by triangulating our ideas and seeking alternate histories and views of events. These tasks illustrate Skinnell's epistemic nature of archival research as we engage in new orientations and interpretations of collected materials.

ILLUSTRATION #2: RECOGNIZING COAUTHORING OPPORTUNITIES—AND SOME CHALLENGES

If we accept that epistemic possibilities for archival research include "seeing who we are in the archives, who we imagine what we (and our students) can be, what knowledges we can make in and from and for the archives, and what we can change beyond the archive(s)," then we can "profoundly [reshape] how we come to an old task" (Skinnell xiii). My second illustration examines another possibility for approaching side-by-side coauthoring associated with archival work, the group publishing assignment built into the syllabus (not an outgrowth of successful student work as in illustration #1). This approach does come with a few wrinkles that teachers need to consider as we write with students. In the intervening years since Lunsford and Ede asked "[i]n what ways, if any, does co- or group-authorship affect the way we view the traditional rhetor-audience relationship?" collaborative research has become as commonplace as individually authored scholarship. However, when applied to teacher-student coauthoring, rhetor-audience relationships remain complicated. When students produce coursework, the primary audience is usually the instructor since students write for a grade. In publishing, audiences include the more traditional triumvirate of editor, reviewers, and finally readership (with the payoff equaling conventional publication). And, fundamentally, all rhetor-audience relationships take on additional/unique qualities when archival research is involved; readers don't always have access to the materials cited by archival researchers, so ethical issues and critical matters of trust become heightened.

In the following side-by-side coauthorship, the instructor provides the infrastructure for an article (writing the introduction and justification for the research, providing context and segues, and drafting conclusions and implications) while the students contribute the meat of the essay (examples and illustration of concepts from their primary investigations). During the 2020 pandemic, when the split-level GSU Archival Research Methods class unexpectedly went online, students and co-teachers made lemonade from challenging circumstances; we pivoted from the syllabus and instead wrote about our experiences in a chapter titled "Doing Archival Research at Home," published in Laura Gray-Rosendale and Steven Rosendale's *Go Online!: Reconfiguring Writing Courses for the New Virtual World*. I submitted the chapter proposal for consideration, and once it was accepted I drafted the outline and contextual framework; students supplied discussions and illustrations addressing the opportunities and challenges they faced while learning how to investigate ephemera, letters, oral histories, and community records solely online. Paola Hernandez, for example, initially wanted to investigate US policies and security measures designed to ban immigration, but the scope of this project proved daunting without physical access to records. She explains how she adapted her final project to include a history of green cards based on digitized materials; she then supplemented her research by collecting border crossing narratives from personal contacts and family members (Gaillet, *Go Online!* 89).

We all read one another's sections and commented on the structure and content of the piece. The collection editors described our contribution thusly: "Gaillet and her students draw from both interdisciplinary scholarly research about working with archives as well as scholarly research about online learning, exposing the many ways in which their experiences might inevitably shape future iterations of this course as well as archival work in general" (Gaillet, *Go Online!* 10). As in this example, many side-by-side projects illustrate the varying practices of acknowledging writing partners and contributors. Book publishers and editors suggest a range of alternatives that include co-named authors, citations and references to student contributions listed within an essay, and appendices attributed solely to a student author. Teachers must understand up front that attribution practices vary widely in side-by-side coauthoring (as well as other examples of coauthoring found in this volume), and that the teacher may not control the byline.

Predating the published article now in print, students contributing to the *Go Online!* essay also presented their archival projects and takeaways from the course experience in a 2021 South Atlantic Modern Language Association roundtable session, "Archival Research in the Time of Pandemic" (Gaillet). The course co-teachers served as chair and respondent for the session, and all participants coauthored/edited the panel proposal/abstract—determining ways in which the component segments of the panel (and ultimately the essay) would work together (much as contributors to a collection often do when they have first presented their work at conferences). The panel helped us solidify the article, offering another layer to coauthoring and publishing that models the work of academic writing/publishing. Admittedly, adding these assignments to a writing course requires additional planning and labor. Prior to the start of the course, the teacher must find appropriate calls for papers, and ultimately the submissions don't move forward unless accepted by the publication editor or conference organizers. Students learn valuable lessons through the process of coauthoring, editing, and submitting their work for publication (whether accepted or not), but if the proposal is rejected, the teacher isn't left responsible for delivering a final project.

Finding external publishing opportunities demands increased effort and foresight on the part of the instructor, requires negotiating with publishers sometimes way in advance of the term's start, and runs the risk of failure if enrolled students lack interest or don't possess required writing skills. For these reasons, I include large-scale publishing assignments only when the topic dovetails with my own research interests and expertise. I recommend talking with the editor/publisher up front, clearly stating that the piece is coauthored with students but that the instructor will fill in content gaps and serve as final editor/guarantor of the project. This approach works particularly well in special topics or specific methods classes, ones in which students signed up for the course because they understood the narrow focus of the class and were invested in the subject matter.

While coauthoring does come with special considerations and requires extra layers of planning and execution, the effort pays off. In my experience, course coauthoring projects are invitational, serve as a heuristic for research stemming from unique *(First Person)*[2] perspectives, and provide new orientations to existing archives given researchers' distinct positionalities. Group publications also illuminate pathways for addressing Graban and Hayden's dual focus on encouraging collaboration with archivists and engaging in reflective research practices that "both stem from and contribute to a critical understanding of what to do better" as we craft and revise archival assignments (5). Coauthoring with students can help bring together many of these issues, particularly as we adopt external CFPs' research and writing guidelines that closely align with our specific course goals and aims. The required collaboration needed to prepare a manuscript for acceptance and publication shifts course pedagogy from top-down authoritative teaching toward cooperative interpretation of artifacts and primary materials, analysis of relevant published scholarship, consideration of stakeholders, a rhetorical analysis of the kairotic moment for submitting work, and discussions about the shape and form of the deliverable.

ILLUSTRATION #3: BLURRY SIDE-BY-SIDE COAUTHORSHIP, A RIFF ON INCLUDING STUDENT WORK IN TEXTBOOKS

Illustration #3, coauthoring in textbooks, highlights a layered, coauthored approach to student research and publishing in first-year and lower-division writing courses. Providing sample illustrations in pedagogical publications doesn't usually count as coauthoring with students. Instead, we often consider the teacher as editor and the student as contributor (and sometimes coach) in this scenario. Typically, in crafting a textbook, the teacher seeks permission to reproduce existing work *after* the student writing was drafted and submitted for course credit. In other words, students weren't deliberately writing with public circulation in mind when they initially created assignments and, therefore, weren't simultaneously focused on tasks of content production, method, *and* publication conventions while researching and drafting. Recognizing that archival research naturally lends itself to circulation and that the archival research process becomes more focused when composing with a target audience in mind, I began seeking opportunities for beginning college writers to publish. The coauthoring textbook illustration below uniquely addresses recurring issues in this chapter, including ways to acknowledge students' contributions when coauthoring with teachers, opportunities for disrupting status quo teacher-student coauthoring practices, and paths that lead to multidirectional benefits for coauthoring partners.

As Michelle Eble and I cowrote *Primary Research and Writing: People, Places, and Spaces*—one of the first undergraduate textbooks devoted to primary and archival research praxis—we quickly realized the need to include student writing samples to illustrate ways to engage in this often unfamiliar work (for teachers and students alike). To facilitate this goal, students in archive-based writing courses were informed up front that once the class was completed, they might be asked if they wanted to contribute to a textbook grounded in archival investigation. Participation was completely voluntary and occurred after the course ended (a typical approach to textbook writing). We kept in touch with former students who expressed interest in contributing to the book, discussing with them the uses and placement of their writing, sharing section and chapter drafts where their writing would appear, and offering opportunities to revise for publication. That practice may fall only slightly outside the norm for textbook writers, given that this work was the first of its kind and relied more heavily on student examples than most textbooks do. A cadre of students diligently stuck with this project, well beyond the end of their classes, and the text includes abundant writing examples collected from numerous sections of writing courses. These student samples (short paragraphs and exercises, research anecdotes, and full-length final projects) are annotated to indicate ways to incorporate/cite archival research and to blend secondary and primary sources in traditional research papers. While not *(First Person)*[2] coauthors with us, our student collaborators in this original archival textbook project did come to see themselves as public and academic scholars with agency, illustrating hallmarks of Lisa Ede's important scholarship that includes calls for mutual respect among collaborators and "critiques of single authorship and the academic norms that support it," as well as explorations of the significance of editing as "a form of textual mentoring" (132–35). However, chapter 4, "Becoming an Authority on a Topic," represents a departure from the textbook norm, showcasing elements of student Bob Brennan's innovative project through a (blurry) coauthored chapter.

Bob—a nontraditional returning student—and I coauthored this chapter embedded within the larger text. This chapter addresses a multitude of issues typical of researched writing, in addition to special considerations associated with archival investigation. Through this extended example, students and their teachers learn how to write about what they (think they) know, address unanticipated/inevitable dead ends in archival research, adjust research questions, rely upon both archival ephemera and secondary scholarship, and corroborate/refute memories of specific events through triangulation of published information and interviews (Gaillet and Eble, 85–106). In an interesting side-by-side arrangement, I coauthored with Bob, particularly when excerpting and introducing portions of his research, including elements of visual rhetoric and analysis, and working with the publisher to ensure that this chapter met the overall goals of the project. Bob was the subject matter expert, teaching me about a specific event and the significance of its aftermath; I was the pedagogical expert in teaching students to write with archives. While our approach may not pattern traditional approaches to coauthoring, we co-crafted this unique chapter (nested within a typical textbook), one that not only appends his beautiful essay as a student example but also parses his research strategies as a form of praxis throughout the chapter. Lunsford and Ede wonder, "How might the ethics of coauthorship be examined and defined?" and how coauthors might share responsibility for the final product in instances of group authorship, such as a textbook. They ask, specifically, "In cases of group authorship, where does the responsibility lie?" ("Why Write," 156). Their questions of ownership, responsibility, and oversight become magnified when applied to teacher-student collaborations or any coauthoring project where one partner has decision-making authority over another. In other words, how do we flatten unequal distribution across coauthors when the teacher secured the contract or publishing assignment, when the writing/work is simultaneously graded in a course *and* targeted to an external readership? Furthermore, in archival research, the investigators must ethically and accurately portray the voices of community members, collaborating with community stakeholders to ensure accountability and truthfulness in reporting their findings (as Bob did in "Becoming an Authority on a Topic"). Chapter 4 of *Primary Research and Writing* demonstrates a nonconventional way to foreground these concerns when coauthoring with students.

Conclusion

In "Why Write ... Together?" Lunsford and Ede ask, "Is the emphasis on or weight of various cognitive and rhetorical strategies different when coauthoring than when writing alone?" (156). Yes, and these shifts in writing and revision processes are amplified when applied to coauthoring with students in the archives, given the ethics of working with materials that readers can't easily access. Students and teachers regularly engage in solo research and writing: students in completing course work and teachers either publishing individually or with peers, among other scenarios. However, combining those roles and tasks in coauthoring may be quite intimidating for students and teachers unaccustomed to or uncomfortable with stepping out of prescribed classroom roles—both as coauthors *and* as archival researchers. This chapter suggests ideas for coauthoring with students and offers nuts-and-bolts ideas of how to get started through side-by-side coauthoring with primary materials. However, before initiating these collaborations, we need to think about why and how these acts hold promise, including for increased advancement opportunities and personal fulfillment issues associated with publishing (for teachers and students), to ethically expand existing scholarship to include a wider range of voices overlooked in the archives, to prepare students for advanced academic and work-place research and writing, and to seek ways to move through and beyond cultural stalemate and division by examining oral histories and archival holdings of communities not fully represented in existing scholarly conversations. The field of rhetoric and composition does not solely glorify the single author, evidenced in the numerous multi-authored and coauthored works that routinely win the field's top awards and prizes. But for students, the quandary now associated with undergraduate coauthoring lies in convincing students that this cooperative act can be meaningful and productive, given their wariness of forced collaboration stemming from years of overreliance upon and undertheorized uses of this pedagogy. As Laurie Grobman and Joyce Kinkead note, "[W]e as a faculty have not articulated to our students the methodology of inquiry in our fields except as injunctions in our classrooms to 'write a paper'" (x). Providing archival, side-by-side, coauthoring opportunities not only addresses these dilemmas, but encourages publishing by introducing students to circulation moments connected to their experiences, local circumstances, and community memberships.

Keeping a concrete reader and venue in mind while engaging in primary investigation aids students in formulating both research questions and a focused research plan, two issues that often sidetrack even experienced researchers when working in the archives. I share numerous examples of academic scholarship and community case studies with students in discussing the value of primary investigation (including my own published collaborative work) before inviting them to write with me, special collection librarians, and community collection curators. The final disseminated products may vary greatly. For example, in advanced archival methods classes, students regularly coauthor with stakeholders to create and publish finding aids for local collections and uncatalogued materials housed in community museums and libraries. Other students have worked side by side with community archivists they met while completing the site visit assignment, with administrators at their places of worship, or with work supervisors to coauthor publicly available histories of community organizations/businesses and cocreate public exhibition catalogs. In several instances, onsite archival assignments led to internships and jobs that included coauthoring public-facing or pedagogical materials with supervisors. In these signature experiences, the combination of acquiring archival investigation skills and cowriting with teachers/supervisors provided students a gateway and the confidence to engage in other public-facing coauthoring.

Lunsford and Ede's forty-year-old claim that "writers in the humanities have tended to ignore coauthorship, both in writing and teaching, while colleagues in the sciences and professions have long used it as a major mode" ("Why Write," 157) still holds true when applied to cowriting with students. Given recent college-to-career initiatives designed to attract and retain students; increased internship opportunities for humanities students; and broader understandings of the value of primary research in workplace writing, "which holds such potential significance for coauthoring," the contemporary question applied to coauthoring with students "may be not 'Why write together' but 'Why *not* write together?'" ("Why Write," 157).

Works Cited

Bahde, Anne, Heather Smedberg, and Mattie Taormina, editors. *Using Primary Sources: Hands-On Instructional Exercises.* ABC-CLIO, 2014.

Brereton, John, and Cinthia Gannett. "Intergenerational Exchange in Rhetoric and Composition: Some Views from Here." *Composition Studies*, vol. 49, no. 1, 2021, pp. 119–24.

Comer, Katie, Michael Harker, and Ben McCorkle, editors. *The Archive as Classroom: Pedagogical Approaches to Digital Archive of Literacy Narratives.* Utah State UP, 2019.

Daniel-Wariya, Joshua, and Lynn C. Lewis. "The Possibilities of Uncertainty: Digital Archives as Cunning Texts in a First Year Composition Curriculum." *Pedagogy*, vol. 20, no. 1, 2020, pp. 141–48.

Day, Kami, and Michelle Eodice. *(First Person)²: A Study of Co-Authoring in the Academy.* Utah State UP, 2001.

Ede, Lisa. "Review of *Stories of Mentoring: Theory and Praxis* by Michelle F. Eble and Lynée Lewis Gaillet." *Peitho*, vol. 18, no. 2, 2016, pp. 130–35.

Enoch, Jessica, and Pamela VanHaitsma. "Archival Literacy: Reading the Rhetoric of Digital Archives in the Undergraduate Classroom." *College Composition and Communication*, vol. 62, no. 2, 2012, pp. 216–42.

Ferriero, David S. "Scanning the Past to Make Access Happen." *Prologue Magazine*, vol. 46, no. 2, 2014. https://www.archives.gov/publications/prologue/2014/summer/archivist.html.

Gaillet, Lynée Lewis. "Doing Archival Research at Home." *Go Online!: Reconfiguring Writing Courses for the New Virtual World*, edited by Laura Gray-Rosendale and Steven Rosendale, Peter Lang, 2022, 85–96.

Gaillet, Lynée Lewis, and Michelle F. Eble. *Primary Research: People, Places, and Spaces.* Routledge, 2016.

Gaillet, Lynée Lewis, and Jessica A. Rose. "At Work in the Archives: Place-Based Research and Writing." *Writing Spaces*, vol. 4, Parlor Press, 2021, pp. 124–44.

Graban, Tarez, and Wendy Hayden, editors. *Teaching through the Archives: Text, Collaboration, and Activism.* Utah State UP, 2022.

Greer, Jane, and Laurie Grobman, editors. *Pedagogies of Public Memory: Teaching Writing and Rhetoric at Museums, Memorials, and Archives.* Routledge, 2016.

Grobman, Laurie, and Joyce Kinkead. "Introduction: Illuminating Undergraduate Research in English." *Undergraduate Research in English Studies*, edited by Laurie Grobman and Joyce Kinkead, National Council of Teachers of English, 2010, pp. ix–xxxii.

Hayden, Wendy. "And Gladly Teach: The Archival Turn's Pedagogical Turn." *College English*, vol. 80, no. 2, 2017, pp. 133–58.

Hayden, Wendy. "Gifts of the Archives: A Pedagogy for Undergraduate Research." *College Composition and Communication*, vol. 66, no. 3, 2015, pp. 402–26.

Kirsch, Gesa, Walker Smith, Caitlin Burns Allen, and Romeo García, editors. *Unsettling Archival Research: Engaging Critical, Communal, and Digital Archives.* Southern Illinois UP, 2023.

Lueck, Amy J. and Nadia Nasr. "Unsettling Archival Pedagogy." *Unsettling Archival Research: Engaging Critical, Communal, and Digital Archives.* Southern Illinois UP, 2023, pp. 283–99.

Lunsford, Andrea, and Lisa Ede. "Collaborative Authorship and the Teaching of Writing." *Cardozo Arts & Entertainment Law Journal*, vol. 10, no. 2, 1992, pp. 681–702.

Lunsford, Andrea, and Lisa Ede. "Why Write . . . Together?" *Rhetoric Review*, vol. 1, no. 2, 1983, pp. 150–57.

Skinnell, Ryan. "Foreword: The Archives of Epistemic Possibility." *Teaching through the Archives: Text, Collaboration, and Activism*, edited by Tarez Samra Graban and Wendy Hayden, Southern Illinois UP, 2022.

"#SuffrageSyllabus." *The Long Nineteenth Amendment.* https://long19.radcliffe.harvard.edu/teaching/suffrage-syllabus/.

9
Scenes from behind the Scenes

Fostering Reciprocal Faculty-Undergraduate Coauthorships via Feminist Communities of Practice

VANESSA KRAEMER SOHAN, JENNIFER PEÑA,
XUAN JIANG, AND GIOVANNA RODRIGUEZ

This chapter provides a glimpse behind the scenes of faculty-undergraduate coauthorship at a Hispanic-serving institution (HSI). We share our experiences as two faculty members (Xuan and Vanessa) and two student coauthors (Jennifer and Giovanna), providing narratives that explain how faculty-undergraduate coauthorship has the power to disrupt traditional conceptions of scholars and scholarship and provide equity and opportunities to first-generation, multilingual, and marginalized faculty-student coauthors, who can see themselves as active participants in academic scholarship (still largely a monolingual space, e.g., Ruiz and Sánchez). Given the lack of institutional support for the time and labor required to develop ethical coauthoring relationships, we build on existing scholarship on communities of practice (CoPs) for undergraduate research to call for establishing feminist CoPs, which provide respectful or relational and reciprocal frameworks to support undergraduate coauthorship between faculty and students. In our scenes, we explore how we have negotiated complex linguistic, cultural, and professional identity construction and unequal power relationships throughout the coauthoring process. Our stories describe the successes and challenges we faced as we sought to develop feminist CoPs, including established institutional CoPs (the writing center and the undergraduate journal) and more informal CoPs in and beyond the institution. We argue that the most effective feminist CoPs engage in reciprocal forms of collaboration targeted at achieving greater access, equity, and social justice; amplify undergraduate students' agency; and support the creation and development of CoPs.

Institution

Florida International University (FIU) is a large urban R1 HSI with a diverse student population: sixty-five percent Latinx, twelve percent Black, ten percent white, and three percent Asian (Robertson 687–688). Besides its racial/ethnic diversity, the 56,000-student population includes twenty percent first-generation students, fifty-seven percent Pell grant recipients, and ninety-four percent commuters ("First Generation Initiatives"). Significant demographic disparities between faculty and students remain, and unfortunately, students do not often see themselves reflected in the faculty (Robertson 687). Although FIU has had some success diversifying its faculty, it has done so among less secure, contingent faculty positions (Robertson 706), including Xuan's as a faculty administrator.

Framework

Our chapter builds on the work of scholars who point to the collaborative and reciprocal nature of faculty-undergraduate coauthorship (Crawford et al.; Fishman et al.; Godbee et al.; Mina et al.; Rounsaville et al.). Given that our institution is an HSI, we are invested in understanding the power of coauthorship for marginalized students. In Larracey et al.'s exploration of the value of undergraduate research (UR) for marginalized students, they argue that Lave and Wenger's concept of communities of practice (CoPs) can serve as a heuristic that helps faculty and students understand the centrality of "relationality and community" and "reciprocity" in UR, particularly in humanities-based UR contexts (Larracey et al. 3). Larracey et al.'s focus on UR directly translates to faculty-undergraduate coauthorship—a collaboration that fosters mentorship and depends on relationality, community, and reciprocity. In this brief literature review, we seek to define CoPs and then explore how a feminist framework (Foss and Griffin; Shanahan) overlaid with the heuristic of CoPs can help us better understand the reciprocal, relational, community-based nature of faculty-student coauthorship. To that end, we propose feminist CoPs as a way to better understand our coauthorship experiences.

We adopt Lave and Wenger's definition of CoPs as "groups of people who share a set of problems, or a passion about a topic, and who deepen their knowledge and expertise in this area by interacting on an ongoing basis" (4). As Wenger argues, everyone belongs to several CoPs in and beyond educational institutions (6). CoPs can exist within and outside of institutions and organizations, and their success depends on their ability to "generate enough excitement, relevance, and value to attract and engage members" (Wenger et al. 50), as membership is based on participation (Wenger 66). Ann Johns differentiates between CoPs and discourse communities by explaining how discourse communities "focus . . . on texts and language, the genres and lexis that enable members throughout the world maintain their goals, regulate their membership, and communicate efficiently with one another" (51). CoPs add to this definition by providing a framework that highlights a "complex collection of individuals who share genres, language, values, concepts, and 'ways of being' . . . often distinct from those held by other communities" (52). We have chosen the term *CoPs* because of the focus on the complexity of intersecting practices and values provided by this framework.

Wenger highlights four key, mutually constitutive areas related to learning in CoPs: *meaning, practice, community,* and *identity*. Through CoPs, members better understand how their lived experiences enable them to make *meaning* in the world; members' conversations help situate their *practice* in social and historical contexts and direct them toward common goals; the *community* assigns value to mutual endeavors and affirms the skills members bring; and members explore *identity*, "how learning changes who we are and creates personal histories of becoming in the context of our communities" (Wenger 5). Our scenes highlight Wenger's four components and underscore the reciprocity and connection fostered by CoPs, which we have found disrupt some of the traditional power relations between faculty and students. As Larracey et al. point out, CoPs foster "deep connections with others through shared histories and experiences, reciprocity, affection, and mutual commitments" (Wenger qtd. in Larracey et al. 12). Similarly, Palmer et al. argue that the learning and mentoring engaged in by undergraduate and faculty coauthors underscore the "inherent cultural, historical, and institutional context of learning within a community of practice" (4–5). Palmer et al.'s emphasis on the learning and mentoring benefits of CoPs sets the tone for valuing CoPs for minoritized individuals, including some of us as coauthors.

In our faculty-undergraduate coauthorships, we've found that such work reaffirms the knowledge and expertise students bring as legitimate, thus highlighting the importance of building on existing and developing new CoPs with students and enabling them to contribute to deepening knowledge of *all* participants in CoPs. This is reflected in a testimonial article by Hochstetler, who shared her growing professional identity as a former undergraduate writing tutor, foregrounding her later "participation in the professional conversations in English education" as a faculty member (43). Hochstetler notes that graduate students are "often deemed more appropriate partners" than undergraduate students for research work (43), which speaks to the untraditional and scarce coauthorships between faculty and undergraduate students. When opportunities to participate in UR are available to minoritized students, they can then work with mentors to "enhance work-related skills that can better prepare them for their future careers and interpersonal relationships" (Castillo and Estudillo 2; Larracey et al.). Our coauthorships highlight the need to validate undergraduate students' linguistic and cultural resources, as we will see in our stories below.

Understanding CoPs through a feminist framework highlights the asymmetrical power relations at work in faculty-student coauthorships. Coauthorship as a form of UR promotes learning experiences that come out of a feminist dedication to "transgressing boundaries" that exclude and silence undergraduate student writers (Shanahan xvi)—particularly those from marginalized communities. Our dedication to inclusion aligns with our belief in the value of faculty and students' lived experiences to the coauthorship process. Faculty and students who bring their everyday experiences to the research enterprise and build on and establish CoPs enable, enhance, and expand the impact of coauthorship opportunities. This process redefines what counts as legitimate knowledge and whose voices can and should contribute to meaning-making.

Methodology

To understand how we participate in feminist CoPs coauthorship, we employed collaborative autoethnography (CAE), a method that allows researchers to capitalize on the power of story through their own written accounts as a way of "knowing and teaching" (Lapadat 589). Researchers' lived experiences become data as it "expands and opens up a wider lens on the world, eschewing rigid definitions of what constitutes meaningful and useful research" while also helping "us understand how the kinds of people we claim, or are perceived, to be influence interpretations of what we study, how we study it" (Ellis et al. 275). CAE "reclaims voices and aims to break silences by introducing insiders' perspectives on societal issues" (Visse and Niemeijer 305). Our study was strengthened by employing CAE, as it combined collaborative and critical views with individual perspectives through self-reflexivity and feminist collaboration (Roy and Uekusa 388).

In this sense, the current chapter is an extension of Foss and Griffin's invitational rhetoric, which involves a reciprocal relationship between listeners and rhetors to achieve mutually "greater understanding of [an] issue" (5), a goal that informed our data collection. A key component of our application of invitational rhetoric as a frame for our scenes of collaboration and coauthorship is Foss and Griffin's notion that rhetors and listeners "contribute to the thinking about an issue" collectively (79). In the scenes of mentorship and coauthorship described in the current chapter, the concept of inviting people in distinct positions (such as mentor, mentee, faculty member, administrator, and student) and with different power relationships to share their experiences and have those experiences contribute to coauthored scholarship reflects the potential for invitational rhetorical relationships to promote "appreciation, value, and a sense of equality" (79). Aligning with the principles of feminism and the goals of invitational rhetoric described by Foss and Griffin, we thereby sought to establish coauthorship and mentorship "rooted in equality, immanent value, and self-determination" (5).

Our data collection was conducted through both writing scenes on the authors' respective coauthoring experiences in the same institution and sharing narrative accounts via Google Drive. When meeting virtually, we "capture[d] researchers' present thoughts and perspectives as well as their past" by sharing our lived stories and responding to each other (Chang et al. 78) through dialogic interactions and written comments to continue our inquiry, metaphorically peeling layers of data to approach the core to better understand ourselves and our shared narratives. In doing so, we were able to identify not only relationality and reciprocity among our coauthoring experiences "constituted in interaction with context, time and place" (Visse and Niemeijer 305), but also how our CoP experiences connect with and advance the existing literature.

Our narratives focus on several key scenes during the process of planning, writing, revising, and editing coauthored scholarship, and as we sought to work within and establish CoPs at the individual, departmental, and institutional level. These scenes expose how we have negotiated complex linguistic, cultural, and professional identity construction and navigated unequal power relationships (including student-student, student-faculty, writer-editor, and faculty-administrator) throughout the coauthoring process. Through CAE, collaboration becomes more accessible in that researchers are also participants and findings more contextualized and generalizable.

Scene One: The Writing Center and Beyond (Xuan and Jennifer)

Xuan, at the time of writing this chapter, was a writing center administrator (WCA) and contingent English instructor at FIU. Xuan started the faculty-undergraduate collaboration journey in her undergraduate class as an inviting announcement, along with other academic opportunities. Although the call was extended to everyone, three Hispanic female students showed stronger interest and earned their coauthorship in four academic publications from 2020 to 2022. Jennifer has three coauthored publications with Xuan; as one of the undergraduate coauthors then, Jennifer moved on to her master's at FIU and is now a doctoral candidate at University of Miami with no gap year, building on the research foundation she accumulated as an undergraduate student.

Those signed-up undergraduates showed strong drive in drafting manuscripts and making their voices heard. They were impressively competent at contributing ideas, connecting literature to their knowledge, and employing rhetorical moves in academic writing. Their motivation was contagious and their contribution was impactful, which resonates with Fishman et al.'s emphasis on reciprocal benefits—"persistence, productivity, and academic success"—of both mentors and mentees (159).

These undergraduate coauthors' understanding of the word *research* has grown, and their roles in academic writing have changed from readers to writers. Jennifer and other undergraduate coauthors experienced benefits of UR, which include metacognitive explorations such as identity shifts through CoP engagement as student collaborators perceive themselves from knowledge consumers to contributors (Palmer et al. 5). Beyond thinking of research as an abstract concept or working on research projects only in course contexts, faculty-student coauthorships can provide an opportunity for students to envision themselves as scholars who can do public-facing work. Encouragement and guidance from a faculty mentor can demystify the research and publication processes and connect students more directly to this kind of faculty work.

Such coauthoring was possible in Xuan's context for at least two reasons: First, the writing center (WC) scholarship is emerging, with undergraduate journals of both creative and academic writing. And second, the WC course and context has helped Xuan establish the space as a CoP for coauthoring. Xuan acknowledged students' time and labor by booking the hours of interested students so that they could write on the WC's dime. As Larracey et al. write, "Part of UR's work is to demonstrate to students that they can and do make important contributions to our collective disciplinary knowledge despite histories of exclusion" (11). One way to acknowledge the importance of students' contributions is to value students' labor from the start by recognizing their financial, mental, and emotional labor involved in such writing, which also helps marginalized students who may typically lack the material resources to engage in long-term writing projects.

In this CoP, Xuan's experiences align with Godbee et al.'s coauthoring journey, having observed students beginning to "see themselves as writers with the ability and even responsibility to write for action in the world" (5). With Xuan as her faculty mentor, Jennifer (as an undergraduate student at the time) was equipped to approach later scholarly work with an understanding of the steps involved in presentations, proposals, and publications. The projects gave Jennifer early exposure to the various stages of the research process, which may not be explicitly taught to students and can become part of the hidden curriculum of "how to do, write about, and talk about research" and "how to navigate complex bureaucracies" (McCrory Calarco 2). As a current doctoral student, Jennifer looks back on her experiences with her mentors during her years as an undergraduate and master's student as reference points for these processes. Jennifer has used examples from her work with Xuan and other collaborators when talking about research with her students who are new to research, extending the reach of that early mentorship.

Scene Two: Discussions of Authorship Order (Xuan and Jennifer)

Undeniably, faculty-undergraduate coauthoring may face various challenges within and beyond CoPs. One such challenge was about authorship order among Xuan, Xuan's mentor, and Jennifer in 2019. Xuan, the first author, led the drafting of a book chapter and felt the need to have Jennifer contribute her voice as a local bilingual student. Jennifer was not part of the proposal but was then invited to contribute to the full manuscript. Jennifer synthesized existing literature with her own standing for the piece. Xuan initiated the discussion and negotiated Jennifer's authorship with her mentor, a senior white male professor, which was beyond her comfort zone of her intersectional identities as a middle-aged Asian female novice faculty member. The mentor was hesitant in the beginning but slowly gave in after reading Jennifer's contributions and listening to Xuan's advocacy. The discussion was complex in the sense that more authors than the two willing parties were involved, and so were intersectional identities and unequal power relationships.

In a journal article coauthored by Xuan, Jennifer, and other two undergraduate students at FIU, mentorship played a pivotal role toward self-advocacy for Jennifer. The coauthorship was between people with multiple roles: a faculty member and three students who were also coworkers. Acknowledging that Jennifer had contributed consistently to the project over the drafting and revising periods, Xuan encouraged her to advocate for herself in the upcoming authorship order conversation, through which Jennifer learned to keep track of and be confident about her level of contribution to a coauthored work, which was important preparation for future collaborations. Being fully aware of the power dynamics involved with professional and individual identities, Xuan initiated the authorship conversation by stating her intention of being the last author, which set a respectful and candid tone. This conversation and its result were an exemplary trial in that they countered the status quo of scientific scholars' authorship—women are more likely to fail to negotiate authorship successfully (Edwards et al.).

This CoP has benefited Jennifer and other student coauthors and empowered Xuan. Xuan, as Jennifer's mentor and coauthor for years, was invited to Jennifer's master's thesis defense and introduced as her "research mentor" by Jennifer (Vanessa chaired Jennifer's thesis). As a contingent faculty member and unofficial mentor of a graduate student, Xuan, having heard Jennifer's introduction, felt more legitimate and motivated to continue with her mentorship and coauthorship with students. We believe that storytelling between mentors and mentees is an important part of sharing knowledge and contributing to growth within mentorships and beyond, as those stories can then be passed on to future mentees. Palmer et al. call for such commitment and continuity with the logic that "commitment to identity development of young adults in the academy then becomes a commitment to future leaders who can embrace change" (12).

Scene Three: Navigating University Bureaucracies (Vanessa and Giovanna)

As a student in Vanessa's upper-division spring 2019 writing course focused on translinguality and transmodality, Giovanna completed projects describing her experiences negotiating language, identity, and culture. In fall 2019,

Giovanna visited Vanessa's office hours to discuss continuing her research and get advice about her struggles to remain enrolled and engaged at FIU. In the meantime, Vanessa proposed a contribution for volume two of *Deep Reading, Deep Learning* (Sullivan et al.). The editors expressed interest in Vanessa seeking out a contribution from one of her students, and Giovanna agreed to expand her final research project into her own chapter.

Vanessa and Giovanna's scenes describe how their work together drew upon CoPs in and beyond the university as they worked to address issues of access to resources. Their collaboration affirms how CoPs provide "inventive ways of engaging students [and faculty] in meaningful practices" and "access to resources that encourage participation" (Wenger 10). CoPs helped Vanessa and Giovanna "identify with particular learning trajectories" around publication, including "actions, discussions, and reflections that make a difference to the communities that they value" (10). In their work together, Vanessa and Giovanna sought to develop a reciprocal, ethical faculty-student coauthoring relationship that foregrounds their lived experience and works to resolve the material and systemic challenges student and faculty writers face.

Looking back, Giovanna needed supportive CoPs *inside* of the university to complement her learning from *outside* of the university—CoPs that would recognize the lived experiences and resources she could bring to the university. Despite Giovanna's desire to succeed, the university's financial aid bureaucracy presented numerous challenges. When Giovanna graduated from high school, she faced many financial struggles and so chose to start at a less expensive local two-year college. As a first-generation student, she often felt alone; while she received emotional support from friends and family, she didn't have any guidance about the bureaucratic issues she faced. After transferring to FIU, she was incredibly stressed—unsure if she was making the correct decisions for herself around her finances, her major, her minor, how much to push back against university administrators who told her "no," and who to contact as she tried to untangle paperwork related to financial aid.

As one of Giovanna's informal faculty mentors, the roadblocks Giovanna encountered frustrated Vanessa as a faculty member and graduate advisor. Vanessa felt powerless in a system that should work better for students, especially at an HSI where administrators tout their dedication to student retention and success and often cite the importance of financial aid support systems to the success of first-generation students (see Rehr et al.). When navigating Giovanna's questions, Vanessa reached out to her CoPs in and beyond the English Department. However, like Giovanna, she lacked access to the resources she needed, in part because her colleagues dealt with these kinds of systemic issues on an individualized basis. The lack of collective understanding for a community-based solution speaks to the need to establish CoPs for first-generation students like Giovanna who face issues of access to institutional resources, retention, and success.

Giovanna found the resources, in part thanks to the connections she made with professors and administrators and her ability to draw upon the resources provided by her diverse community of friends outside of the university. Her friends let her couch surf and provided her with food, and with her peers and professors at the university who helped her identify less-visible scholarships and write letters of support—all forms of mentorship and collaboration necessary to her success. Although Giovanna wishes she could have had a more well-defined CoP at FIU for first-generation students like her, with labor and luck, she was able to apply the social-emotional resources she had developed in her CoPs to navigate these challenges. She was ultimately able to graduate in 2021.

Scene Four: Writing and Revising (Vanessa and Giovanna)

While Giovanna was facing these ongoing issues, in spring 2020 she and Vanessa began work as coauthors to collaboratively build out Giovanna's chapter based on her class research surveying coworkers about linguistic shame. Vanessa also contributed her own chapter on translingual reading practices and wrote a brief essay response to Giovanna. The process proceeded smoothly for Giovanna; she felt she maintained the scope and purpose of her project in responding to the editors' comments despite her unfamiliarity with the publishing process and expectations. She had no idea how long the process would take—exacerbated by the COVID-19 pandemic. Although Vanessa brought prior publication experiences to their coauthorship, she had never composed with an undergraduate and felt similarly uncertain. They helped one another throughout the process through a reciprocal, collaborative mentorship, building a small but successful CoP together. Their work ultimately encouraged Giovanna to pursue her graduate degree and Vanessa to seek out other institutional CoPs, connecting with Xuan and Jennifer in FIU's writing center, and later working with Xuan to build more CoPs, such as the *FIU Undergraduate Research Journal* (https://fiuurj.fiu.edu/).

Throughout the process, Vanessa and Giovanna developed a reciprocal coauthoring relationship that enabled them to navigate editor-coauthor power dynamics while maintaining their agency. In their meetings and brainstorming sessions, Giovanna and Vanessa were able to provide one another with feedback to clarify their arguments and continue to build on the coauthoring relationship they had already developed. Given Giovanna's status as an essential worker during the pandemic and her struggle to overcome the institutional and bureaucratic challenges outlined earlier, Vanessa negotiated a less time-intensive revision plan with the editors, a key part of any academic publication process. As the faculty coauthor with more experience, Vanessa felt it was important for her to use her position to advocate for Giovanna. Vanessa and Giovanna developed their arguments in conversation with one another. For example, the editors asked Giovanna to describe her own experiences with linguistic shame. In Vanessa and Giovanna's revision discussions, Giovanna recounted examples of teachers privileging Standardized Academic English and discouraging her and other students from viewing their language, identity, and culture as resources. However, rather than focusing on a shameful moment, she flipped the script on the editors' suggestion by focusing on the power of a positive comment she received from an elementary teacher on a personal essay: "This is why I became an English teacher." That piece of praise stuck with her as an example of a rare piece of positive feedback, reinforcing her and Vanessa's argument about how monolingual ideologies limit students—an argument they both ended up highlighting in their chapters for the collection.

Although the publication process took longer than Giovanna expected, she felt it was worth it when the print copy arrived and she was able to celebrate with the same family and friends who made up the CoPs necessary to her ultimate success in graduating and in completing her chapter. Vanessa was also incredibly relieved to see the final copy, in part because her and Giovanna's coauthorship took place during the COVID-19 pandemic—their work together kept Vanessa engaged in research and student collaboration during a time when she felt isolated from so many of her students. These experiences led both Giovanna and Vanessa to see the importance of students and faculty establishing CoPs to advocate for one another and provide similar positive and reciprocal coauthoring opportunities.

Conclusion

As Wenger argues, CoPs provide a vocabulary for understanding "learning [a]s an integral part of our everyday lives" (8). Our experiences with coauthorship reiterate how integral "everyday" learning is and how important it is to recognize the challenges that undergraduate coauthors are experiencing, as well as the diverse linguistic, cultural, and social resources they bring to our collaborations. In using collaborative autoethnography to tell our stories to one another during the writing process for this piece, and in the product we've shown you here, we hope to demonstrate the value of CoPs to the success of faculty-undergraduate collaboration. As we've shown, our CoPs enabled us to find ways to meaningfully practice coauthorship in a way that reinforced our everyday lived experiences and identities—a fundamentally feminist act. The CoPs we developed have been vital to the development of successful, sustainable, and reciprocal mentoring relationships that have come out of the above coauthoring experiences. We have listened to and learned from one another in ways that disrupt traditional understandings of the one-sided benefits of such coauthorships: both Xuan and Vanessa feel they have grown exponentially as mentors, scholars, teachers, and administrators because of these experiences.

Jennifer and Xuan's reciprocal, collaborative coauthorship indicates that there can be a synergic impact for contingent faculty who are perplexed with their professional identities and the future students of mentees who later have teaching roles. Mentorship of undergraduate students has the potential to have a ripple effect among those students who go on to teach. Worth noting here is Palmer et al.'s (7) finding that relationships with faculty members had the most important influence on their undergraduate participants' self-perceptions when compared to their relationships with other types of mentors (such as graduate students and peers). While it may be productive for some students to be encouraged by graduate students and peers in their research pursuits, faculty-student coauthorships enable the development of long-term mentorships that can play a major role in students' self-perceptions of themselves as researchers. Jennifer and Giovanna can attest to the value of such mentorships on their self-perceptions, including their ability to see themselves as current MA/PhD students.

The coauthorship process solidified Vanessa's belief in the importance of empowering students to publish their own stories in and beyond our classrooms, and the need for developing systemic responses to the challenges individual students face, which can be supported through CoPs in and beyond the institution. Given the context of Giovanna and Vanessa's collaboration—during the pandemic—both benefited from one another's support, but Giovanna in particular lacked material support for her coauthorship. Vanessa found ways to garner financial support by participating in a faculty research grant during the summer, such funding did not exist for Giovanna. Because of the pandemic, their collaboration often felt as if it was happening in a vacuum (a lengthy process exacerbated by pandemic-related publishing delays). Vanessa's experience highlights the need to create supportive CoPs for coauthorship that can support faculty *and* students during such challenges.

Xuan and Vanessa's approach to coauthorship continues to evolve from solely focusing on one-to-one models of mentorship to a more collaborative, interdisciplinary, intra-institutional model: a brand-new CoP. Over the past two years, they have worked together to establish and coedit the first interdisciplinary *FIU Undergraduate Research Journal (URJ)* at their institution. The process of starting a peer-reviewed journal run with and for students not only took advantage of the existing CoPs at FIU's writing center but also drew upon other interdisciplinary CoPs at the university. In Xuan and Vanessa's experience developing and publishing the first issue of the FIUURJ, they have sought to build out the infrastructure that enables the development of more CoPs and thus move away from "the one-to-one burden of traditional UR models by emphasizing collaboration and community" among faculty, administrators, and students engaged in UR (Larracey et al. 15). Jennifer also heard about the journal. On the day of saying goodbye before moving to another institution for her doctoral program, Jennifer brought a cross-stitch with "FIUURJ" on it. Xuan has kept this handmade piece in a salient space of her office. Just like the stitch, the three have been weaving together in the ongoing tapestry of authorship and friendship, and the tapestry evolves with more individuals involved.

Xuan and Vanessa's collaboration of founding FIUURJ answers the call by Larracey et al. for "administrators, mentors, and institutional leaders" to "consider ... building new UR programs or reimagining existing opportunities in partnership with multiple institutions or within one institution" (14). Such work, Xuan and Vanessa have found, offers opportunities to not just replicate the benefits of CoPs like FIU's writing center but develop a broader network of "reciprocity and respect" at their institution—one that hopefully will have the institutional staying power to impact additional students beyond those they can reach individually.

Works Cited

Castillo, Yuleinys A., and Antonio Estudillo. "Undergraduate Research: An Essential Piece for Underrepresented Students' College Success." *PURM: Perspectives on Undergraduate Research and Mentoring*, vol. 4, no. 1, 2015, pp. 1–15.

Chang, Heewon, Faith, Ngunjiri, and Kathy-Ann C. Hernandez. *Collaborative Autoethnography*. Left Coast Press, 2013.

Crawford, Anne E., Peyton Galloway, and Jane Greer. "Drawing Hope from Difficult History: Public Memory and Rhetorical Education in Kansas City." *College English*, vol. 82, no. 3, 2020, pp. 255–81.

Edwards, Hannah A., Julia Schroeder, and Hannah L. Dugdale. "Gender Differences in Authorships Are Not Associated with Publication Bias in an Evolutionary Journal." *PLoS One*, vol. 13, no. 8, 2018, e0201725. https://doi.org/10.1371/journal.pone.0201725.

Ellis, Carolyn, Tony E. Adams, and Arthur P. Bochner. "Autoethnography: An Overview." *Historical Social Research/Historische Sozialforschung*, vol. 36, no. 4, 2011, pp. 273–90. https://www.jstor.org/stable/23032294.

"First Generation Initiatives." *Florida International University*. https://firstgen.fiu.edu. Accessed 6 Mar. 2023.

Fishman, Jenn, Katherine Hovland, Ali Leonhard, and Sunaina Randhawa. "Conducting Consequential Research: The Access Writing Project." *Pedagogy*, vol. 22, no. 1, 2022, pp. 159–63. https://doi.org/10.1215/15314200-9385590.

Foss, Sonja K., and Cindy L. Griffin. "Beyond Persuasion: A Proposal for an Invitational Rhetoric." *Communication Monographs*, vol. 62, 1995, pp. 2–18.

Godbee, Beth, Jessica Bazan, Megan Glise, Ariel Gonzalez, Katelyn Quigley, and Brittany White. "Stretching beyond the Semester: Undergraduate Research, Ethnography of the University, and Proposals for Local Change." *PURM: Perspectives on Undergraduate Research and Mentoring*, vol. 3, no. 2, 2015. https://epublications.marquette.edu/english_fac/302/.

Hochstetler, Sarah. "From Consuming to Producing: The Potential of Preservice Teacher Scholarship in English Teacher Preparation." *Language Arts Journal of Michigan*, vol. 27, no.1, 2011, pp. 43–46. https://doi.org/10.9707/2168-149X.1835.

Johns, Ann M. *Text, Role and Context: Developing Academic Literacies.* 1st ed., Cambridge UP, 1997. https://doi.org/10.1017/CBO9781139524650.

Lapadat, Judith C. "Ethics in Autoethnography and Collaborative Autoethnography." *Qualitative Inquiry*, vol. 23, no. 8, 2017, pp. 589–603.

Larracey, Caitlin, Natalie Strobach, Julie Lirot, Thai-Catherine Matthews, and Samanda Robinson. "'A Place to Be Heard and to Hear': The Humanities Collaboratory as a Model for Cross-College Cooperation and Relationship-Building in Undergraduate Research." *Innovative Higher Education*, 2022. https://doi.org/10.1007/s10755-022-09612-x.

Lave, Jean, and Etienne Wenger. *Situated Learning: Legitimate Peripheral Participation.* Cambridge UP, 1991.

McCrory Calarco, Jessica. *A Field Guide to Grad School: Uncovering the Hidden Curriculum.* Princeton UP, 2020.

Mina, Lilian, Megan McAfoose, Megan Moulden, and Shannon Zilavy. "Class-Based Research in the English Composition Class." *Perspectives on Undergraduate Research and Mentoring*, vol. 3, no. 1, 2013, pp. 1–13. https://eloncdn.blob.core.windows.net/eu3/sites/923/2019/06/Mina-et-al-3.1.pdf.

Palmer, Ruth J., Andrea N. Hunt, Michael R. Neal, and Brad Wuetherick. "The Influence of Mentored Undergraduate Research on Students' Identity Development."

Scholarship and Practice of Undergraduate Research, vol. 2, no. 2, 2018, pp. 4–14. https://doi.org/10.18833/spur/2/2/1.

Rehr, Tori I., Erica P. Regan, Zayd Abukar, and Jacquelyn C. A. Meshelemiah. "Financial Wellness of First-Generation College Students." *College Student Affairs Journal*, vol. 40, no. 1, 2022, pp. 90–105.

Robertson, Douglas L. "Equifinality, Equity, and Intersectionality: Faculty Issues in Pursuit of Performance Metrics." *Innovative Higher Education*, vol. 47, 2022, pp. 683–709. https://doi.org/10.1007/s10755-022-09594-w.

Rounsaville, Angela, Esther Milu, and Joel Schneier. "Contributive Knowledge Making and Critical Language Awareness: A Justice-Oriented Paradigm for Undergraduate Research at a Hispanic-Serving Institution." *College English*, vol. 84, no. 6, 2022, pp. 519–45.

Roy, Rituparna, and Shinya Uekusa. "Collaborative Autoethnography: 'Self-Reflection' as a Timely Alternative Research Approach During the Global Pandemic." *Qualitative Research Journal*, vol. 20, no. 4, 2022, pp. 383–92.

Ruiz, Iris D., and Raúl Sánchez, editors. *Decolonizing Rhetoric and Composition Studies: New Latinx Keywords for Theory and Pedagogy*. Springer, 2016.

Shanahan, Jenny Olin. "The Transformative Power of Undergraduate Research in Writing Studies." *The Naylor Report on Undergraduate Research in Writing Studies*, edited by Dominic DelliCarpini et al., Parlor, 2021, pp. xi–xvii.

Sullivan, Patrick, Howard Tinberg, and Sheridan Blau, editors. *Deep Reading, Deep Learning: Deep Reading Volume 2*. Peter Lang, 2023.

Visse, Merel, and Alistair Niemeijer. "Autoethnography as a Praxis of Care–the Promises and Pitfalls of Autoethnography as a Commitment to Care." *Qualitative Research Journal*, vol. 16, no. 3, 2016, pp. 301–12.

Wenger, Etienne. *Communities of Practice: Learning, Meaning, and Identity*. Cambridge UP, 1998.

Wenger, Etienne, Richard McDermott, and William M. Snyder. *Cultivating Communities of Practice: A Guide to Managing Knowledge*. Harvard Business School Press, 2002.

SECTION III

Consequences of and Reflections on Coauthoring

10
Destabilizing and Restabilizing Hierarchies in Faculty-Undergraduate Coauthoring

Abby M. Dubisar

Complexities arise when faculty research, write, and publish with their current and former undergraduate students. These complications may go unacknowledged or be hidden, as the coauthoring process yields a complete and finished peer-reviewed work, evidence of successful academic partnership. Faculty mentors move on to other projects and undergraduate authors graduate and pursue other goals. This collection offers an exigence to reflect on the process of coauthoring to acknowledge its untold stories, inviting considerations regarding how undergraduate student-faculty coauthored projects implicitly involve hierarchies regarding the benefits that coauthors derive. As someone who thrives by learning from undergraduate students in my classes, coauthoring with my students beyond our classroom context—which results in publications that I then teach in future classes—has enabled me to foster the joy I experience in teaching with building my publication record.

Digging into my own experiences as a faculty mentor and coauthor in such undertakings, I engage here some of the constraints and challenges regarding how hierarchies are subverted and maintained as faculty write with and support students, questioning how impact occurs. As an invitation to other faculty to do similar consideration, I offer a context for discussing how such writing partnerships can both destabilize hierarchies and risk re-entrenching those same hierarchies. Based on research on collaborations between undergraduates and faculty (Blackwell and Martin; Grobman; Grobman and Kinkead), as well my experiences publishing and mentoring publication with eight undergraduate students in three separate contexts after they were students in my classes, I identify moments in the research, writing, and publishing processes when the continuum between mentor and coauthor shifts and changes by drawing on project origins, publication motivation, reviewer feedback, and the afterlife of publications. This chapter is not coauthored, a choice that reflects its focus on my faculty perspective. If I had potential coauthors to write this chapter with me, I would have approached them to invite their perspectives on how hierarchies are de- and restabilized. However, I currently do not have any potential coauthors, including past coauthors, who are interested in analyzing and theorizing about issues of coauthorship and the complex hierarchies within them.

In what follows I ask readers to notice the fluidity of impact within faculty-undergraduate coauthoring projects, especially those that result in normative academic publications. Further, this chapter offers recommendations to take up in coauthoring contexts that destabilize hierarchies. These recommendations include being transparent with students about how such coauthoring may unevenly benefit contributors. In what follows I ultimately argue that while these power differentials can be productively troubled, doing so is an ongoing and recursive process that can be obscured by academic norms unfamiliar and uninteresting to many undergraduate researchers.

Hierarchies in Coauthorship

My motivation for coauthoring with undergraduate students began when I wanted wider audiences to learn from my students and their projects. I teach two undergraduate courses most frequently: Gender and Communication, a twenty-five-person, 300-level course that fulfills my university's US diversity requirement and thus invites a wide range of majors, and Analysis of Popular Culture Texts, a thirty-person, 200-level course that fulfills an advanced communication requirement for a variety of degree programs as well as degree requirements for students majoring in English, speech, and technical communication. As a feminist rhetoric scholar, I can structure some aspects of these courses around my expertise. I am thus especially excited when students choose to pursue topics that build upon and further my own research interests, an occurrence that can be rare since such a wide variety of majors take my classes.

My R1 job requires teaching, research, and service. While I am evaluated on all three components of my job, peer-reviewed publications are expected at a regular clip to remain "research intensive" and be deemed "meeting expectations" in my annual review. Coauthoring with undergraduate researchers is, to me, a satisfying combination of all three work roles. I find a kinship with scholars such as Laurie Grobman and Joyce Kinkead who describe undergraduate research (UR) as bringing together "our passions for teaching and research," a synergy that can be rare (xi). I assign projects relevant to writing studies in my courses and notice how some students choose topics that happen to be related to my research that we could expand together if they wish. Then, if they are interested, I mentor them through the process in a way that can be fun, work- and time-intensive, and possibly acknowledged by my employer as valuable. And when coauthoring results in a peer-reviewed publication in my field, I have evidence of meeting expectations for what my employer deems the most important part of my job, which benefits me.

My job requirements do not necessarily value UR as an end in itself, a hierarchy I subvert by writing and publishing with students. As a teacher, I find myself both proud of my students' projects and annoyed that these projects become trapped within the classroom platforms and spaces for which they were initially created. Doubled up with these feelings of joy and pride is my conviction that writing studies scholars can and should assign projects that the broader field would be interested in and from which they could learn. Coauthoring with undergraduates puts into practice the writing studies belief that high-impact practices can shape and change our field, a broader mission to which I wish to contribute. As an instructor, I want my students to be part of that impactful spread of undergraduate influence on our field and publishing with them seems like a reliable way to build that impact. That said, this influence is incomplete and inequitable, as it is shaped by my own biases regarding which student projects fit expectations for the field of writing studies and my own research agenda. Further, my own interactions with students guide my impulses to pursue research together with them. Our coauthoring begins from their ideas and classroom behavior, not my desire to invite an undergraduate researcher to join me in a project I am pursuing.

In the remaining pages I describe three completed projects and one project underway to discuss how hierarchies shift and change in coauthorship between me and my student coauthors. I organized these examples based on my level of involvement and how my role changed across coauthoring contexts. In the first example of publication I characterize my coauthors as a group of students who contributed to a scholarly project I lead, joining their class projects together to create an argument about students' conceptions of remix. My role shifts considerably in the final publication example where the opposite happened: the student's project reached publication more independently from me and I composed an instructor reflection for the final version. I characterize these shifting roles throughout this essay, and I complicate those roles with details of the coauthoring as I describe each project. After detailing the coauthorship contexts and the fluidity of hierarchy maintenance and subversion, I turn to actions and recommendations that these experiences prompt me to make.

Coauthorship as Faculty-Led: Rhetorical Analysis with Video

In 2017 six undergraduate students and I published a journal article: "Haul, Parody, Remix: Mobilizing Feminist Rhetorical Criticism with Video" (Dubisar et al.). This article built on my previous remix research (Dubisar and Palmeri) and my work in feminist rhetoric and video (Dubisar, "Embodying"). Its publication began in fall 2015 when several students in my popular culture analysis course created final video projects that both applied and demonstrated feminist rhetorical criticism. The videos did so in ways I was eager to promote further by publishing them and writing about them with the student authors. While I teach seven types of rhetorical criticism in this course, the nine students I asked to pursue publication with me all composed feminist analysis in ways that excited me. I was struck by how the students took up very recent popular culture texts and critiqued them in rhetorical terms in fewer than three minutes, with the collage and multi-source genre conventions expected by YouTube audiences. In response to my invitation, six expressed interest in writing with me after the class ended.

I chose *Computers and Composition* as a publication venue because I knew that Dr. Kris Blair, editor, is committed to publishing feminist research. I made this selection without any input from my student coauthors. I thus destabilized the classroom hierarchy of student-teacher by asking the students to write with me but reestablished it by making the first major decision and not taking the time to teach the students how to select a venue for initial submission or seek their input from a range of venues I could have curated. This process also destabilized the grade-based hierarchy of assessing student projects, as I had essentially communicated to these students that their work exceeded the "value" of a top course grade, since it was worthy of broader attention from audiences beyond our class. Deeming their work worthy of publication, however, reentrenched my assessment of their work since I positioned myself as the first gatekeeper to the publication of their work.

At the time I was a few years away from applying for tenure and promotion, knowing that to meet the requirements I needed to publish. Thus, I anticipated and fostered a coauthoring opportunity with these students to both enhance my research profile and make more public my own role as a proud teacher of these students. I was invested in being a coauthor on the publication for these reasons, shepherding the students' exceptional work to an audience who would be impressed. Further, I wanted to bring these student projects together, as their meaning was enhanced by joining them as a collective, a perspective only I had as the teacher. My six coauthors were enrolled in two different sections of my course, so they did not already know one another, and my role was thus to bring them together based on the similar themes of their projects. To interpret and frame the projects for the *Computers and Composition* audience, I wrote all the new content of the article, reentrenching my role as the leader, whereas the students did not revise their video projects and their written portions were slightly revised from the reflective pieces they wrote about the video assignment for our class. Thus, another way I maintained my authority role in the teacher-student hierarchy was both inviting the students to write and publish with me ("your work is special!") and simultaneously telling them that it would be almost no work for them ("publishing is easy!"), as they had already produced the writing and video composing.

I thus reestablished the hierarchy of me being the only one who knew the norms of academic publishing and wrote the new content for a community of readers to which I belong, not legitimately mentoring my students into the complexities (and perhaps more boring aspects) of academic publishing. To get to the final version of the publication, I responded to reviewers, communicated with the editor, and did all the other attendant work related to publishing. I emailed my coauthors along the way with updates, but none had any questions or a desire to play a more active role in moving the article to publication. They thus seemed comfortable with the hierarchy of me maintaining my instructor role and theirs as students, not needing to complete any work or contributions unless directly asked. This dynamic conformed to my expectations and aligned with my description of how our work together would play out. Such a dynamic highlights a very limited view of coauthorship, in which subordinate contributors play their role, but do not shape the entire project. In the revision process I was asked to bring in my instructor perspective more fully in the article by commenting on each student-coauthor's project, a request made by the editor and reviewers that also buttressed—in fact required—I firmly stabilized my role as the lead author and knowledge-producer of the article. After the publication came out, I ran into one of my coauthors and, as we talked about the essay, she said, "I'm glad that worked out for you," a statement that reflects how this publication benefited me more than the student-coauthors, and the student's understanding of that fact. The comment surprised me and initially stung a bit, but the student was right. The article's publication benefited me by enhancing my research profile, showing a trajectory of my work that continued from earlier publications on remix and video, and offered evidence of my effective pedagogies that lead to student projects worthy of attention by members of my field. Because my R1 colleagues do not often understand undergraduate students as potential coauthors and researchers, this publication also set me apart from my colleagues as a researcher-teacher who writes and researches with novices and seeks to "uplift" her students in a unique and potentially impactful way, however apocryphal that understanding of impact may be.

Coauthorship and Colearning: Communicating Elective Sterilization

In 2018 I pursued coauthorship with an undergraduate student, an opportunity that also arose from classroom interactions and assignments and an endeavor I initiated in the context of a college-wide UR award in which students earn money for conducting research with a faculty mentor. As a result of our work together, Sara Davis and I published a "persuasion brief" in *Rhetoric of Health and Medicine* in 2019 entitled "Communicating Elective Sterilization: A Feminist Perspective." We chose this genre because it is intended to reach practitioners as well as academics. We felt an urgency to reach audiences beyond academic readers (Davis and Dubisar). Davis also presented a poster at the undergraduate research symposium on campus (the only student from my department and one of a few humanities students), and we were interviewed by the *RHM* editor for a video published on the journal's website ("Author Interview").

We met in 2017, on the first day of my fall Gender and Communication course. Every semester I open by asking students to think of a time when they noticed gender, culture, and communication overlapping and I invite students to describe the examples that come to mind. Davis's description of her efforts to have an elective tubal ligation—which would permanently prevent future pregnancies—catalyzed a rich first-day discussion about access to reproductive healthcare, doctor-patient communication, and gendered double standards for elective sterilization. Her experiences in that context also informed her final research presentation for the class, which exceeded the assignment's expectations regarding depth and demonstrated the widespread issue of people being denied permanent birth control because their medical providers refused to perform the procedures, told patients they would regret being sterilized, and more.

Davis's research prompted me to think about the rhetorical implications of these doctor-patient interactions and how patients use persuasive strategies to access the care they need. The spring after Davis took my course, my college initiated a donor-based funding competition for undergraduate research, an award that yielded hourly pay for an undergraduate to conduct research. I sent the call for proposals to Davis and when she expressed interest I suggested we meet. Davis asked if we would work together on the research and writing the award would fund and, via email, this is how I described what we would do if awarded: "We would work together to work on the sterilization topic more, with the goal of co-authoring an academic journal article and possibly presenting at a conference. So I would be your mentor and both write and research with you. We could consider interviewing practitioners in Ames as well as collecting a wider sample of pamphlets. We can talk more about it in person if you'd like." While we did not formally interview any practitioners and we did not present at a conference together, our project did proceed as I described in the 2018 email.

Our proposal was accepted, and we were funded: Davis would research and write for the two hundred funded hours over the summer, totaling $2,400 in compensation, and I would receive $500 in professional development funding as her faculty mentor/coauthor. The proposal included two writing projects: (1) a personal essay that Davis would author and I would provide feedback on but that she would be the single author of and write about her experience and (2) a coauthored academic journal article in the field of rhetoric. Davis's project created for our class had both personal and research-based components so both would be expanded into these two new projects. And since I was familiar with *RHM*'s persuasion brief format, I asserted it as the top publication venue for the academic project. Following that decision, Davis initiated the articulation of our coathoring roles when she emailed me:

> I wanted to ask you before I started working on the academic piece. Now that we maybe have an idea of where we are going to be sending it, how would you like to divide the work? I didn't want to start on anything before I knew what you had in mind because that is the one, we are going to write together. Like I mentioned, my idea regarding the RHM journal maybe could do with how providers should respond to and approach patients so that they sound

less condescending or skeptical (that is making the patient feel at ease and comfortable asking questions rather than projecting guilt and uncertainty on the patient). How would you like to proceed there? (Davis, "Re: Academic Portion")

I had already emailed *RHM* editors to query their interest in our project, which is reflected in my response to Davis that I sent twenty minutes after she wrote to me:

> This is a great question and a really important one. I think I should take the lead on the rhetoric part of the piece, but I'm not exactly sure what that will look like yet. I definitely plan to write the section of the literature review regarding how rhetoric research has addressed reproductive justice/contraception and why/how elective sterilization is a feminist/justice issue. Does that sound ok? . . . My hope is that we'll hear from RHM soon with an outline or directions on how the article should be organized. You're such an awesome collaborator to be thinking about these questions already. I'm so glad we get to work together on this! (Dubisar, "Re: Academic Portion")

Our coauthorship proceeded in this way, with Davis asking me questions about next steps and seeking feedback and me responding, with both of us working through to-do lists that we generated together. We thus had the normative coauthor negotiations of discussing how the work would get accomplished and exchanged, as well as what we would each accomplish. I took the lead on contextualizing her topic in rhetorical studies while Davis researched the literature review on communication about elective sterilization as well as gathering and analyzing the primary materials of pamphlets and online writing of patients disclosing their experiences asking to be sterilized. For example, on May 18 Davis emailed me about a thesis she had found and was going to read that day. I wrote back with enthusiasm and two other sources for our literature review. By May 29 we had received positive feedback from *RHM* about our idea. Davis wrote to me in response:

> I'm so glad you found this publication and that we can go ahead and move forward! I've been working on reading through all of the popular articles this weekend, and have half of the bibliography done haha, so I'll upload what I've got finished and you can see the different articles I've read and what they're about. I think in terms of timeliness, we're going to be on point. I highlighted the sources that I'm most interested in using due to their immediate relevance. . . . I also worked on my first revision of the creative nonfiction

piece and uploaded that to the folder as well. Yay! Let me know what you'd like to do next :) (Davis, "Re: Fw: Persuasion")

Our planning, writing, and revising correspondence continued in this manner. We met a few times, not as often as we probably would have had it not been summer, and emailed a lot. Our emails are rich with enthusiasm and joy over the project in addition to planning tasks.

Throughout the various stages of the research and writing process I had to diligently destabilize the faculty-student hierarchy to continually position Davis as the lead researcher. One aspect of that diligence included justifying humanities research as labor. The college-level deans who promote the funding opportunity did not understand how I would count Davis's research and writing hours over the summer since she would not be working in a lab or clocking in at a physical research site. I was committed to Davis earning all the funding available and was able to justify her hours and connect them to the research activities underway. Even securing funding for an undergraduate student to conduct research felt like a subversion of academic research hierarchies, compensating students for work that often goes unpaid (or that only faculty get paid to do in these occasions). There was also a brief and tense period early in our work together when the difference between Davis's pay being income or a scholarship would potentially harm her eligibility for healthcare benefits. While this was resolved in a positive way that did not cause Davis harm, I did not have any way of anticipating that such an award could lead to that impact, making my undergraduate student coauthor vulnerable through a research award. Additionally, when the journal contacted us to interview us for their website, a faculty colleague of mine was mistakenly emailed instead of Davis, as they share the same surname and a first name, spelled differently. The emailer assumed my coauthor would be a faculty colleague over the possibility that the student in the email directory was my coauthor, an oversight that was easy to correct yet aligns with our normative expectations for knowledge-making in the academy.

The afterlife of this publication also demonstrates the de- and reestablishment of hierarchies. My university ran a story about our coauthorship, which focused on the research itself and Davis's findings about how elective sterilization is communicated (Hunt). The story includes a photo of Davis doing research activities, sitting at her laptop with sterilization brochures, a depiction that was important to me since undergraduate research is so often pictured as students in labs using pipettes or gazing intensely at beakers. The article also accurately portrayed the research project as Davis's, an important detail that aids understandings of undergraduate researchers as scholars with their own research questions, not always assistants joining a faculty member's existing project.

As a result of this project, I have been contacted a few times by journalists who are writing about elective sterilization, especially in the context of the Supreme Court overturning *Roe v. Wade*. With her permission, I forward such requests to Davis, who now works full-time as a public-school teacher, for her to decide whether to respond to or not. One journalist who contacted me for fact-checking regarding the continued accuracy of our research seemed dismayed that I was not the expert on the project. While I am personally invested in access to reproductive healthcare, since elective sterilization is not the focus of my research agenda my professional expertise ends with what I learned through coauthoring with Davis. *RHM* has asked me to review a few publication submissions about contraception and attendant issues, which I am happy to do, applying my expertise from feminist rhetoric, but acknowledging that I am not a medical rhetoric expert. Thus, my service requests have expanded due to this coauthorship with Davis, reestablishing academic hierarchies since Davis's position as a public-school teacher does not necessarily meet the expectation for an *RHM* reviewer. To date this article has been cited in seven other publications, the most recent of which offers the "first empirical evidence of the potential outcomes among childfree women seeking sterilization" and it makes me proud to see our work cited in this context and the evolving research on elected sterilization (Lemke et al.).

Publication Venues Shaping Coauthorship: Video Games and Environmentalism

In 2021, I suggested one student, Mica Meader, submit her final video project to *JUMP+*, the *Journal for Undergraduate Multimedia Projects*. This publication venue is a rich treasure trove of student-authored artifacts, as it provides effective examples of dynamic projects that arise from coursework and students' articulations of those projects through a written student reflection. It is also an example of how undergraduate web-based publications reorient faculty-student coauthorship interactions. My experience with Meader and *JUMP+* revealed that fluid boundaries can develop around autonomy over student work, publication preparation and revision. Here I found myself contributing as a former instructor to a student-drive project since it evolved out of my class, and the labor and credit was Meader's since I did not have a coauthoring role like I had in previous projects. This time I wrote an instructor reflection, as *JUMP+* expects.

Meader was enrolled in my fall 2021 Analysis of Popular Culture Texts course and, like several of her classmates, made a "play-along" video for the final video project, applying critical concepts from our course to a video game as they play and record the game, editing the gameplay video to align with their argument. Meader's video uses an environmental justice–oriented perspective to analyze *Animal Crossing: New Horizons*, an incredibly popular game (Meader). The play-along genre accommodates pairing her commentary and analysis with actual play of the game, allowing her to show how the game demands players practice deforestation and colonization to win. This video genre, popular on YouTube and other platforms, yokes together a student's video game literacy with their analytical skill.

I especially wanted Meader's video to be published since she is an English major and I want audiences to know that women English majors actively critique the very games they expertly play, a troubling of the hierarchy of who we imagine when we hear the term *gamer*. My own research does not include video games, so I did not see Meader's project as an opportunity to coauthor. I also did not think Meader's video needed any revision, as it was a perfect analytical unit from my view. Our teacher-who-encourages and student-who-creates hierarchies were maintained as Meader submitted her video and consulted me with questions along the way. When she received revision suggestions, contextualized in reviewers' excitement about her project, she asked me to help her navigate what to revise and how. Meader did the bulk of the labor to bring this project to publication, which was unpaid and largely accomplished over the summer. She consulted with me along the way.

As a moment of coauthorship, this example is more fluid. The way Meader and I worked together to create the final publication conformed to the way *JUMP+* asked us to both contribute. In this case my role fits expectations for faculty service and mentorship, as faculty are expected to support students in broadening the reach of their academic work and supporting them along the way. I wrote a short instructor reflection, as *JUMP+* requires, which will not "count" when my research productivity is assessed, of course. In my narrative regarding my service activity, I can describe mentoring Meader as a form of service, but that is the least valued part of my job.

After I notified my department staff that Meader's video was published and available online, they posted about this publication on social media. I asked the staff member who does so to revise the post to include the fact that the project arose from the specific course on popular culture analysis. So, while *JUMP+*'s choice to publish Meader's video and the work she did to revise it and bring it to publication reflect her solo authorship as the video's creator, I attempted to make my role more apparent by linking it to my course. Meader's publication fulfills my goal of bringing students' work to public audiences, making the most of the proud teacher role.

Future Projects

What I described here are three very different coauthorship contexts. All these interactions taught me that I want to continue to learn from undergraduates beyond classroom contexts and do so by pursuing research together, all the while being as transparent as I can be about benefits. One challenge endemic to these projects is the timing of these coauthoring opportunities, as students are often in their junior or senior years when I meet them and initiate writing together. Currently, I am coauthoring with a student who will graduate in three months, a very short amount of time to conduct our work together. My coauthor, Tracie Martinson, is a student from my fall 2022 popular culture course. She was awarded funding from the same competition that Davis won. Martinson analyzed the 2021 Busch Light/John Deere "for the farmers" campaign, taking up the bespoke beer can and case box art featuring John Deere tractors, as well as considering implications for corporate philanthropy with food and beverage products. Our project, entitled "Beer Farmers," includes analyzing how the campaign harnesses nostalgic, white masculinity, implicitly recentering whiteness through agricultural iconography and agrarian myths (Singer et al.).

My research in feminist food studies prompted me to be enthusiastic about this topic when Martinson began pursuing it for a written project, an analytical debate paper. I offered Emily Contois's article on hard seltzer as a gender-neutral beverage as a model for this student, the type of analysis we could write together. For this round of awards, Martinson earned $1,500 for one hundred hours of work on the project during the spring semester. We will have a publication drafted by the time Martinson graduates and the funding period is over. We have talked about how she will likely have to do some unpaid work as the article works its way through the publication process, which she understands. She also applied to present at our campus undergraduate research symposium and will use some of her paid hours from the award to work on her slides and presentation for that context. When Davis won the same award, she was paid twelve dollars per hour and Martinson is currently paid fifteen dollars per hour, a positive change that makes the wage more competitive with other work available to students. The professional development funds for faculty mentors are no longer part of the award as they were when Davis won, so this mentoring work is a normative part of their job, as it would be without the award.

Implications and Recommendations

To close I want to turn from my reflective critique of the coauthorship contexts I offered here toward a set of recommendations or suggestions for myself and other teacher-scholars in writing studies. As these examples have shown, complexities occur at every stage of UR coauthorship. Embracing them and being transparent about them with students can only enrich our interactions as co-researchers and writers, as complicated as they may be. For writing studies teacher-scholars who do want to engage with undergraduate students in coauthorship, I recommend doing so for reasons that benefit *both* students and faculty, that maintain and shift hierarchies between these two roles in productive ways. I also offer additional recommendations and invitations to consider when approaching coauthoring with undergraduate students.

Specifically, I recommend coauthoring with undergraduate students in ways that benefit members of the local campus community, including both administrators and faculty in other disciplines and writing colleagues on campus. Through campus publication and circulation about such work, undergraduate humanities students' projects can gain wider audiences and funding for such work could be maintained during constrained budget periods, and potentially increase.

Second, I recommend writing studies teacher-scholars coauthor with undergraduate students to facilitate students' contributions to the writing studies field. Doing so makes apparent the work writing faculty do to design assignments that align with conversations taking place within our field, positioning students as knowledge-makers in writing studies and faculty as learners from student work. This process also offers faculty coauthors the delight of introducing students to our field and its many research avenues, as well as offering an expanded audience for students' ideas beyond campus, which they may not know are available to them.

Additionally, I hope writing studies scholar-teachers are open to understanding coauthoring with undergraduates as an end in itself, with its own intrinsic benefits, not a means to graduate education, higher post-graduation compensation, or other "tangible" results. As Kuh, O'Donnell, and Schneider note, "Among the challenges to institutionalizing HIPs are demonstrating the fiscal benefit of increased graduation rates, changing academic reward systems to support faculty and staff involvement in HIPs, and acknowledging HIPs in the institutional data system" (9). Demonstrating these benefits, while significant, is beyond many faculty members' capacities and pursuing coauthorship is worthy, regardless of demonstrable benefits that institutions may value. To the best of my knowledge, none of my coauthors have pursued graduate education in the humanities and prompting them to do so is not my intent.

I further recommend that scholar-teachers in writing studies embrace fun amid the complexities of coauthoring. My motivation comes from the fun of carrying out these research pursuits that students begin into new spaces beyond the classroom, in relaxing into a faculty role that is still advisory but not as performative as teaching, when I am contending with a group of students instead of just one or a select few. I recommend faculty conceive of coauthoring as an opportunity to focus on the student and their interests in a new way, cheering them on and joining in when necessary.

I invite writing studies scholar-teachers to teach the publications that result from coauthorship. I teach all three of the publications I have detailed here, which has several advantageous rhetorical purposes: it shows current students that their ideas can find audiences outside of classroom contexts; it validates the course and its content as relevant to broader academic conversations; it boosts my ethos as a teacher who is invested in her students' ideas; and it enables me to talk about how and why writing matters and holds implications outside of the arbitrary nature of classroom assignments that are written on tight deadlines, under constraints. On a more practical level, doing so also pushes on the problematic practice of using "models" of student writing in class, as I can offer current students the ideas of past students for assignments I still teach but in a published form that can still generate ideas for current students. Additionally, student coauthors know their work will be read by audiences after it is published in these contexts, as they have consented to its publication. Thus, I can "recognize students as authors whose work is worthy of study and vest authority in their words and expertise," as Paul Anderson and Heidi McKee note in their study of the ethics of teaching student-authored texts (60) with the students' consent granted through the publication process. I hope students in classrooms across the country are also reading their work.

I also encourage writing studies teacher-scholars to acknowledge the inherent complexity of coauthorship. Faculty can be intentional and honest with undergraduate students about why they want to coauthor, codesigning a writing plan in which all contributors communicate their goals, their time commitment, and what they hope to get out of the interaction. Especially in contexts where students are not being compensated financially, not earning academic credit, and may not benefit from academic publication, discussing the work before it begins helps everyone articulate their expectations and anticipate challenges.

Being deliberate about destabilizing hierarchies when possible is also a recommendation that I hope writing studies scholar-teachers will consider. In this essay, for example, referring to my coauthors such as Davis by surname affords coauthors the same naming convention as other scholars cited in academic writing. I am grateful to Eric Darnell Pritchard for leading me to understand how using surnames reflects status (53). Other practices could include inviting student coauthors to address faculty by their first name, not by Doctor or Professor as they may in the classroom. Faculty can also ask students to suggest where their meetings take place, and when, not assuming that meetings will take place in the faculty member's office or a place convenient to the faculty member. Student coauthors can also initiate the writing tools and platforms that they use with faculty coauthors, as faculty adjust their norms to write together more equitably.

Ultimately, as I consider these recommendations in the contexts in which I work and conduct research, I am prompted to keep in mind the importance of not coopting students' ideas and research efforts for my own gain. I continue to seek ways to coauthor with undergraduate students so they can benefit from this high-impact practice, and in doing so I put into practice Kathleen Blake Yancey's claim: "Undergraduate research in English studies offers all of us new ways of seeing, new ways of making knowledge, and new ways of sharing that knowledge" (252). These coauthoring relationships detailed here have transformed my sense of self as a teacher and researcher. Such coauthoring holds the potential to transform our field and who it enfranchises to create knowledge.

Works Cited

Anderson, Paul, and Heidi McKee. "Ethics, Student Writers, and the Use of Student Texts to Teach." *Teaching with Student Texts Essays Toward an Informed Practice*, edited by Joseph Harris, John D. Miles, and Charles Paine, Utah State UP, 2010, pp. 60–77.

"Author Interview with Dr. Abby Dubisar and Sara Davis." *YouTube*, uploaded by Rhetoric of Health and Medicine Journal, 9 Mar. 2019, www.youtube.com/watch?v=RxPGP-ypez4.

Blackwell, Christopher, and Thomas R. Martin. "Technology, Collaboration, and Undergraduate Research." *Digital Humanities Quarterly*, vol. 3, no. 1, 2009. http://www.digitalhumanities.org/dhq/vol/3/1/000024/000024.html.

Contois, Emily J. H. "White Claw and Gender Neutrality: What Hard Seltzers Reveal about Alcohol Advertising's Long Journey toward Gender Inclusion." *Advertising & Society Quarterly*, vol. 23 no. 2, 2022. https://doi.org/10.1353/asr.2022.0014.

Davis, Sara. "Re: Academic Portion." Email to the author. 10 May 2018.

Davis, Sara. "Re: Fw: Persuasion Brief on Elective Sterilization?" Email to the author. 29 May 2018.

Davis, Sara, and Abby M. Dubisar. "Communicating Elective Sterilization: A Feminist Perspective." *Rhetoric of Health and Medicine*, vol. 2, no. 1, 2019, pp. 88–113.

Dubisar, Abby M. "Embodying and Disabling Antiwar Activism: Disrupting YouTube's 'Mother's Day for Peace.'" *Rhetoric Review*, vol. 34, no. 1, 2015, pp. 56–73.

Dubisar, Abby M. "Re: Academic Portion." Email to the author. 10 May 2018.

Dubisar, Abby M., Claire Lattimer, Rahemma Mayfield, Makayla McGrew, Joanne Myers, Bethany Russell, and Jessica Thomas. "Haul, Parody, Remix: Mobilizing Feminist Rhetorical Criticism with Video." *Computers and Composition*, vol. 44, 2017, pp. 52–66.

Dubisar, Abby M., and Jason Palmeri. "Palin/Pathos/Peter Griffin: Political Video Remix and Composition Pedagogy." *Computers and Composition*, vol. 27, no. 2, 2010, pp. 77–93.

Grobman, Laurie. "The Student Scholar: (Re)Negotiating Authorship and Authority." *College Composition and Communication*, vol. 61, no. 1, 2009, pp. W175–196.

Grobman, Laurie, and Joyce Kinkead, editors. *Undergraduate Research in English Studies*. NCTE, 2010.

Hunt, Angie. "Changing the Conversation about Elective Sterilization for Women." *Iowa State University News Service*, 28 May 2019. https://www.news.iastate.edu/news/2019/05/28/sterilization.

Kuh, George, Ken O'Donnell, and Carol Geary Schneider. "HIPs at Ten." *Change: The Magazine of Higher Learning*, vol. 49, no. 5, 2017, pp. 8–16.

Lemke, Jillian, Debra Mollen, and Johanna Soet Buzolits. "Sterilized and Satisfied: Outcomes of Childfree Sterilization Obtainment and Denials." *Psychology of Women Quarterly*, vol. 47, no. 4, 2023. https://doi.org/10.1177/03616843231164069.

Meader, Mica. "Environmental Justice in Animal Crossing New Horizons." *JUMP+*, vol. 12, no. 1, 2022. https://jumpplus.net/issue-12-1/environmental-justice-in-animal-crossing-new-horizons-12-1/.

Pritchard, Eric Darnell. "'Like Signposts on the Road': The Function of Literacy in Constructing Black Queer Ancestors." *Literacy in Composition Studies*, vol. 2, no. 1, 2014, pp. 29–56.

Singer, Norie Ross, Stephanie Houston Grey, and Jeff Motter. *Rooted Resistance: Agrarian Myth in Modern America*. U of Arkansas P, 2020.

Yancey, Kathleen Blake. "Afterword." *Undergraduate Research in English Studies*, edited by Laurie Grobman and Joyce Kinkead, NCTE, 2010, pp. 245–53.

11
Telling Our Own Stories

Coauthoring with Students to Advance DEI Pedagogy

LAUREN S. CARDON AND BRANDY MARTINEZ

When we decided to coauthor this chapter, Brandy Martinez was finishing up her senior year as an English major and serving as president of the University of Alabama chapter of Sigma Tau Delta, an international English honor society; Lauren S. Cardon had just finished her coauthored book (with Anne-Marie Womack), *Inclusive College Classrooms: Teaching Methods for Diverse Learners*. Drawing from our experiences as student and researcher, respectively, both of us had collaborated on a DEI pedagogy panel for the Sigma Tau Delta Annual Convention. During this panel, Martinez was able to link educators' choices to the forms of exclusion she experienced as a Mexican American first-generation student with a disability navigating the challenges of life and learning at a flagship university. It was during this panel that Cardon saw the potential for a coauthored contribution. One of the challenges she had encountered when conducting research for her book was the absence of narrated lived experiences. Such narrative accounts are needed in pedagogy scholarship, which has tended to rely on quantitative data and at times generalized results without accounting for subjective and experiential diversity. As we discussed coauthoring a contribution to this volume, we found we had to navigate a host of challenges to ensure an equitable writing process as well as open communication,

https://doi.org/10.7330/9781646427796.c011

given the differences in our positions. We decided to center the contribution on Martinez's narrative, provided in the form of a counterstory. Through her counterstory and our coauthoring process, we discuss how faculty and student coauthorship can provide a means of addressing a gap in pedagogical scholarship, yet for this coauthoring to be equitable and meaningful, both authors must address the inequities in the relationship and find a means of drafting and communicating that addresses these inequities.

In coauthoring this piece, we suggest that showcasing narratives by students from underrepresented groups has the potential to accomplish several goals in DEI research. First, this practice provides an important humanizing dimension to scholarship on DEI pedagogy, in which we often work with quantitative data. While important, quantitative research risks reducing students to numbers rather than considering their emotional and psychological responses to these practices, as well as their lived experiences.

Second, this approach promotes agency for students who want to be part of these conversations. Disability rights activists invoke the South African mantra "Nothing about us without us": in this context, as James Charlton explains, the mantra refers to the need for "people with disabilities ... to proclaim that they know what is best for themselves and their community" (3). Certainly this mantra applies to students with disabilities in an academic context, and it might be extended to encompass students from other underrepresented groups. In participating in these conversations about members of their own communities, students from these groups work against an academic paternalism that reinforces institutional hierarchies.

A third goal of this approach is that it creates what Martinez calls a "doorway" for other students to share their stories through coauthorship. With more students sharing their experiences, we can learn from a collection of voices that inflect the direction of DEI pedagogy while establishing inclusive practices for coauthorship between students and faculty.

Scholarship on coauthoring tends to focus on two main areas: (1) coauthoring with other scholars and the process and practices that entails and (2) coauthoring with graduate students as a form of mentorship and a means of introducing them to scholarly publication. Drawing from the tenets of critical race theory, in this essay we discuss how to navigate process and power differentials in student-faculty coauthoring, and we illustrate why narrative accounts are a needed source of expertise in scholarship on DEI pedagogy. Ultimately, we argue that given the proper context and intentionality, coauthorship can be a productive and valuable means of promoting undergraduate counterstories to shape DEI teaching practices.

In the first section, we address the initial challenges of establishing our plans to coauthor, particularly in navigating the power differential as student and faculty member. We then provide a brief critical framework on counterstorytelling and the ways that this practice has informed our coauthorship. Martinez then shares her counterstory, which illuminates issues of exclusion students face when navigating the college experience, as well as how such narratives can generate meaningful conversations about institutional and pedagogical changes. In the last section, we reflect on the counterstory and offer suggestions for modeling opportunities for student-faculty coauthorship.

The Problem of Representation

BRANDY MARTINEZ

When I was invited to be on the DEI panel for Sigma Tau Delta, I saw it as an opportunity to make recommendations based on my own experiences in the classroom as well as to provide a platform that might allow other students to tell their stories. However, I was initially reluctant. I worried that the audience would think of my experience—a relatively privileged one—as the standard one for all students with similar backgrounds. My story is my own. It can't be tokenized or represent every other Mexican American student's story.

Yet sometimes privilege is a call to action: "If not me, then who?" After all, I have the privilege of being a college student. I have the privilege of being able to make my education a priority. I have privilege that others like me have to fight for. As I discuss in my counterstory, my experience at the DEI panel felt productive, and the conversation expanded beyond the event, into an opportunity to coauthor with my professor. It became an opportunity to share my experiences of navigating college and managing issues of access and inclusion, both in and beyond the classroom.

Dr. Cardon reached out to me about coauthoring as an extension of the conversations our panel brought forth.[1] For me, it was initially daunting to coauthor with my professor. Early in the process, I expressed that I felt like, as a student, my contributions would be far inferior to hers. Despite any reassurances she gave me, it was impossible for me to get over the student/faculty sense of hierarchy. Communicating this to Dr. Cardon, however, enabled us to keep an open dialogue and find the most productive ways to work together throughout the writing process. To soothe some of my doubts, Dr. Cardon approached me with the idea of recording our conversations about my experiences. Then she would transcribe those conversations, and I would make edits. I would later learn that our approach is a popular one for coauthoring scholars, one Day and Eodice refer to as "co-invention"—a drafting process that involves working together through multiple stages including talking, researching, analyzing, revising, and editing (23).² This process made becoming a part of this project feasible for me, especially when considering the workload I had as an undergraduate student. Overall, Dr. Cardon's ability to understand my concerns, both in terms of our dynamic and my workload, helped me feel more confident that I could contribute meaningfully to a coauthored project.

LAUREN S. CARDON

I felt conflicted approaching Brandy after our DEI panel, mainly because I worried that, as a student, she would feel obligated to say yes regardless of her interest or comfort level. Ultimately, I broached the subject as a conversation, highlighting the ways that her insights could inflect a larger pedagogical conversation. When researching *Inclusive College Classrooms*, I noticed the dearth of student input on inclusive teaching practices in the college classroom. Some studies incorporated student surveys, and some students published pieces in undergraduate journals or on websites like the Humanities, Arts, Science and Technology Alliance and Collaboratory (HASTAC). Yet my coauthor (Womack) and I kept returning to the overall lack of narrative accounts, of shared lived experiences, particularly from students historically marginalized by the American university system.

How can we make up for the absence of student voices in publications about DEI pedagogy? As Brandy pointed out, these stories are intersectional and individualized, and yet, these narratives have a lot to teach practitioners: they help us envision the human impact of our teaching practices in terms of how they include and exclude. Circulating and publishing such narratives, however, means finding ways to create opportunities for those students with stories to share. The burden of publicizing these stories cannot be placed solely on students from marginalized groups, for these are often the students least likely to speak up as well as those more likely to be silenced in dominant discourses. Moreover, given that many academic publishers view work coauthored with undergraduates as less credible or professional (Plakhotnik 348), it's no surprise that many students doubt their ability to pursue such opportunities even when their contributions meet more traditional conventions.

At the same time, faculty cannot simply approach students from minoritized groups out of the blue and ask them to coauthor, for this practice carries hazards of tokenization, intimidation, and the subordination of students' narratives to fulfill our own publishing agendas. These challenges became part of our conversations as well, and we discuss ways to address them later in this essay.

Student Narratives as Counterstories

LAUREN S. CARDON

Scholars of critical race theory (CRT) introduced the concept of the counterstory, which Daniel Solorzano and Tara Yosso define as both a means of "telling the story of those people whose experiences are not often told" and "a tool for exposing, analyzing, and challenging the majoritarian stories of racial privilege" (36). When we only encounter the experiences of students from dominant groups, those experiences become normalized and reinforce traditional practices. Yet when we encounter the narratives from "those on the margins of society" (Solorzano and Yosso 36), we are compelled to recognize conflicting experiences of the same practices.

One challenge of using counterstories to inflect pedagogical scholarship is that this practice breaks with conventions of disciplinary publication. Historically, peer-reviewed publications have tended to center a voice read as objective, a clinical expert in the field able to keep emotions and subjectivity out of the discourse. As Aja Y. Martinez explains, CRT methods push back against this supposed neutrality because it invisibilizes the experiences of BIPOC and undermines experiential knowledge as a form of expertise. Instead, CRT "recognizes that experiential knowledge of people of color is legitimate and critical to understanding racism that is often well disguised in the rhetoric of normalized structural values and practices" (3). One problem, unfortunately, is that even when academic institutions and educators seek to make such experiential knowledge more visible, it's often only within socially sanctioned channels—DEI symposiums or panels, for example. Rather than sidelining these narratives and other forms of experiential knowledge, educators, journals, and administrations need to center them and allow them to inform institutional and pedagogical change. In addition, both Martinez and Gloria Ladson-Billings note that single narratives aren't enough, as Brandy's own reluctance suggests: "[T]here is diversity within experience," observes Martinez (183).[3]

Critical pedagogy scholars like bell hooks set a precedent for using counterstory to challenge traditional practices and myths about student learning. In *Teaching to Transgress* (1994), hooks begins with a counterstory about her experience of predominantly white institutions. After schools were integrated, she recalls, "[g]one was the messianic zeal to transform our minds and beings that had characterized teachers and their pedagogical practices in our all-black schools. Knowledge was suddenly about information only. It had no relation to how one lived, behaved. It was no longer connected to antiracist struggle" (3). The educational environment hooks describes is one that has been normalized and for many is still viewed as effective. It's the same practice that Paolo Freire described as the "banking model"—an instructor delivers knowledge to students that gets deposited in their minds, which they then regurgitate on a test. But hooks's experience of this environment, particularly when contrasted with her experience at a Black institution, reveals its flaws: the way this model stifles critical thinking, keeps students isolated, and implies that knowledge is static rather than something to be evaluated, debated, and challenged.

hooks's response reveals one important function of the counterstory: it can challenge assumptions about best practices. Counterstories can also serve other purposes, as Solorzano and Yosso note: they can foster a sense of community among underrepresented groups; they can help "those at the margins of society" recognize new opportunities and feel connected to others; and they can become instructive, showing that "by combining elements from both the story and the current reality, one can construct another world that is richer than either the story or the reality alone" (36). Similarly, in talking about such narratives as being a "doorway," Brandy suggests that each narrative that gets published is an opportunity for others to see themselves in the discourse.

In the next section, Brandy shares her counterstory, a narrative of her experience transitioning from her hometown to a college campus at a predominantly white institution (PWI). We decided to include her entire counterstory both as a means of affirming this form of CRT methodology and as a recommended coauthoring practice to ensure the narrative is preserved as the storyteller intends, rather than potentially being repurposed or retrofitted to align with the coauthor's claims (in this case, the faculty member's), or to suit publication conventions. Brandy's counterstory speaks to her journey toward belonging on campus, as well as her reservations about participating in a professional panel and coauthored publication. She includes her takeaways from the coauthoring experience; I include mine in the final section.

Counterstory: Meaningful Conversations

BRANDY MARTINEZ

Participating in the Sigma Tau Delta panel and reflecting on my journey as a student has been an opportunity to think about my experiences with exclusion and belonging—in my hometown, on campus, and as part of an academic community.

I grew up in Fort Payne, Alabama, a small southern town with a large Hispanic community. Growing up, I questioned my identity. I was never "Mexican" enough to my classmates of Mexican descent in high school, and my white classmates rarely acknowledged my heritage—instead they treated me as an "exception." They would make stereotypical comments about Hispanic people and then look at me and say something like, "but you're not like that." I internalized some of these comments; later in college I would find myself thinking things like, "I have to be successful in what I do because I am the only person of color from my school that got to go to UA"; "I am representing my community and that means I have to over excel"; or "My success only means something if I make some grand contribution."

Once I started at the University of Alabama, where there's a lack of Hispanic representation, these internalized ideas would affect my sense of belonging as well as my performance. These feelings were often reinforced by my peers. I have had people during my time at UA comment on how I don't sound like I speak Spanish, or they'll make those same harmful generalizations I heard in high school. This struggle of not being "___ enough" contributed to negative feelings I have had about my performance in academia. I felt like I had to perform perfectly or else people would know I was struggling, and I'd reinforce those beliefs. As someone who struggles with mental health, this pattern became paralyzing—resulting in late assignments, not being able to start on a paper, and not participating in class.

This sense of exclusion would have felt more manageable if it were limited to the classroom. But I felt it everywhere. Growing up, I went to the same Catholic church for over twenty years. I always thought of church as a place where there were people who looked like me. I remember being young and seeing the tops of black hair and darker skin when I looked around during service. But when I joined a campus ministry, it was a different experience—no one looked like me. In class and other social settings, I often didn't know where to sit—I found myself scanning classroom after classroom for someone who either looked like me or seemed friendly and approachable. I felt ostracized from the other women in my dorm. Their parents were doctors and lawyers, while my dad worked at a rug factory and my mom at a poultry factory. When the women in my dorm would talk about their parents' jobs, I wouldn't say anything—not because I was ashamed, but because I knew there would be this awkward silence. I didn't want anyone feeling sorry for me; I'm proud of my upbringing and my hardworking parents.

These scenarios would build up and contribute to my overall feeling of isolation. Faculty and administrators think that those feelings of exclusion relate specifically to the classroom. What they're not seeing is how those feelings of isolation and insecurity can affect every part of the campus experience, from the classroom to the dorm to the churches to the social experiences, making it even harder to be successful.

That pressure can also translate to self-confidence issues in the classroom. I see, for example, that I'm the only Hispanic student in the room, and sometimes that makes me feel like I have something to prove. If I'm going to raise my hand and say something, it has to sound eloquent; it has to sound smart. And even if I do say something, I always feel like the next student's comment is more professional, sophisticated—just at a higher level than my own comment. As a student with ADHD, I felt additional pressure because of my struggles with time management, staying engaged, and learning at a different pace than a majority of my classmates. I was constantly concerned I would have a hard time forming fluid and cohesive thoughts to share with my peers and professors. I was worried that if I chimed in during class, I would have completely misunderstood the conversation or the topics we discussed.

It's hard to pinpoint an exact moment when I started feeling less isolated and more a part of a college community, but I have felt conflicted about the relative privilege that has gone into my own sense of inclusion. I'm not saying I didn't work hard to get to where I am, or that I didn't put all my effort into the opportunities I've had. However, I have to recognize that many of the opportunities I was granted during college relied on me knowing the right people and being comfortable approaching them. Juggling the guilt and excitement I would experience whenever I got to be involved in a project was difficult, and I would often feel intense doubt and anxiety. Was I *actually* meant to be here? Questioning myself and my abilities further intensified leading up to the Sigma Tau Delta panel.

Before attending the Sigma Tau Delta convention, I had a deeply instilled perception of the academic world: To make important contributions to your field you have to have pages and pages of qualifications and experience. To be heard and believed you have to be an expert on the topic. I doubted myself leading up to the convention. After all, I'd only recently started working on building up my experience through campus and community involvement, internships, meetings, and networking. I was completely convinced that even though I've lived out and experienced the very same keywords we would be discussing at the panel, that what I had to say was somehow less valid.

I also didn't know the other students going on the trip with me, but I had heard of them and knew that they were talented and intelligent. Three of the four were white women who already knew each other. Knowing what I knew about my peers, I was scared. I thought that I wouldn't fit in, and that I would feel anxious the entire time. To add to my stress, knowing Dr. Cardon's qualifications and knowledge on DEI made me feel uncomfortable speaking on a panel with her at first. I believed that my attending the convention was pointless.

Though I got over some of the worries I had regarding those coming on the trip with me, I was still nervous about the panel itself and the validity of me being there. Watching my peers present their essays and poems only fueled my anxiety. They were all the center of attention for each presentation. They had to stand behind a podium, and they were asked questions about their writing style or research. I kept hearing words that I'd been hearing in class thrown around—assimilation, structuralism, othering—and I panicked. I interpreted it as a reaffirmation that I had to sound smart, fluent in academic jargon. If I wanted to impress people I needed to thoroughly plan what I wanted to say.

The night before our panel, I met with the other presenters. I got there an hour early, and I started doing as much research as I could. The pressure of time counting down was getting to me. I looked up synonyms, antonyms, and definitions, watched videos, and even started scripting out what I needed to say. However, doing the research wasn't necessary. I already knew how to change my speech to be "academically appropriate." Again, I just kept telling myself that I needed to sound intelligent or else no one would take it seriously. I felt like I was spiraling. Not only that but I had just gotten done watching four others present and sound like impressive professionals.

The panel I participated in was different from what I had envisioned. Unlike the other panels, which were divided between audience and presenters, for ours the chairs were set up in a circle to make audience participation more inviting; you couldn't tell who was on the panel and who was in the audience. Early in the conversation, I could tell that no one on that panel questioned my presence or my qualifications and abilities, a fear I'd had in the back of my mind for weeks leading up to the event. The setup and this sense of acceptance gave me a push that I had been needing.

As I started sharing my ideas and experiences, I saw my new friends all giving me reassuring head nods of approval, and people (both faculty and peers) taking notes on what I had to say. I talked about the lack of diversity I saw at the convention and among members of the organization. I talked about how I thought the panel was an excellent first step at addressing diversity, but I feared people would feel it was enough, when really we needed to do more. I talked about my fear of being tokenized. I shared things that professors do in the classroom that have made me feel excluded (like having strict attendance policies and using lecture as the only instructional method) and those that have made me feel more included in the learning experience (like when professors put thought into their diversity statements and take the time to highlight them during class; when the learning experience is discussion-based; when the instructor establishes an approachable, caring tone and attempts to connect with students). I realized there was so much I had to say, and that this was a conversation I needed to be a part of.

On the way home from the convention, I felt accomplished; I felt like I contributed something important, and I realized that I wanted to have more conversations like the ones I had on the panel. It's like after participating I realized that my narrative was valuable not only because people could learn from it but also because there are people like me who don't get a shot at detailing their story.

A few months after the conference, Dr. Cardon approached me about coauthoring based on my comments at the panel. I was grateful for the opportunity, but I very quickly became anxious and overwhelmed. Not only did the topic of the essay seem intimidating but also I realized I would have to dissect intersectional aspects of my life. My main concern was that I would inaccurately convey the experience of a first-generation Mexican American college student. I was worried I would be inauthentic, and I didn't even know if I fully understood my own experiences. Not only that but years of academic insecurity made me reluctant to give my insight. None of it felt good enough, but I was also protective of what did feel good enough. Even once we started and Dr. Cardon repeatedly reassured me, I experienced a constant stream of internal turmoil.

That began to change as a result of our conversations once we started drafting. Rather than a typical professor/student interaction, it felt like two people genuinely interested in how inclusion works and what we could learn from each other. These conversations humanized the process, made it feel less like an academic assignment and more like something I could meaningfully contribute to.

Through discussions with Dr. Cardon, I can see how my own experience struggling with belonging on campus could translate into insights for instructors. For example, I would want instructors to see how issues of inclusion can extend to dorms, extracurricular activities, places of worship, and other spaces; how disability accommodations give a narrow picture of the challenges students might be navigating; and how issues of mental health might impact student engagement. Generally speaking, I would like to see instructors design their classes with empathy, with that understanding that students have different needs and abilities.

I now look at being on the conference panel at Sigma Tau Delta as a doorway for other people to be able to share their stories and recommendations—whether through panel collaborations like mine or through a coauthoring experience like this one. But then that calls for faculty, administrators, and editors to be more open to hearing and publishing these stories. I feel like the more that we take in different narratives, the more we see diversity as something natural, not something that we have to think about.

As a first-generation Mexican American student with a disability, I want to not only make the case for providing platforms that allow students to tell their stories through coauthoring but also make recommendations based on my own experiences in the classroom. I am hoping that in coauthoring with Dr. Cardon, we can stimulate conversations about student-professor relationships in the college setting. I also hope that we can help pave the way for making pedagogy more inclusive and equitable.

Key Takeaways

LAUREN S. CARDON

In coauthoring with Brandy, I initially envisioned a conversational exchange in which she would contribute her experiences and together we would extrapolate lessons for instructors about DEI teaching methods. However, as we worked together, I realized a complication for the faculty/undergraduate coauthoring approach, particularly as it relates to DEI issues and counterstorytelling: how to establish these partnerships in the first place.

One concern that Brandy kept coming back to was the issue of tokenization that might emerge from collaborations like ours. Our coauthorship emerged organically: Brandy was one of several students who wrote a letter for an English major recruiting campaign in which she self-identified as a first-generation student. Because of this letter and her involvement with Sigma Tau Delta, when I received an invitation for myself and a student to participate in a DEI panel at the convention, I immediately thought of Brandy. At this time, we had an established relationship and had already talked about her experiences as a first-generation student. After hearing her remarks on the panel and talking with her about them on the car ride home, a coauthored publication seemed like an appropriate, mutually beneficial next step. However, I learned through our conversations that despite our preexisting relationship, Brandy was concerned at each phase that she was being invited to participate not based on her merits but solely because of her identity. It wasn't until later that Brandy felt more comfortable with the publishing opportunity as well as our coauthoring process.

Brandy's concerns speak to an important takeaway for faculty interested in pursuing coauthoring opportunities in the interest of promoting minoritized student voices in DEI scholarship: faculty have to be mindful in how we pursue these partnerships and with whom we pursue them. One option, as we demonstrate, is to build on a preexisting relationship. Faculty involved with student organizations, or whose students are already active in vocalizing ideas about DEI practices, might approach a student and inquire whether they might be interested in a coauthored publication. Another option is to approach students through an established infrastructure within their department or institution; for example, Bates College has introduced a Short Term Course Redesign program in which faculty and students partner to redesign courses (Hubley and Burns); similarly, Bryn Mawr and Haverford established the Pedagogical Partnership program (now adopted by over seventy institutions) to promote semester-long conversations between students and faculty about ways to enhance teaching methods and promote inclusion. These programs embody benefits for faculty as well as students; for example, students often learn to share "power—and responsibility—with faculty," experience "stronger connections to departments and institutions," and develop "confidence in and capacity to articulate their perspectives" (Cook-Sather et al. 3). Faculty involved in these programs can draw from an existing infrastructure to approach students about coauthorship opportunities.

Our experience coauthoring illustrates other challenges for faculty-student coauthored work. First, even once the coauthoring partnership is established, both participants need to be aware of a power differential, particularly when the student is enrolled in the instructor's course. The instructor needs to ensure that the student has a way to say no, assert dissent, and abandon the project. This can be challenging, as in some cases even if the instructor asks the student direct questions, the student may feel compelled to say what they imagine the instructor wants to hear. Along these same lines, it's the instructor's job in these coauthoring practices to establish a basis of trust. The trust is not just a matter of maintaining confidentiality; it's also a reassurance about the process, about making the student feel safe by being open and honest, and about giving the student a final say in how their own narrative is presented.

This last element is especially difficult when incorporating counterstories. Many scholars, myself included, have been indoctrinated into an institutional context in which personal narrative defies academic conventions. It is hard to be comfortable with the shift in tone and discourse entailed by the juxtaposition of traditional scholarship and counterstories. While Brandy and I edited one another's sections, I tried not to touch her counterstory unless it was a matter of clarity. In earlier drafts, I found myself interrupting her content to explain (or as we came to call it, "professor-splain") takeaways from her experience. In a sense, coauthoring with an undergraduate, while it entails aspects of mentorship, is every bit as much a dialogic process as coauthoring with other faculty: for successful coauthorship, faculty also have to listen, learn, and trust. We have to be humble and even silent when our students are telling their stories.

The process is therefore central to the success of these coauthoring experiences. While faculty have our own share of time management challenges, we need to prioritize the student's circumstances. In our case, Brandy found working together in my office the most productive. She preferred to vocalize her ideas through conversation and then have me transcribe her responses. My assumptions about how people work sometimes interfered with this process, as I assumed Brandy would want some time on her own to review our work; however, even later in the process she expressed feeling more confident and productive when we were working together. The coauthoring process, I've found, is an extension of a lesson I've learned about teaching: how to question my assumptions and to some extent my own authority, with the underlying belief that faculty can learn from our students just as much as they can learn from us—if not more.

Notes

1. LC: For the sake of this article, I initially encouraged Brandy to use my first name (using my title made it feel less like an equitable coauthorship). However, she was more comfortable referring to me with my title and preferred that I use her first name.
2. This stage of talking is critical to successful coauthoring, according to Day and Eodice; when coauthors engage in dialogue, "their thinking is audible and several pools of knowledge combine in a virtual space to create a deep lake of possibilities from which choices of what is to be written down are made" (128).
3. Coauthoring with students is also subject to the same challenges of other forms of coauthored scholarship; for example, Wendy Bishop notes how the humanities has historically privileged single-authored work, whereas STEM fields and others value coauthored scholarship (55).

Works Cited

Bishop, Wendy. "Co-Authoring Changes the Writing Classroom: Students Authorizing the Self, Authoring Together." *Composition Studies*, vol. 23, 1995, pp. 55–61.

Charlton, James I. *Nothing About Us Without Us: Disability Oppression and Empowerment*. U of California P, 1998.

Cook-Sather, Alison, Melanie Bahti, and Anita Ntem. *Pedagogical Partnerships: A How-To Guide for Faculty, Students, and Academic Developers in Higher Education*. Elon University Center for Engaged Learning, 2019.

Day, Kami, and Michele Eodice. *(First Person)²: A Study of Co-Authoring in the Academy*. UP of Colorado, 2001. https://doi.org/10.2307/j.ctt46nxhs.5.

Freire, Paulo, with Myra Bergman Ramos, translator. *Pedagogy of the Oppressed*. 30th anniversary ed., Bloomsbury, 2012.

hooks, bell. *Teaching to Transgress: Education as the Practice of Freedom*. Routledge, 1994.

Hubley, Doug, and Jay Burns. "Five Stories from Short Term's Innovative Practitioner-Taught Courses and Course Redesigns." *Bates College*, 9 Jun. 2016, https://www.bates.edu/news/2016/06/09/short-term-showcase-2016/.

Martinez, Aja Y. *Counterstory: The Rhetoric and Writing of Critical Race Theory*. National Council of Teachers of English, 2020.

Plakhotnik, M. S. "Co-Authoring with Undergraduate Students: An Emerging Process from the Semi-Periphery of the World of Science." *Learned Publishing*, vol. 35, no. 3, July 2022, pp. 332–40. https://doi-org.libdata.lib.ua.edu/10.1002/leap.1469.

Solorzano, Daniel G., and Tara J. Yosso. "Critical Race Methodology: Counter-Storytelling as an Analytical Framework for Education Research." *Qualitative Inquiry*, vol. 8, no. 1, Feb. 2002, pp. 23–44. https://doi.org/10.1177/107780040200800103.

12
Charting a Pathway from First-Year Composition to Academic Publishing

SHIRLEY E. FAULKNER-SPRINGFIELD, KAYLA MOORE,
AND CHARITY RIDDICK-MULLEN

Shirley

Scholarly activity establishes the intellectual and professional credibility of students and faculty. When writing studies faculty engage in scholarly activities, they become models who foster the possibilities for their students' own scholarly activities. However, modeling is not enough in today's competitive climate where the voices of historically underrepresented students of color are still missing from academic scholarship. While science, technology, engineering, and mathematics (STEM) faculty does an outstanding job of coauthoring scholarship and of generating science-based funding with STEM majors, writing studies faculty falls short of providing consistent coauthoring and research opportunities for writing majors and themselves. Karen Jackson posits that "[w]hile teaching, research, and service are the major components of our functions, like most HBCUs, teaching takes precedence" (138). I accept Jackson's conclusion that teaching is a priority for English faculty at historically Black colleges and universities (HBCUs) because when our proposal for this edited collection was submitted, I was teaching four sections of first-year composition at North Carolina Central University (NCCU), an HBCU in southwestern North Carolina where Jackson is a professor of English. Though I bore a heavy teaching load, I attempted to coauthor with undergraduates, so I could promote access, equity, and justice in writing studies scholarship. The primary objectives of this coauthoring project are to use a first-year composition course as a bridge to connect historically underrepresented students of color to an academic publishing opportunity and to serve as a mentor text for African American students at HBCUs.

We are three African American women: the writing professor who taught the first-year composition course and two undergraduate students who were enrolled in the course. Today, we are positioned at two HBCUs in North Carolina: North Carolina Agricultural and Technical State University (Shirley) and North Carolina Central University (Kayla and Charity). In this chapter, we discuss the results of our labor: our successes, our struggles, and our reasons for coauthoring with writers in different disciplines. We argue that writing studies faculty should coauthor with undergraduate students of color to augment their critical literacies and competitiveness and to promote justice in academia, in the professions, and in the wider society.

How Did We Get Here? Methodology and Pedagogy (Shirley)

This project began with my informal observation of forty-three students in two of my honors first-year composition courses at NCCU. My hope was to identify coauthors for a scholarly publication about students' research projects that linked their communication skills to their educational and career goals. During the first week of the spring 2022 semester, I introduced students to their semester-long research project. The theme of the course was "Becoming." The theme reflected NCCU's mission statement that claims to prepare students for leadership roles and a global marketplace. One assignment objective was for students to learn that while NCCU's objective is to meet the needs of a local job market, it also strives to produce globally competitive students. Hence, the assignment called on students to explore three philosophical questions: Who are you? Who are you becoming? and How are you becoming who you are becoming? To answer these questions and their research questions, students analyzed NCCU's mission statement, their departments' mission statements, and their degree requirements. One key component of the assignment was for students to interview one professor in their department about students' degree and career requirements and to focus on their writing requirements first. After discussing the assignment with students, I solicited coauthors. But no one volunteered. Had my words fallen on deaf ears? Will students realize the importance of this writing project after they interview professionals in their disciplines about their writing requirements? Why do I value this assignment? These questions populated my mind while I explored reasons my recruitment effort resulted in deafening silence.

My next step was to identify students who demonstrated the intellectual and emotional capacities to complete the coauthoring project. These essential attributes include critical thinking, problem-solving, teamwork, collaboration, professionalism, a strong work ethic, effective oral and written communication, leadership, honesty, creativity, ambition, emotional intelligence, and curiosity. In April, I examined my list of prospective coauthors. Armed with an invitation, I emailed, called, and texted eight students: two Hispanic males (Early College), one Hispanic female (Early College), two African American males, and four African American females. Although these potential coauthors exhibited skills and characteristics that educators and employers value, the Hispanic males and one African American female felt their writing skills were inadequate for scholarly writing. The Hispanic female did not respond to my invitation. The African American males declined without explanation. One African American female accepted my invitation but was not in an environment conducive to teaching and learning. However, Kayla Moore and another African American female whom I will refer to as Valencia positively responded to my invitation. Shortly thereafter, Charity Riddick-Mullen joined our writing group after reconsidering my invitation.

Because our writing process was progressing slowly, I emailed my coauthors on November 3 and requested their sections of the manuscript and a Zoom meeting. During the meeting, I learned that our progress was impeded by academic obligations: Kayla was preparing for four examinations; Valencia was preparing for five examinations, and Charity was studying for four examinations. Their academic requirements necessitated a pause in our project until the semester concluded. At NCCU, the final examination schedule was from November 30 to December 8. Kayla showed initiative by emailing her portion of the manuscript to me on November 6 before she became fully immersed in final exam projects. At N.C. A&T, exam week was from December 5–9. Although the final exam period began on December 5 on my campus, most students completed their final projects before the Thanksgiving holiday started, resulting in a 48% increase in writing center appointments in November. Additionally, in December, the writing center co-located with the library to offer writing and information literacy assistance in one location. These significant changes occurred during my first semester at N.C. A&T.

Moreover, my follow-up emails and texts to Valencia and Charity went unanswered until Charity finally responded on January 28, 2023. She expressed regret for not replying sooner and stated that her classes had "been distracting and overwhelming." Charity's stress was palpable: it leaped off the page. On January 29, I tried to lighten the situation by saying, "Thank you for responding to my email even if it is two months late. LOL! It is good to hear from you." I emphasized that her classes must be a priority and invited Charity to a Zoom meeting to discuss her schedule. Charity informed me that she had applied her usual method of writing in solitude. I could only speculate about the impact of her choice. Had her decision led to feelings of isolation, frustration, and demotivation? Charity decided to remain on the project.

In February, through Zoom meetings and email messages, we became busy editing the manuscript. On March 14, we submitted it to Laurie and Jane, and on April 11, they informed us that our manuscript had been accepted with major modifications. Before we revised the manuscript, Valencia withdrew from the group without warning, leaving us confused and unsettled.

Nevertheless, determined to establish a strong presence in writing studies scholarship, Kayla, Charity, and I tirelessly forged ahead. However, two weeks before the manuscript was due, Kayla's grandfather died. Although Kayla intended to write through her grief, I encouraged her to take a brief hiatus—take some self-care time—to initiate her healing process. As a Black woman mentor and "othermother," it was my responsibility to teach my mentees that Black women's mental health matters. Occasionally, I also sought refuge from the demands of directing a writing center, managing this writing project, and teaching writing. During the spring semester, I taught Standard American English (SAE) to undergraduate students while demonstrating to Kayla and Charity that book editors' linguistic preference is SAE.

Recruiting and retaining coauthors proved challenging for three primary reasons: (1) many students did not self-identify as writers capable of producing a scholarly product; (2) some students concluded they did not have the time to invest in a writing project that did not result in extrinsic rewards such as a grade; and (3) none of the forty-three students were English or writing majors and could not see how coauthoring with a writing professor would advance their careers. Nonetheless, my efforts to manage this writing project with two of my former students were rewarded when we learned that our chapter would be included in this collection.

Resisting and Capitulating: Scholarly Writing Ain't Easy (Charity)

I was among the students who initially declined Shirley's invitation to coauthor this chapter. Throughout my academic journey, I have never considered myself a writer, and this self-perception influenced my decision. Writing papers to achieve decent grades or pass courses was never a challenge for me; therefore, merely receiving "good" grades became my primary goal in school. Furthermore, as a high school student, my writing experience was limited to research papers. After I matriculated to college, I learned that my writing lacked structure, complexity, coherence, clarity, and succinctness. Despite these shortcomings, many of my high school teachers and college professors praised my content and gave me good grades, so revising was not my priority. Ultimately, my academic writing experience had not prepared me to identify as an academic writer.

The most significant factor that contributed to my reluctance is best articulated by H. R. Leggette when he asserts that "[s]tudents often write for one audience—their instructor" (108). Those instructors' objective is to ensure that their students are able to apply the lessons they have learned. However, to coauthor meant that I would write with the objective of having instructors learn from me, which is troublesome. In addition, the possibility of my writing being read by a global audience induced tremendous stress in me. Fortunately, my sister who is a psychology major eavesdropped on my phone conversation with Shirley and convinced me to become a coauthor on this project. She summed up Leggette's argument that "[students] need to learn how to write for a broader audience. . . . If students are not expected to defend their argument to a large audience, they will never move from knowledge telling to knowledge transforming" (108). My sister emphasized the importance of being a part of a writing opportunity with an established educator and with my peers who are invested in learning. My sister insisted that the opportunity would develop my collaboration skills and strengthen my networking prospects. In addition, she explained that I would enhance my writing skills since the chapter would go through several revisions and reviews.

Even after agreeing to become a coauthor, I remained skeptical about my writing abilities. Subsequently, my skepticism turned into frustration: I feared my mistakes would jeopardize our opportunity for publication. Then the inevitable happened. Our manuscript was accepted with modifications, but my anxiety about my writing skills shrouded our achievement. While I appreciate constructive criticism, the thought of editors continuously scrutinizing my writing, requesting revisions, and posing more questions began to dampen my enthusiasm. I understood their intentions were to ensure the best possible outcome but that understanding did not eliminate the persistent doubts I harbored about whether I was the right choice for this task. These doubts led to questions such as Am I capable enough? Why did I agree to write this chapter? How am I going to approach this writing task as a nonwriter? and Why was I chosen?

It was not until I started reading scholarship on coauthoring that my anxiety decreased and the questions stopped replaying in my mind. As I delved deeper into this writing project, I was driven to enhance my writing skills and to equip myself for opportunities beyond college. As a psychology major, I am expected to conduct research, collect and analyze data, read various texts for comprehension, and enter into scholarly conversations. Writing from a psychological framework, Traci A. Giuliano explains that many publishers require "large sample sizes" and other tasks that would challenge student writers. Unlike quantitative methodologies prevalent in psychology, this coauthoring opportunity allowed me to approach the writing process from a narrative-based perspective, which is an excellent model and starting point. Moreover, in "Guiding Undergraduates through the Process of First Authorship," Giuliano maintains that faculty should "mentor undergraduates through first authorship" (11). Though we did not initially identify a first author, I found Giuliano's article helpful since all of us took on the role of first author. Additionally, throughout our writing process, whenever I felt the urge to give up, Shirley offered words of encouragement that instilled a sense of perseverance within me. Her guidance and writing support made me feel more confident even when doubt crept in. She never let me believe that I couldn't make a valuable contribution to this chapter. Furthermore, whenever confusion arose, she readily made herself available for discussions and thoroughly addressed our questions and concerns. I genuinely believe that without Shirley's guidance, I would have left the writing group.

Coauthoring: A Natural Phenomenon (Kayla)

After spending a year in one of Shirley's first-year composition courses, I instantly accepted her invitation to coauthor with her and some of my peers. Shirley's invitation was an indication of my performance in her class: I was earning exceptional grades, meeting course learning objectives, and fostering my leadership skills. Therefore, an opportunity to highlight the voice of an academically competitive African American female in a scholarly publication motivated me. Besides, this writing project elevated my competitive edge by placing me one step ahead of my peers who declined Shirley's invitation. Additionally, I knew it would allow me to collaborate with other historically underrepresented students as I had done during group projects and presentations that exposed me to different ideas and cultures. Perhaps my most salient reason to form a partnership was to demonstrate to a professional audience what collaboration among historically underrepresented students is like.

Equally important, my two first-year composition classes prepared me for this professional writing experience. During the fall 2021 semester, I experienced an academically challenging yet pleasurable immersive experience in my writing course. The rigorous learning environment was enjoyable: it was in-person, unlike the COVID-19 pandemic-induced online courses I completed during my senior year of high school. Those courses demotivated me and stifled my voice. In contrast, Shirley's writing course was designed to engage my peers and me in friendly competition; in other words, she wanted us to be inquisitive and take risks. Sometimes, when my peers struggled to respond to Shirley's questions, I reframed her questions in a way that most undergraduate students might understand and moved the discussion forward. The rigor of the writing course and the genuine interest and dedication Shirley showed in improving my writing skills persuaded me to enroll in her second writing course that led to this coauthored chapter. Shirley expressed that she would help improve my writing, and she provided me with reasons to strengthen my writing skills. For instance, in the second course, she designed a research assignment that asked us to research the requirements of our majors and potential careers particularly our writing requirements. While learning my degree requirements, the class allowed me to be as involved as possible. For example, I actively engaged in all class projects such as strengthening my leadership skills by leading class discussions, improving my interviewing skills by participating in mock interviews and giving honest feedback to my peers, and developing my writing skills by engaging in drafting and revising activities. In her discussion on preparing undergraduates for first authorship, Giuliano writes that faculty should "[p]rovide good writing instruction throughout the curriculum" (2) to prepare them for coauthoring projects. Shirley's writing assignments were clearly written, linked to our learning outcomes, and revised several times with Shirley's guidance. As a business administration major, it is incumbent upon me to become an effective communicator and scholarly writer. My participation in this professional writing project significantly contributes to achieving those goals.

Organizing, Researching, and Writing (Kayla and Charity)

To form a strong partnership and to enhance our technology literacies, we integrated more technology into our revision process. Shirley is six miles from one of us and thirty miles from the other, so technology closed the geographical gap that hindered us from meeting in person. However, technology could not close the gap created by untimeliness. In April of 2023, the editors invited us to revise our manuscript, and similar to when the proposal was approved, we were preparing for examinations. Additionally, one of us was beginning a new job in May and preparing for a week-long cruise in June. The other one was preparing to resume a summer position and was transitioning from a much-needed self-care break.

After a month of inactivity, Shirley sent us an email that included a clear set of responsibilities. To ensure we produced a high-quality product, Shirley established guidelines and guided us through them until we completed this chapter. Brian Payne and Elizabeth Monk-Turner encourage faculty who coauthor with students to shepherd those students through the entire writing process. Furthermore, Reed et al. maintain that "[c]oauthorship improves the quality of student writing, models collaborative behaviors, develops leadership skills, and is a useful teaching strategy, particularly for adult learners" (22). Reed and her coauthors discuss best writing practices for adult learners who "bring their own experience to the learning environment, and [who] learn by solving real-life problems" (22–23). We believed their practices applied to us, and like our class project, our coauthoring project is grounded in a theoretical framework designed to promote learning through research, synthesis, problem solving, active engagement, and reflection (Reed et al.).

For the most part, Shirley shifted authority to us while mentoring and nurturing us. In her email, she informed us that we should create a writing and revising timeline based on the editors' feedback, conduct research on researching and coauthoring with undergraduates, and create an outline that identifies each author's responsibilities. The path Shirley built for us is reflected in Payne and Monk-Turner's four steps that result in successful faculty-undergraduate coauthoring projects: (1) faculty must identify student writers; (2) tasks must be clearly determined; (3) all writers should be involved in producing and agreeing upon guidelines that will help the team meet its objectives; and (4) student writers should produce most of the work at the beginning of the project, so faculty can complete the project if any students cannot complete the work before the project is published. Moreover, in the same email, she identified the names of four articles and two books about coauthorship with undergraduate students. Kayla could not access the articles using our school's library databases as her secondary education experience had not equipped her with college-level information-literacy skills. In high school, Kayla used Google Scholar to conduct research. While composing this chapter, she taught herself how to use the library database and unfortunately learned that we did not have access to the sources Shirley had identified. Therefore, Shirley emailed two articles to us. Later, using her library's database, she taught us how to access the scholarship. Then, following the instructions in the email, Kayla took the lead on the project, created a Google Drive folder and populated it with a chapter outline, a task list, and a writing and revising timeline. In a Google Doc, we created an outline using the editors' feedback, analyzed their comments, and discussed how the feedback might move our draft in the direction they had identified. This strategy deepened our understanding of the concept called "audience expectation." On Mondays, between one and three hours were dedicated to developing the chapter in Google Drive after we had worked on it individually by annotating the chapter, discussing our own feedback, and identifying future tasks. Additionally, reading new scholarship on authorship better positioned us for our roles as coauthors and made us feel more confident. We used the technology and the documents to keep us on track while we learned how to manage this large writing project.

Once we were settling into our normal lives, we communicated across other platforms such as Zoom and cell phones. We agreed to use Zoom as our primary meeting platform because we could easily share documents and verbally communicate in real time. In one meeting, Kayla informed us that she felt uncomfortable editing Shirley's writing. Kayla's admission opened a conversation about Payne and Monk-Turner's observation regarding coauthoring with students. The authors maintain "that students may be resistant to critiquing a professor's writing," so they "must be told that they can give critical feedback to faculty members on these projects" (para. 23). Our conversation eased Kayla's discomfort by eventually corroborating her belief that critiquing Shirley's writing would nurture her own writerly self as peer review improves our writing and critical thinking skills. As Charity listened to the conversation, she identified two primary reasons for her reluctance to critique Shirley's writing. Charity doubted whether she possessed the knowledge and authority to offer valuable feedback on Shirley's writing, and Shirley was still the authority figure and writing expert who had much to teach us about writing though we were coauthors. We had finally divulged our secret that it was difficult to collapse the hierarchy even after applying our authorial voices and executing authority in all other matters related to revising this chapter. In fact, one conclusion we drew was to use Facetime when working without Shirley. Besides, Shirley does not use Apple products, and we identified sections of the chapter that didn't require Shirley's immediate input. Our aim was to develop our ability to coauthor a document for a target audience, become more self-reliant, and work together without constant faculty guidance. By seeking assistance from each other, we gained fresh perspectives that were invaluable in shaping our ideas and identities as professional writers. Writing with each other created a more open and relaxed atmosphere that was free from Shirley's scrutiny. Though sometimes we devalued Shirley's watchful eye, her guidance resulted in our success.

One lesson Shirley taught us about generative artificial intelligence is to rely on our own intellectual abilities to think critically about writing and researching. Shirley experimented with ChatGPT 3.5, a generative AI, by requesting articles written by professors at HBCUs who had coauthored with students though she was aware that the complex algorithm lacked the ability to accurately respond to the complex prompt she had designed for it. Nonetheless, ChatGPT's first response yielded five articles. After requesting the chatbot to "Regenerate," its second response yielded six articles. Shirley attempted to verify the sources by searching three universities' databases, Google Scholar, and the internet. All the sources were bogus; ChatGPT had hallucinated. It was important for us to learn how to responsibly use chatbots, to learn that generative AI tools are designed to produce answers to queries by any means, and to learn that they were programmed to write in SAE though they are multilingual. Additionally, Charity integrated ChatGPT 3.5 into her writing process to ensure that her writing was concise and formal. Prior to feeding her work to ChatGPT, it was very informal. To help her writing meet what she considered "publication standards," Charity relied on ChatGPT to strengthen her writing. However, she learned that chatbot produces redundant, decontextualized prose, so she revised the AI-generated content and maintained authorial control of her writing.

Finally, to help us think globally about academic writing, we analyzed "Co-Authoring with Undergraduate Students: An Emerging Process from the Semi-Periphery of the World of Science." When the article was written, Maria S. Plakhotnik was teaching at "a high-ranking Russian university" (334). Plakhotnik's curriculum is taught in English, but "almost all students are native speakers of Russian, and non-native speakers of English" (334). Learning that we and some non-English-speaking Russian students are similarly situated surprised us. Plakhotnik's coauthors who do not write in English are less likely to produce manuscripts for publication consideration. Plakhotnik asserts that "[s]ome journals and publishers openly state in their policies that they do not accept work authored by students" (338) because students produce substandard work. Thus, Plakhotnik's coauthors ranked the journals that would likely publish their work (337). In the United States, some academic publishers accept work coauthored with students, but like Russian publishers, they caution authors to ensure that their writing adheres to the rules of SAE, the primary language of domestic and international scholarly discourse. Ultimately, the integration of modern technology into our writing process resulted in a more methodical writing process, a smoother distribution of authorial responsibilities, and a space where we could candidly express our feelings about coauthoring and writing in general.

What Did I Learn While Writing with Kayla and Charity? (Shirley)

As an African American woman compositionist and justice advocate, research is germane to my identity and positionality. I am passionate about helping underrepresented students of color experience authority as academic, professional, and community writers. Hence, I undertake critical pedagogical strategies and research methodologies with underrepresented students of color that cast them in a role of authority figure. The seminal idea that took root in my mind in 2010 grew into this coauthoring project. My first attempt to coauthor with undergraduate students was during the fall of 2010 at NCCU when first-year college students in one of my composition courses engaged in a letter-writing exchange with high school students in an English course. Initially, the college students found no value in collaborating in a letter-writing project with high school students though ninety-nine percent of them had just graduated from high school. Eventually, all of them except one accepted the challenge to write letters but not to coauthor with me. Though the research project resulted in a single-authored rhetorical analysis of college students' letters, the college students and I engaged in a collaborative writing practice. That pedagogy comprised brainstorming, drafting, and revising their letters to high school students. In addition to helping college students meet traditional first-year composition and community-service learning objectives, the project was designed to introduce high school and college students to an actual audience who would respond to their writing.

Like that collaborative writing project, this coauthored project was challenging and rewarding. Kayla and Charity fostered a deeper appreciation within me for coauthorship and mentorship opportunities with undergraduate students of color. This project taught me to trust undergraduate students like Kayla and Charity to manage parts of a writing project such as this one. Kayla self-identifies as a writer and a leader. According to academic standards, Kayla epitomizes a "gifted student," and her inquisitiveness manifests in her thinking and writing process and in her leadership skills. In contrast, Charity did not identify as a writer, yet she possesses grit and a willingness to learn how to strengthen her academic writing skills. I saw something in Charity that she could not see in herself: a writer and a leader. She had actively participated in class, led a class discussion on how to create a table of contents in Microsoft Word, and produced good writing that improved after she moved it through a rigorous revision process. Despite her accomplishments, she resisted the identity this writing project imposed upon her because she has "never considered [her]self a writer." Cognizant of the type of emotional support she needed to push through this project, Charity called upon writing center staff and her family to guide her through her writing process. Charity reminded me that writing is a social activity that comprises both academic and nonacademic communities of practitioners who support writers (Lave and Wenger).

What would I do differently next time? To better acclimate undergraduate students of color to a historically White, heteronormative, ableist dominated discourse, I would implement the following plan: (1) annotate the proposal, (2) meet with writers for no less than two hours to discuss the proposal, (3) establish clear written guidelines early in the process, (4) design a weekly writing schedule that would include thirty minutes for addressing questions and establishing goals and two to three hours for writing, and (5) select potential undergraduate coauthors early in the semester and mentor them on authorship. As Guiliano and her mentor put it, "'[T]he best undergraduates are often better than graduate students' because they are 'not only very bright, but often are more intrinsically motivated—if you hold them to high standards, they will meet or exceed them, and you can publish great work with them'" (2). While I wholeheartedly agree with Guiliano and other faculty who coauthor with students in writing studies, I must add that we should carefully define the term *writer*. Countless students of color have not been trained to self-identify as academic writers. Many African American students write in African American English (AAE), and too many educators perceive the dialect as an obstacle to learning SAE. Those educators focus on grammatical errors instead of on those students' content and their potential to skillfully switch between AAE and SAE. In turn, many of those students conclude that they cannot write because educators have repeatedly communicated to them that they speak as they write and that they are incapable of writing in academic English (Gilyard; Jordan; Kirkland; and Richardson, "African American" and "PhD"). Historically, an academic writer has been one who produced a formal style of writing ascribed to White students who have attended elite private and public schools that immersed them in SAE. Those students receive invitations to coauthor with professors because they require less writing instruction, making them more efficient and desirable collaborators.

Final Words (Charity)

While Kayla and I reflected on how this project has benefitted us beyond our writing classroom, a few key points stood out regarding my identity as a writer and writing teacher. Prior to that discussion, I had not assessed this project's influences on my pedagogy at a summer camp where I teach writing. As a summer camp group leader of fourteen second graders, I have assumed an authoritative position similar to many faculty members who coauthor with students and who teach writing in general. For instance, during "Wonderful Writing" sessions that are held twice a week, my students write about topics they choose such as their favorite animals, summer camp activities, or future careers. I noticed that when students pursue their own agenda, a genuine sense of passion is maintained, and when students are passionate, they tend to generate substantial and "meaningful knowledge" (Mina et al, 3). To help my students produce clearly structured writing, I started designing clear writing guidelines, as Shirley had done. This coauthoring experience has also taught me the importance of reviewing and editing with my students. Now, when I notice common spelling and punctuation mistakes in students' papers, I guide them in sounding out misspelled words and practicing the correct use of periods until they grasp the concept. Finally, this coauthoring experience boosted my confidence as a writer and justice activist. I'm thrilled about the possibility of this chapter inspiring African American female students to conduct scholarly research and coauthor with their professors. Equally important, I encourage them to embrace their vulnerabilities and the power within them. Surely this writing project will enhance my graduate school and employment prospects, add credibility to my research and ideas, and elevate my academic reputation as a credible writer and researcher.

Final Words (Kayla)

This coauthoring project taught me how to work well under pressure. While completing this project, I served in a part-time leadership position at a summer camp. During a typical eight-hour shift, I interacted with eighty to one hundred rising first- and second-grade students, supervised eight to ten staff members who worked directly with campers, and informed parents of incidents and updates. Among a task-filled job that compelled me to be present in many ways, I still had to write, and write effectively. My writing consisted of completing programming templates, disciplinary forms, incident reports, and coaching cards as well as composing messages to staff. Most of my writing was reviewed by my supervisor before being read by my target audience, but some of my writing served as documentation for camp records. To ensure I wrote effectively, I took copious notes and stored them until I could return to them and begin the documents. Whenever I could step away from campers and staff, I completed those documents and revised them as I had learned to revise this chapter. Otherwise, I would not have met my objectives of completing documents for my supervisor's review.

To write for this project, I took notes at work when ideas presented themselves to me and weaved them into the chapter after I returned home. I worked eight hours a day during the week, so the majority of my writing was produced primarily on weekends. Giuliano contends, "[I]t may take some creativity to find the time and space for writing, as in 'writing weekends'" (3). I felt the pressure from my own self-motivation and my coauthors to ensure I produced most of my writing and rewriting on the weekends. Consequently, one job taught me how to improve the other.

My greatest takeaway from this coauthoring experience was the support I received from my coauthors when I needed it the most. While deeply immersed in the routine of working during the week with my coworkers and working on the weekends with my coauthors, I lost my grandfather and subsequently lost my motivation to write. During my painful loss, my coauthors consoled me with encouraging actions and words, and they reassured me that I was capable of completing this chapter with them. Shirley and Charity continued to develop the chapter in my absence. With heartfelt appreciation, I finally put my finishing touches on a scholarly publication project that has motivated me to become even more innovative in academia and beyond.

Works Cited

Gilyard, Keith. *Voices of the Self: A Study of Language Competence*. Wayne State UP, 1991.

Giuliano, Traci A. "Guiding Undergraduates through the Process of First Authorship." *Frontiers in Psychology*, vol. 10, 2019, pp. 1–5.

Jackson, Karen K. "Don't Knock the Hustle: HBCU Writing Center Life." *Academic Exchange Quarterly*, vol. 17, 2013, pp. 135–41. https://rapidintellect.com/AEQweb/t5406z3.pdf.

Jordan, Zandra L. "Evaluating Essays across Institutional Boundaries: Teacher Attitudes toward Dialect, Race, and Writing." *Race and Writing Assessment*, edited by Asao B. Inoue and Mya Poe, Peter Lang, 2012, pp. 97–109.

Kirkland, David. *A Search past Silence: The Literacy of Young Black Men*. Teacher College P, 2013.

Lave, Jean, and Etienne Wenger. *Situated Learning: Legitimate Peripheral Participation*. Cambridge UP, 1991.

Leggette, H. R. "Faculty Define the Role of Writing in the Social Sciences of Agriculture." *NACTA Journal*, vol. 59, no. 2, 2015, pp. 104–10.

Mina, Lilian, Megan McAfoose, Megan Moulden, and Shannon Zilavy. "Class-Based Research in the English Composition Class." *Perspectives on Undergraduate Research and Mentoring*, vol. 3, no. 1, 2005, pp. 1–13. https://eloncdn.blob.core.windows.net/eu3/sites/923/2019/06/Mina-et-al-3.1.pdf.

Payne, Brian, and Elizabeth Monk-Turner. "Benefits of Writing with Students." *Academic Exchange Quarterly*, vol. 9, no. 1, 2005, pp. 282–86.

Plakhotnik, Maria S. "Co-Authoring with Undergraduate Students: An Emerging Process from the Semi-Periphery of the World of Science." *Learned Publishing*, vol. 35, 2022, pp. 332–40.

Reed, Cynthia J., Mary-Claire McCarthy, and Bonnie L. Briley. "Sharing Assumptions and Negotiating Boundaries: Coauthorship as a Tool for Teaching and Learning." *College Teaching*, vol. 50, no. 1, 2010, pp. 22–26.

Richardson, Elaine. *African American Literacies*. Routledge, 2002.

Richardson, Elaine. *PHD to Ph.D.: How Education Saved my Life*. Parlor P, 2013.

13
Creative-Critical Coauthoring

Definition and Demonstration

SANDY FEINSTEIN, NICOLAS FAY, FAITH ISEMAN,
ASHLEY OFFENBACK, CHRISTIAN D. BRENDEL,
RACHEL JENSEN, AND JENNIFER MURET-BATE

In 1995, the year I (Sandy) submitted a paper with three of my students, one of whom was Jennifer Muret-Bate, I could find no models of students coauthoring with one another and their English teacher. At the time, I was teaching a course in multicultural literature, and the makeup of the class at the small, rural Methodist college in Kansas reflected the local community: they were white, Christian, native speakers of English. Expanding the conventional approach to multiculturalism to find a way to personalize the subject, each of us, including the teacher, chose readings we felt reflected our culture. This experience served as the basis of the article we coauthored together. While the proposal I submitted to the editors' call for papers was duly formal and conformed to disciplinary expectations, my interests even then bridged literary scholarship, pedagogy, and creative writing. As I would learn years later, Wendy Bishop, at roughly the same time, would describe cowriting in her creative writing class, which she framed as an anomalous approach in English studies as well. My experience as a creative writer first induced to teach the subject in 1981 would influence how I read and taught literature as Bishop's experience as a creative writing teacher informed how she taught composition: through pedagogic experiments in collaboration; hybridizing of forms; radical appropriations; and pushing at the conventions of how to make meaning. Over time, teaching both creative writing and literature would increasingly narrow the distance between the two disciplines for me: creative writing itself, thus, became a critical act and useful pedagogy for engaging students in early literature, my field, by providing an alternative means for representing what was understood, whether of texts or themselves. There was then no theoretical underpinning for integrating creative writing into literature classes.

A year later, I taught my first course with a scientist, which prompted me to begin integrating the research tools and methodologies of chemistry into my literature and writing courses as well: moving beyond the classroom into the field or "labs," which would offer another means for teaching observation, argument, meaning, and critical thinking (Feinstein, "Peripatetic," "Collaborative," "Reading and Writing," "Going Outside"). Designing these alternative approaches to writing and reading was my form of creative criticality, which would be theorized nearly twenty years later as creative critical (Franks et al.).

When I began teaching literature in 1980, there was no theory for applying creative writing to literary texts or, for that matter, theorizing creative writing or its teaching in general. Indeed, when I was in graduate school (1975–1980), one of the tensions in English departments among composition instructors, literature teachers, and creative writers was the varying degrees to which each saw theoretical approaches as applicable to their areas of expertise. Creative writing was a thing apart, a historical view of which is provided by recent discussions of the creative critical approach (McFarlane et al.; Clifton). The question asked, or anticipated, even as recently as 2014, was "What use is theory?" (Parker).

Nearly ten years later, the scholarly creative critical website (2023) introduces itself with an assertion regarding the blurring of the eponymous terms, followed by a series of questions:

> The twenty-first century has seen the erosion of any sharp distinction between the "creative" and the "critical." Can criticism itself aspire to be creative? Does creative writing have a critical force? Or should we dispense with these terms altogether.

These were questions I had answered for myself and began to address in articles about the time the journal *CounterText* was founded (2015), well after coauthoring with Jennifer, Christian, Rachel, and Ashley. This journal, like the creative critical website, makes the argument for approaching texts in ways not typically associated with critical analysis. Its "domain," as the editors explain, is broad, being "the post-literary... in which any artefact that might have some claim on the literary appears" and thus "allows for vital and challenging migrations and mutations of the literary" (Callus and Corby). A quick MLA or Google search reveals, however, the challenges of distinguishing a theory that uses such key words in English studies—namely, "critical" and "creative." *CounterText* tends to embrace more experimental incorporation of the creative critical, eschewing explanations for the approach, where others, such as *Text*, unpack and explain what the creative work is doing critically (cf. Frank et al.).

Of my coauthors here, only Nicolas, in his last semester, was directly introduced to creative critical as a pedagogic construct. His exposure came initially in a cross-disciplinary course called Creativity, from which followed a coauthored submission (Feinstein et al., "Admissions") to a special issue of *Text* focused on the creative critical. Nevertheless, *all* of us here have assigned or engaged in a variety of pedagogic experiments involving creative constructions as critical acts that ultimately led to coauthorship, the earliest of the publications involving Jennifer who, as an English teacher herself now for over twenty years, reflects on how her experience proved foundational to her teaching. Ashley's coauthoring experience, by contrast, has exerted its impact more recently, after she decided to attend graduate school to become an English teacher, a direction not at all on her radar when she was a graduating senior in the honors seminar, Why Literature Matters (2013). At the time, she was set on a career as a professional writer, which prompted me to change her assignments from the traditional English papers to what would now be called critical creative assignments, as she explains. Christian and Rachel would devise responses more in line with their immediate plans to attend graduate school, one in linguistics, the other in criminology, which their narratives address; yet they, too, would shape their critical responses in alternative forms, including posters and music, among other creative reformulations.

The pandemic provided a unique opportunity for incorporating creative performance into critical readings and representations of the Arthurian Legend, as Faith and Nicolas explain. Faith, a communications major now in business, initially felt overwhelmed in the Arthurian course, which started with the making of masks—compared to medieval armor—before meeting in person in an outdoor amphitheater. She and Nicolas developed an appreciation for medieval literature during this challenging time for education, an experience they reflect on in our coauthored article for *Passionate Humanities*.[1] Another course, creative writing, that she and Nicolas took the following semester, still under COVID restraints, also incorporated critical creative pedagogies without identifying them as such. For example, their assigned poems and short fiction began first with classical narrative poetry and prose followed by collaborative exercises intended to facilitate individual and joint writing projects.

Coauthoring to publish, however, was not part of any of the course requirements; rather, it was offered as a choice that extended the course beyond its official conclusion and, in so doing, provided a transition from one kind of education (institutional, credit-based, hierarchical) to another (voluntary, shared, egalitarian). In the courses themselves, all students were invited to be coauthors, but, except for the first one with Jennifer, expressing an interest in doing so was to be deferred until final grades were submitted.

Each cowriting experience has reinforced my ideal of education as continuous and unrestricted by artificial boundaries, be they geographic (the classroom), temporal (class hours), or assessment-constructed (grades). It also provided a model of a process engaged by professions, whatever the field: begin, discuss with others, develop, revise, submit, and, if writers, publish. As such, coauthoring highlights other missing elements of higher education: the integration of creativity to enhance knowledge acquisition, the building of an intellectual community, and personal development including career preparation. Having moved well beyond the time and space of the classroom, our views on the impact of coauthoring follow in the form of a creative critical response.

An Eptalogue, a Post-Modern Symposium

> Concerning the things about which you ask to be informed I believe that I am not ill-prepared with an answer.
>
> —Plato, *Symposium*

Persons of the Eptalogue
Sandy
Jennifer
Nicolas
Christian
Rachel
Ashley
Faith

Scene
A Remote Learning Space

NICOLAS

In many ways, the conditions surrounding my first time writing collaboratively were incompatible with the nature of collaboration itself. As a sophomore during the COVID-19 pandemic, the fall 2020 semester marked a return to a new kind of normalcy designated by isolating guidelines. In the few classes not delivered through a virtual format, masking and social distancing were effective in hindering the spread of the virus but also proved to be challenging barriers to classroom communication. An exception to this was a course on Arthurian literature in which projects and exercises were designed to facilitate connection and interaction, and where we used collaborative problem-solving to transcend constraints. Even after retreating to our screens for the final weeks of the semester, student-led lessons and a collaborative final extended the ethos of connection that had been established. After the class concluded, Sandy extended an invitation to coauthor a paper in which we would use our classroom experiences to, as the journal prompted, "justify the existence" of the humanities within academia, and "find new ways to advertise our strengths to the public." Loose guidelines and an initial draft of an introduction were emailed to the students who accepted the invitation, but the direction of the article could only be determined after each of our sections were completed and compiled. Sandy's email concluded, "I'll try to make all the parts fit together—and may make in the future—but I'm open to suggestions. I also identify what I might add after you have completed your drafts. Again, suggest away (or just do it)." And so, from our respective locations, we "just did it." We wrote separately, yet together, all working toward a common goal.

FAITH

The *blank canvas* supplied by Sandy at the conclusion of our semester served as a challenging opportunity for me, as I would have no idea the mental and creative exercise I was about to embark on. The open-ended nature of our prompt was unique in the sense that we as a team would not be able to converse and develop a structure for our piece in person; we had no indication of the perspective that the other would provide for their new or familiar relation to Arthurian literature, the study of the humanities, and how it had affected us. This was my first experience in academic writing outside the practice of homework, let alone coauthoring—but when we began to submit what we had written it was quite interesting to see varied perspectives of the same shared experience, which gave our collective piece authenticity. As I began writing down my thoughts, similar to my final writing submission to Sandy, I became anxious that what I had to say did not hold any value or worth. I continued to question my voice and my perspective on humanities, *where do I even start? I recently declared my major—does my experience even matter?* So I decided to start from the beginning of my relationship with literature, and from there explain how it shaped my thought processes, exercised my ability to empathize, and provide why I believe that the study of humanities is important. Looking back, that whole exercise prepared me for the rest of my college career—how to engage in a manner that is uplifting and helpful in the learning process. I saw the effects of my coauthoring experience pour into my professional career: learning new tasks, becoming a sponge for knowledge, engaging with my team through varied experiences, opinions, etc. I had no idea the impact this experience would have on me—I must have enjoyed it . . . here I am once again!

NICOLAS

The open-endedness of Sandy's email statement freed us to write in ways that were reflective of our individual viewpoints, voices, and styles, and alleviated the pressure to conform to our notions of academic writing (an early line in Sandy's email read "feel free to respond 'creatively' in your section—with images, and/or 'creative' writing, etc."). By combining our stories, we were able to create something interesting and unexpected: narratives of lived experience interacting with scholarly form.

This initial encounter with creative elements in collaborative scholarship served as a precursor to coursework and coauthoring experiences where the import of creativity was made explicit. In a class succinctly and aptly titled "Creativity," the idea of experimentation and playing with form as a viable—and even vital—form of scholarship was given a label: creative critical. This approach was introduced through prompts and projects designed to cultivate new and different ways of seeing. These activities were often collaborative, crossing interdisciplinary boundaries and encouraging us to find new applications for our skills and interests.

CHRISTIAN

I think we're on the same page: "making" is best done collaboratively—best for both the product and the makers! As a linguist, I may be biased—I'm intimately entangled with the gravitational pull of long-dead stems, ancient arguments, and ongoing conversations—but our reality is filtered through language, and language is itself coauthored. In a never-ending dialogue across time, the collaborative actions of language users have coauthored the resources—words—we use to express our thoughts. For language, this process of change is generally subconscious, the behavior of a system evolving in no particular direction through the inevitable participation of human-brained iterators. *Conscious* coauthorship is an extension of this phenomenon: rather than a set of discrete, unconnected writings, I've experienced coauthorship as a continuous conversation, variously featuring both familiar and novel interlocutors who introduce and refine the metaphors used to understand reality. Every coauthored paper—or e-mail, or serendipitous conversation—is a slice of a fundamentally indivisible process of refinement of understanding.

NICOLAS

Exactly—what I initially saw as disjunct pieces of writing were elements of a whole that, when brought together, produced a nuanced narrative greater than the sum of its parts. I found this idea to be especially true of interdisciplinary and creative critical coauthorship where seemingly disparate authors, disciplines, and modalities came together to enhance arguments and generate new ideas.

I experienced what you describe as a process of refinement not only within projects and publications but in a general sense as well. Coauthoring familiarized me with processes like writing a proposal, writing within the confines of a journal prompt, revising, and so forth. In these cases, constraints were an additional voice in the larger conversation, posing a question or a scenario for the authors to navigate and respond to. Within these projects, I experienced firsthand one of the threshold concepts of writing studies: writing as social activity with the purpose of bringing about new understandings, "not about crafting a sentence or perfecting a text but about mulling over a problem, thinking with others, and exploring new ideas or bringing disparate ideas together" (Estrem). Writing alongside professors and other students with the creative critical approach exposed me to pedagogical methods that disrupted my notions of authorship and what academic writing could look like, providing a foundation for a kind of scholarship I didn't know was academically viable: embracing both individuality and the way we connect.

FAITH

My hopeless-romantic tendencies play a significant part in my desire to write. This desire was only showcased privately until the day I shifted my major course of study and decided to pursue communication. I selected a pathway that focused on rhetoric, public speaking, nonverbal communication, and writing. In a desperate attempt to prove to myself that I could write, and write well, I leapt at the chance to learn everything I possibly could in my Comparative Literature and Creative Writing courses.

When the opportunity arose to coauthor an article along with Sandy and fellow students, it occurred to me that a great way to improve is to have others workshopping with me. This experience, however, was different from other "group projects" I have been a part of since it occurred during the height of online/hybrid schooling. This hybrid approach to our collaboration occurred through a series of emails and text messages, much like my engagement with my coauthors on this project. What I didn't expect were the periods of waiting for each other's responses, waiting for submissions, and reading several revisions, or the waiting period to hear back from the editors and submit yet another final draft for publishing. I did find, however, that coauthoring wasn't as daunting as I initially thought it might be.

Through this experience, I have learned a lot. I began to keep an open mind, which in my personal experience could prove to be difficult when I'm trying something new. I did my best to lean into the *uncomfortable*; I needed to stretch my "writing muscle" and wouldn't have been able to do so without a push. I even began to notice that the questions I asked myself and my peers changed. For example, prior to one of my many workshops in my Creative Writing course I met with Sandy and asked her to evaluate my workshop piece with the class and not to hold back. This workshop session helped me tremendously on what to improve, and also to recognize that I have grown as a writer. It was during this turning point in the semester that I began to play with the creative critical approach, although I had not identified my work as such. For example, I put together a short film to present autoethnographic research as my final instead, which was later written as a full-fledged paper that I presented in that year's Research & Creativity Conference hosted by Penn State Berks.

Through workshops and other coauthoring experiences, I've noticed changes in the way I approached group projects: my goal shifted to the group dynamic and learning to be in sync with another's vision, and my criticism evolved from judgment to a reflective critique. Critical analysis and out-of-the-box thinking while coauthoring was further developed, especially when writing with others in my class who excelled in genres and/or styles that differed from mine. These experiences have broadened my point of view in approaching a prompt concept, structure, tone, and more. A hybrid written with two coauthors while it could have been stressful, turned into an amusing exercise knowing that my coauthors' additions will eventually resemble my work while being completely unique and yet supportive.

Over time my outlook evolved; rather than approaching it as a daunting venture I began to find the appeal of creating something unique. This outlook has helped me as I transitioned to work in the world of banking, specifically in trusts and estates. The structure of a last testament, will, power of attorney or governing trust document can be quite creative and unique, as it differs from one person or family to the next. The legacy created through these documents can be quite profound if done properly. Legacy planning leads me to engage with many different people and documents: each trust officer has a different way to address clients and handle their business. Having learned how to approach an interaction with the proper critical analysis helps me adapt to what our clients need, how to make them feel heard, and ultimately work with people I may not have much in common with. My experience as a coauthor has helped me grow in more areas than I ever expected: as a writer, communicator, and team player.

ASHLEY

Infusing lessons from literature class with a career in trusts and estates is totally unexpected. Hearing about Faith's experience applying the creative critical approach to her work in banking makes me feel similarly to how I did in 2013: that year, Sandy asserted I could learn about professional writing in a literature class. As a professional writing undergraduate, I was only interested in practical writing skills and was highly skeptical that a literature course had any relevance to my chosen field. By the end of the course, my perspective had been entirely transformed as I realized literature is extremely relevant to me and can be a catalyst for learning about any and every major or career.

My newfound appreciation for the utility of literature resulted because of Sandy's use of the creative critical approach. The success of Sandy's customized and collaborative teaching method is illustrated by my story: She took literature, a subject that I was completely uninterested in and managed to help me understand it while simultaneously teaching me about my (entirely different) major field of study.

How she accomplished this was through individual assignments tailored to the student's major or intended career path. For example, at the time it was my aspiration to be a journalist. When we studied George Orwell's *1984*, the connection was obvious; the work is clearly related to the field of journalism.

Reading *1984* did teach me much about the power and responsibility that lies with journalists simply because of the storyline in the novel.

However, Sandy managed to make other works of literature, with absolutely no content relation to journalism, incredibly relevant to me. When we studied *The Princess Bride*, for example, Sandy and I developed a project that would teach me about both topics: I wrote a mock interview with William Goldman, a book review, and a query letter to *The New Yorker*. For our study of William Shakespeare's *Merchant of Venice*, I wrote social media posts that a theater company could use to advertise their performance of the play. I appreciated these very practical assignments that also allowed me to engage with the texts. I was amazed that Shakespeare and his work written over four hundred years ago could help me learn about journalism in the present day.

Perhaps this method was so effective because it seeks to truly understand the students: considering their academic goals, career goals, personal background, and input to figure out how to help them best learn and engage with the material. It was this teaching method and incorporation of the creative critical approach that motivated me to participate in a coauthoring experience with Sandy and classmates years after the initial course.

RACHEL

Much like Ashley my experience in Sandy's courses allowed me to subvert my interest in my actual major (applied psychology) through literature—I still have saved on some hard drive a mock playbill I created of a comedy on Oedipus's ghost warning Hamlet beyond the grave of his odd family relationships. In my academic experience outside of Sandy's courses, coauthoring was a much more rigid practice with clear-cut expectations and binary conclusions whereas in my professional experience in a policing nonprofit it is often muddled. It is difficult to reconcile this rigor with policing, or any type of public and civil service for that matter, which is messy and achingly human while also forced to adhere to its own flavor of rigid procedures and federal and state legal codes. This, in my humble opinion, is the crux of creative critical thinking, utilizing creative mechanisms to work toward an understanding.

My first experience with coauthoring in 2013 in an article for *Rendezvous Journal of Arts and Letters* was very similar to the writing of this piece. Sandy, Ashley, Christian, and I all communicated from wherever our lives had taken us. For me, it was graduate school and completing my master's degree in criminology (followed by a doctorate recently achieved). In this article I discussed why I chose to teach *Lonesome Dove* by Larry McMurty to my Integrative Arts course peers led by Sandy. The final line of my submission was "As a person however, this course and its design allowed me to explore themes in literature and critically think about them in unique ways that have made me a much better student and scholar." That course and the 2015 submission were both in line with my experience with Sandy. Our learning and coauthorship was unbounded in a way, as a core tenant of her courses was not to direct or "set up" her students, allowing us to poke and prod and push to use creative means to understand the "text" we all taught to one another.

CHRISTIAN

I've talked about informal coauthorship a lot today, but I'm glad you reminded me about our coauthored paper (Feinstein et al., "Why Study Literature?") and the value of these more traditional coauthorship events. I've written several times with the authors in this room (including right now), and these waystones, separated by months and years, have helped me identify my path as a linguist (from undergraduate enthusiast to, most recently, PhD recipient) and continually relocate myself on it. In the paper you mention, I began questioning why should a common "love of knowledge"—philosophy—be semantically (and practically) divided by the modern English words *art* and *science*? Since then, I've continually agonized over this question with my colleagues, across both formal publications—my own research and this reflection itself—and long-form emails with Sandy and breathless discussions with colleagues outside the classroom. Through these group efforts, I try to rediscover the role of scientific research (or is it philosophy?) in a world that feels increasingly unknowable, one which I often feel mocks my attempts to generalize or predict its behavior.

RACHEL

You've hit the proverbial nail on the head; it's amazing how different disciplines such as linguistics and criminology grapple with the same, applied questions. A key aspect I learned in graduate school, which may surprise many of my fellow social science researchers, is that it is not enough to analyze data. Reporting results requires a flair of creativity to understand the story that variables and statistical outputs are telling. Regression tables and log odds, while sound statistical theory, are no good without a creative mind to parse out what that means in regards to people, what it means to them and how it impacts them. While in graduate school, I was a coauthor on a published peer-reviewed article that explored instances of force and resistance in police encounters involving individuals with behavioral health conditions. Coauthoring in this context was much more rigid in its process compared to my past experience with Sandy and others. My 2013 experience built my confidence to think around empirical corners in a unique way, allowing me to think about the data outputs (text) in a meaningful way.

With my academic background and my experiences, I began to view my work as coauthorship through a creative critical lens. I learned that it was not just that I could examine a text but the mechanism of *how* I examined it that mattered. It was the process of coauthorship, actively listening to others and working on incorporating what was important to them into project outcomes. Many of my professional projects bring together police leaders, advocates, community organizers, and others with unique expertise who are passionate about creating safer communities. My role as coauthor was to weave those different voices (creative lens) together to a singular narrative (text).

My coauthorship experiences have now spanned eight years, and I have learned many lessons from both processes in academia and policy and practice. Before I viewed what I had to say as a star in the sky, part of a collective but individualistic. Now I view it as communal, a unique thread in a tapestry.

CHRISTIAN

Coauthorship has certainly changed me too. Before college, my idea of learning was a solipsistic race to imagined mastery. My journey has convinced me that the scope of the term *coauthorship* should not be limited to only published, written texts, but also to less-esteemed exercises in co-construction that happen through engaged pedagogy, both teacher-and-student and student-to-student.

Indulge me as I pull on another loose thread. The Latin *auctōritās*, the progenitor of English "authority," embeds the idea of "invention" ("Auctōritās"), a word whose own etymon *inveniō* denotes a humble "finding" rather than the more contemporary, individualistic notion of "creating" something from nothing ("Inveniō"). Coauthorship can be understood, then, as a kind of together-finding, a co-inventive, constitutive dialogue that defines its topic of inquiry as much as it describes it. Although "sole authorship" is a principal criterion of measuring a scholar's value in various academic fields, the "inventions" discovered through collaboration are real and essential, whether encoded in a coauthored article or arising from unadorned conversations.

I cannot invent anything alone, especially myself.

ASHLEY

As Christian alludes, I also found my coauthoring experience to be impactful on my personal development as I "invented" my own life and trajectory as a young adult. I had just recently finished undergrad in 2015 when Christian, Rachel, Sandy, and I (along with other unnamed classmates) coauthored an article titled "Why Study Literature?" The article was born from a literature course (and international trip) we completed together in 2013.

Reflecting on my original coauthoring experience nearly a decade ago, snapshots of memories come to mind: that initial day as an undergraduate in Sandy's literature class, presenting my portfolio on the last, hiking in the frigid mud of the Slieve League mountains in Ireland, witnessing our article in print for the first time, among many others. Not only were these moments notable in terms of the coauthoring but they were some of my most significant memories period. Sandy's class, the Ireland trip, and the resulting coauthorship have had an immense impact on my life: the writing and related adventures rerouted me to grad school, improved my writing skills, built my confidence and matured my personality as a young adult, to name a few. I've often conveyed the impact of the experience through writing.

It became the inspiration for my graduate school personal statement and writing sample. I wrote about it at length for my goals and dreams paper as part of my graduate study ("Why do you want an MA in English studies and what do you hope to accomplish?"). Before that it inspired a creative piece and a published article on the significance of the honors program. The reason that I continue to write about this experience is because it has had such a positive impact on my life and personal development, for which I am forever grateful and could not have accomplished without the assistance of my coauthors.

JENNIFER

As you have all shared here, I also learned to see myself as a part of a dynamic and interconnected whole through the process of coauthoring. My introduction to coauthoring came in 1994, when I was enrolled in a multicultural literature course with Sandy. The project grew out of an assignment in which each of the students in the class was to choose a book that represented an aspect of their own culture, read the text with the class, and then facilitate a group discussion over the text. Looking back at our class makeup, which was quite homogeneous on the surface, one might not expect much variety in the texts that were chosen; surprisingly, however, we found ourselves reading everything from cookbooks to horror novels. The resulting discussions were rich, and they revealed classmates' diversity and common ground in equal measure. The perspectives and contributions of undergraduate students injected a wealth of heart and personal narrative into an academic assignment arena, which might have otherwise remained a more traditional, academic evaluation of literature. I loved and learned a great deal from the participatory nature of it.

After this assignment, which was one of my earliest experiences in teaching, Sandy invited us to coauthor about our experiences. This coauthored piece was then submitted for publication and chosen to become a chapter of the book *Sharing Pedagogies: Students and Teachers Write about Dialogic Practices* (Feinstein et al., "At Home"). At the time, I had no understanding that what we were doing might come to be described as "creative critical." In a way, I was blissfully unaware that the personalization of studying and writing about literature in which we were engaging was breaking the rules of what academia and creatives would have had us do. In our coauthoring we worked together to produce a creative product that blended an inventive and connected approach to an academic evaluation of text. In doing so, the group embarked on a new learning experience that impacted us personally and guaranteed we would relate to, learn from, and remember the texts and the experience.

CHRISTIAN

Like you, Jennifer, I wasn't explicitly aware of the creative critical approach when I was an undergraduate. The pedagogical and advising style that Sandy practiced allowed me to study historical linguistic topics and methods even as a student at a campus with no formal linguistics courses. When I matriculated at a college without a linguistics major, I quickly realized I didn't know how to achieve my goal—or even what my goal was. Accordingly, my first experiences with coauthorship were not in preparation of a publication but instead conversations with my professors—most often, Sandy—about my projects and assignments, most of which involved an amorphous lens of "linguistics" that I only murkily grasped. Constantly and continually these written and verbal dialogues expanded and crystallized my notion of what "linguistic research," or any research, could be. No mere idle conversations, these collaborative experiences instead coauthored the first drafts of the authoritative definition of linguistics I've held in my mind through my career, a foundational text in my brain as significant as any printed journal article. We found that linguistics was not just a reconstruction of Proto-Indo-European or a syntax tree but an analysis of the connection between demon names in *Paradise Lost*, a consideration of the narratological effect of translation differences on the interpretation of Old French texts, or an honors thesis on the divergence of J. R. R. Tolkien's Elvish languages.

Even in the traditional undergraduate courses I've since taught in linguistics, I recognize my (then-unknowing) adoption of creative critical approaches in my own pedagogy. I recall one time, when exploring speech perception, my students attempted to memorize and recite (for the entire class) song lyrics in languages unfamiliar to them. They discovered for themselves that even monolingual English speakers could more accurately remember and reproduce songs in German than in Japanese—and that lyrics in Simlish (a gibberish entirely unbound by the systemic properties of language) were almost impossible to reproduce faithfully. Through play, those students translated embodied performance to intellectual purchase on concepts like "typological distance" and "phonological similarity." The (inter-)play inherent to these experimental endeavors, building on each other over years, constituted a coauthored definition of my very field, a cognitive "article" that I've mentally cited and built on when I write, and think, ever since, an article that I've shared with my students.

JENNIFER

Sandy's invitation to co-teaching and coauthoring was foundational to my perspective on education. Our coauthoring was an exploration and extension of our co-teaching. As undergraduate students we had a rare opportunity to share in the design and learning of our class. We wrote about what we learned from each other—in content as well as pedagogical areas. This had an absolutely direct impact on my own career trajectory—informing the way I knew I wanted to teach. My engagement and learning from these activities have continued to influence my work as a secondary school educator throughout my career. I had learned that the process of learning is best facilitated when all—the instructor and the learners—are engaged in the learning. That was a lesson I would study further in graduate school through restorative practices, a field that advocates participatory learning and decision-making, arguing that "human beings are happier, more cooperative and productive, and more likely to make positive changes in their behavior when those in positions of authority do things with them, rather than to them or for them" (Wachtel). This lesson, which I first learned in Sandy's multicultural literature class, is one I would apply when I had my own classroom full of at-risk high school students.

Today I see reflections of my own (now long-ago) experience when I assign my students to collaborate with me in writing grant proposals for our school each year. It is gratifying to see them expressing the same pride and eagerness that I remember from my own coauthoring experience. They learn, as I learned, that writing together provides an opportunity for multiple perspectives to come together to create a richer whole. We all learn from each other much more than if we each separately responded to a prompt. We are all the "teacher," and we all learn from each other, and our end product takes on a life of its own far beyond what any of us could have individually imagined.

Our common thread here, if I can borrow Rachel's notion of a tapestry, seems to be that we have all learned something about how to connect and work with people and how to include creative approaches in more conventional situations. This has changed how we evaluate, understand, and respond to real life in fields as diverse as academia, linguistics, banking, and policing. It seems to me that our coauthoring in our classes with Sandy helped us become better humans in the world.

SANDY

In Plato's *Symposium*, one character reconstructs a story he heard from another character who heard it from another. The filtering through different characters over time may be the narrator's way of accounting for gaps in memory, omissions, additions. Here, we are narrators of our own stories, but the potential reconstruction is no less affected by time. The frame of our reconstruction provides a creative critical response to Plato's and the reconciling of narratives that, while not impacted by three different tellers' version of a story, is impacted by the changes between who each of us was when we first published together and who we are now years later as we reconsider the experience.

Those Plato's narrator identifies as participating in the *Symposium* represent a range of voices involved in different disciplines, from historical playwright to statesman. Socrates, Plato's teacher, is the ultimate authority; but Plato is credited with authorship. Perhaps Plato's works may be the first coauthored ones involving a former student and teacher. They may also be the first published creative critical consideration in philosophy. Plato's *Symposium*, moreover, is closer to invention than to what the word may now convey to contemporary academics.

Plato's *Symposium* presents coauthorship as a dialogue with critical purpose. Though accepted as having been constructed by Plato, individual voices are retained, and combined, to come to an understanding of a specific idea—love. It also, perhaps, begs the questions, Did Plato publish with his former teacher or his former teacher with his pupil?

We, too, use our individual voices to reflect on how we began coauthoring with one another as part of an undergraduate education. Since graduation, each of us has developed our own singular voices as teachers. Coming together again, we offer a creative critical demonstration not only of coauthorship but of Platonic love, as learning and collaboration, inconceivable in Plato's multi-voiced representation of the subject.

Note

1. Though accepted by the editors for their anthology and a publisher expressing interest in it (October 6, 2021), including a contract secured (March 13, 2024), on August 13, 2024, one of the editors announced his withdrawal as editor after which another coauthor, expressing surprise by the withdrawal, decided on August 21, 2024 that he couldn't continue the anthology on his own. The then students, Faith and Nic, experienced every step but the final one in the process of coauthoring our article, "Sovereignty, Literature, and Teaching: What do Students Most Desire?"

Works Cited

"Auctōritās." *A New Latin Dictionary*, edited by Charlton T. Lewis and Charles Short. Oxford, 1891.

Bishop, Wendy. "Co-Authoring Changes the Writing Classroom: Students Authorizing the Self, Authoring Together." *Composition Studies*, vol. 23, no. 1, 1995, pp. 54–62. http://www.jstor.org/stable/43501316.

Callus, Ivan, and James Corby. "Editorial." *CounterText*, vol. 1, no. 2, 2015, pp. v–xi.

Clifton, Glenn. "Critical-Creative Literacy and Creative Writing Pedagogy." *University of Toronto Quarterly*, vol. 91, no.1, 2022, pp. 51–66.

Estrem, Heidi. "Writing Is a Knowledge-Making Activity." *Naming What We Know: Threshold Concepts of Writing Studies*, edited by Linda Adler-Kassner and Elizabeth Wardle, UP of Colorado, 2015, pp. 19–20.

Feinstein, Sandy. "The Collaborative Cross Disciplinary Classroom." *Learning Literature in an Era of Change: Innovations in Teaching*, edited by Dona Hickey and Donna Reiss, Stylus, 2000, pp. 99–112.

Feinstein, Sandy. "Going Outside: More than Leaving the Classroom." *Teaching Ideas for University English: What Really Works*, edited by Patricia M. Gantt and Lynn Langer Meeks, Christopher Gordon, 2004, pp. 17–27.

Feinstein, Sandy. "The Peripatetic Approach to Teaching the Gothic." *Thought & Action*, Spring 1999, pp. 39–47.

Feinstein, Sandy. "Reading and Writing, Backward and Forward: Topics, Models, Audiences and Language." *Power and Identity in the Creative Writing Classroom*, edited by Anna Leahy, Multilingual Matters, 2005, pp. 192–202.

Feinstein, Sandy, Carman Costello, Amanda Folck, and Jennifer Muret Bate. "At Home with Multiculturalism in Kansas." *Sharing Pedagogies: Students and Teachers*

Write about Dialogic Practices, edited by G. Tayko and J. Tassoni, Boynton-Cook, 1996, pp. 67–79.

Feinstein, Sandy, Bryan Shawn Wang, Nicolas Fay, Nathan Tam, Niccolas Bernhart, and Kyla Ebersole. "Admissions: A Report from a Pilgrimage to an Alternative University." *Text: Journal of Writing and Writing Courses*, vol. 28, no. special 72, 2024.

Feinstein, Sandy, Tiffany Wesner, Christian Brendel, Lily Cernak, Ashley Offenback, Rachel Jensen, and Sean Geguera. "Why Study Literature?" *Rendezvous Journal of Arts and Letters*, vol. 43, no. 1–2, 2017, pp. 163–74.

Franks, Rachel, Jesper Gulddal, and Alistair Rolls. "Editorial." *TEXT*, vol. 20, no. special 37, October 2016. https://textjournal.scholasticahq.com/issue/3476. Accessed 17 May 2024.

"Inveniō." *A New Latin Dictionary*, edited by Charlton T. Lewis and Charles Short. Oxford, 1891.

McFarlane, Brandon, Alexander Hollenberg, Hyein Lee, and Marco Cibola. "Remaking Critical Theory: A Creative Humanities Process and Intervention." *University of Toronto Quarterly*, vol. 92, no. 2, 2023, pp. 147–81.

Parker, Jan. "Critical-Creative Writing and Theory of/and Practice." *Arts and Humanities in Higher Education*, vol. 13, no. 3, July 2014, pp. 183–88.

Plato. *Symposium*. Translated by Benjamin Jowett, The Internet Classics Archive, 360 BCE. https://classics.mit.edu/Plato/symposium.html.

Wachtel, T. "The Next Step: Developing Restorative Communities." Paper presented at the Seventh International Conference on Conferencing, Circles and other Restorative Practices, Nov. 2005, Manchester, UK.

"Welcome to Creative Critical." *Creative Critical*. https://creativecritical.net/. Accessed 17 May 2024.

Index

Page numbers followed by f indicate figures, and page numbers followed by n indicate notes.

AAPI. *See* Asian American Pacific Islander
Abbot, Sophia, 12
academic personality, development of, 137–38
accountability, 7, 40, 70, 155
Across the Disciplines (Kinkead), 42
activism, 115, 121; community-based, 82; disability rights, 194; supporting, 114; tribal, 108; women's, 148
Advanced Composition (course), 64, 68, 69, 73, 74
African American English (AAE), 218–19
agency, 121; authorial, 8; dimensions of, 51; shared, 66; student, 115
Allen, Marissa Shirley, 42–43
Alvarez, Elsa Angelica, 57, 60
American Educational Research Association (AERA), 128
analysis, 42, 140, 187, 196; critical, 223–24, 229; data, 212; fostering, 116; rhetorical, 180–82; verbal, 70
Analysis of Popular Culture Texts (course), 178
Anderson, Madison, 82, 88
Anderson, Paul, 190
Animal Crossing: New Horizons (game), 187
anthologies, 20, 105, 107
"Archival Research in the Time of Pandemic" (roundtable session), 152

Archival Research Methods (course), 151
archives, 151; coauthoring and, 144, 146–50, 152; collaboration and, 143; community, 143, 150; digital, 144; investigating, 156
arguments, 3, 11, 80, 90, 134, 169, 180, 187, 211, 223, 227, 228; narrative-informed, 137
Art Book Room, 40
artificial intelligence, 216
Asian American Pacific Islander (AAPI), 83, 84, 89, 91
Assessment Institute, 128
Association for the Assessment of Higher Learning Education (AAHLE), 128
authority, 14, 16, 205, 233; academic, 5; realigning, 13; roles, 181

Babcock, Rebecca, 24n2
Beat Generation, 40, 41
"Beer Farmers" (Martinson and Dubisar), 188
behavior, 36, 228, 232, 236; classroom, 179; collaborative, 214
Bell, Annissa, 5
bias, 179; mitigating, 84
Bishop, Wendy, 206n3, 222
Blackwell, Christopher, 178
Blair, Kris, 180
Blancato, Michael, 83

Bloom, Lynn Z., 10
Blume, Kolbie Astle, 39
boundaries, 72, 99; crossing, 108, 162; faculty-undergraduate, 78, 81; knowledge across, 89; university-community, 78, 81
boundary dwellers, 13, 20, 81–82, 88; authorship and, 84; benefits for, 86; coauthoring and, 83, 85, 91; community engagement and, 87; undergraduates as, 82–87
boundary objects, 80, 81–82, 89, 91
boundary spanners: community engagement and, 87; developing, 89–92; role of, 82–83
boundary zone, 10, 79, 80, 84; coauthoring processes in, 87–90
Boyer Commission, 11
brainstorming, 68, 78, 89, 103, 133, 217
Brennan, Bob, 154
bridging function, 89, 90–91
Bromley, Pam, 51
Brown, Renee, 16
bureaucracies, 165, 166–68, 169
Busch Light/John Deere "for the farmers" campaign, 188

Cache Valley Historical Society, 43
CAE. *See* collaborative autoethnography
call for proposals (CFP), 5, 19, 55, 118, 121, 133; research and writing guidelines of, 152–53
Canterbury Fellowship, 104, 106
Carda, Nathaniel, 90
CCC. *See* College Composition and Communication
CCCC. *See* Conference on College Composition and Communication
CCCC Position Statement on Undergraduate Research in Writing: Principles and Best Practices, 11, 69
Center of Education Effective (UC Davis), 127
Center for Teaching Excellence (Pepperdine), 74
CFP. *See* call for proposals
Charlton, James, 194
ChatGPT, 216
Chávez, Karma R., 122
Church, Lois Lake, 53, 54
circulation, 65, 74–76
Clark, Beverly Lyon, 4, 8, 9
coaching cards, 220
coauthor, term, 7–9
coauthoring: benefits of, 49, 233; boundaries of, 21, 82, 84, 87–90; challenges of, 44–45, 49, 150–53; community, 78, 81, 91, 99; complexities of, 71, 190; conversations about, 9–19, 165–66; creative-critical approach to, 19, 22, 228; critique of, 189–90; defining, 4, 7–8, 44; developing, 18, 23, 38, 54, 58, 106, 112, 217; equitable, 69, 73, 206n1; faculty roles in, 36–38, 180–82; faculty-feminist, 60, 115–23, 163; group, 150, 155; hierarchies in, 178–80; as identity affirmation, 137–39; impacts of, 21–22, 225; intergenerational, 13, 149; metaphor for, 95–96; narratives surrounding, 100; nested, 10, 96, 97, 98, 99, 106, 108, 109; parameters for, 8, 37; partnerships for, 44, 45, 144; processes for, 6, 53, 56, 79, 87–90, 91, 128, 133, 149, 169, 177, 194, 205; questions about, 6–7; side-by-side, 144–45, 147, 148–55; successful, 50, 55, 68, 80, 147; teams, 89, 90, 97; textbooks and, 153–55; understanding, 75, 81, 233; value of, 38, 80–81, 90, 109
Coauthoring Advanced Composition (course), 66
"Co-Authoring with Undergraduate Students: An Emerging Process from Semi-Periphery of the World of Science" (Plakhotnik), 216–17
code-switching, 15, 66
colearning, coauthorship and, 182–86
collaboration, 60, 128, 129, 139, 145, 162–63; archival, 143, 155; authentic, 122; benefits of, 227–28; challenges of, 65; coauthoring and, 33, 82, 114, 128, 147, 163, 170; dialogic, 23; feminist, 121; forced, 156; forms of, 160; idea generation and, 68; intersectional/intergenerational, 145; processes for, 21, 80, 128; reflecting on, 238
collaborative autoethnography (CAE), 162–63, 164
collections, 177; orientations/interpretations of, 150
College Composition and Communication (CCC), 3, 4, 8, 15, 24n1, 99, 104, 106
College English, 4, 5, 6, 12, 23, 24n1, 41
College of Humanities and Social Sciences (USU), 32
Committee on Publication Ethics (COPE), 7
"Communicating Elective Sterilization: A Feminist Perspective" (Davis and Dubisar), 182
communication, 40, 184, 191, 226, 231; approaches to, 134; doctor-patient, 182; drafting and, 194; feedback and, 137; initiatives for, 61; nonverbal, 229; open, 193; oral, 209; regular, 35; technical, 32, 41, 102, 178; written, 209

communities of practice (CoPs), 21, 159, 163, 165, 166, 167, 169–70; benefits of, 161; coauthorship and, 171; developing, 162, 168; feminist, 160, 162; successful, 168; value of, 170
community: academic, 84, 96, 199, 218; Black, 83; building, 109; college, 200; diverse, 168; Hispanic, 199; intellectual, 225; learning, 108; marginalized, 162; mutual endeavors and, 161
community engagement, 79, 80, 81, 88, 89, 105; boundary spanners in, 82–83; coauthoring and, 78; collaboration in, 78; decolonizing, 87
Community Literacy Journal, 5
community members, 19, 78, 83, 88, 89, 156; researchers and, 84–85, 155
community organizations, 82, 86, 156
Comparative Literature (course), 229
"Composing Collaborative Feminist Recovery Projects with Scalar" (web text), 104
composition, 98, 104, 105, 136, 143, 155, 213; first-year, 217; teaching, 223; video, 181; well-synthesized, 140
Composition Studies, 5, 98
Computers and Composition, 180, 181
Conference on College Composition and Communication (CCCC), 5–6, 7, 11, 74, 80, 105
confidentiality, 86, 205
connections, 95, 97, 99, 101–2, 114, 115, 117, 119, 121, 122, 130, 132, 168, 226; community, 91; deep, 161; forging, 61; interpersonal, 88; social, 8; threads of, 98
Contois, Emily, 188
conversations: academic, 135, 138, 140, 190; counterstories and, 199–203; generative, 13; multidirectional, 145; pedagogical, 196; virtual, 122
Cook-Sather, Alison, 11, 17
Cooper-Rompato, Christine, 42
CoPs. *See* communities of practice
Council on Undergraduate Research (CUR), 32
counterstories, 194, 195; conversations about, 199–203; incorporating, 205; student narratives and, 197–98
CounterText (journal), 223
course-based undergraduate research experiences, 40
COVID-19, 49, 50, 56, 121, 149, 168, 213, 224, 226
cowriting, opportunities for, 148
Crabtree, Robbin D., 113
Crawley, Emily, 81–82, 86, 88
creative critical approach, 223, 229, 231

Creative Writing (course), 229
creativity, 147, 209, 223, 227, 232, 233, 237; critical, 224–25
Creativity (course), 224, 227
critical race theory (CRT), 194, 197, 198
critical thinking, 116, 117, 209, 223, 224, 235
Crumbley, Paul, 40, 41, 45
cultural historical activity theory (CHAT), 79
culture, 59, 146, 148, 166, 169, 182, 213, 234; building, 38, 40; coauthoring, 32–33; incorporating, 106, 196; linguistic diversity and, 10; maintaining, 105; popular, 180, 188
CUREs. *See* course-based undergraduate research experiences
curriculum, 33, 67, 70, 107; coauthoring, 69; collaboration on, 43; development of, 37, 68, 145; vertical, 146
Currie, Lindsay, 32

data, 37; analysis of, 212; collecting, 140, 212; quantitative, 193
Davis, Sara, 14, 188, 189, 191; coauthoring with, 183–84; elective sterilization and, 13, 182; persuasion brief by, 182; research by, 185, 186; on rhetoric, 184
Day, Kami, 196, 206n2; coauthoring and, 7–8, 16, 147; collaboration and, 6, 14, 147
Dedoose, 80
Deep Reading, Deep Learning (Sullivan et al.), 167
DEI. *See* diversity, equity, and inclusion
Department of English (USU), 20, 32, 33, 38
development, personal/professional, 113, 121, 135, 189, 225
dialogue, 12, 75, 112, 113, 116, 119, 120, 121, 124, 195, 205, 228, 233, 235, 237; collaboration and, 13; generating, 119; internal, 117; meaning-making, 123; multivoiced, 19; scholarly, 107
Dickinson, Emily, 40
Digital Measures, 37
discourse, 10, 33, 107, 114, 161, 197, 198, 205; academic, 19; ableist, 218; dominant, 196; heteronormative, 218; professional, 3; scholarly, 217, 218
diversity, 64, 70, 118; experiential, 193; lack of, 202; linguistic, 10, 15, 24n2; religious, 68; subjective, 193
diversity, equity, and inclusion (DEI), 20, 193, 194, 195, 196; initiatives, 68; issues around, 71, 72; panel, 204; practices, 10, 66–71; research, 17, 73; scholarship, 204; student voices and, 14; symposiums, 197; talking about, 201; teaching methods, 205

"Doing More with Barely Enough" (Zea), 58
Downs, Doug, 8
drafting, 136, 226; communication and, 194; initial, 121, 122; messiness of, 71; original, 123
Dubisar, Abby M., 13, 14, 18, 20, 22, 23, 180
Duncan, Jennifer, 40
dynamics, 82; epistemological, 88; political, 86; power, 16, 64, 65, 70, 87; research, 16

Eble, Michelle, 153
Ede, Lisa, 21, 23, 149, 154, 157; coauthoring and, 144–45, 150; on cognitive/rhetorical strategies, 155; on creativity/originality, 147
Edenfield, Avery, 41
editing, 34, 152, 163, 187, 196, 210, 215, 219; mentoring and, 154
education: analyzing/assessing, 42; higher, 4, 7, 16, 106, 225; undergraduate, 73, 238
Efthymiou, Andrea, 51, 52, 53, 60
Elder, David, 73
elective sterilization, 13, 182–86
Emotions and Affect in Writing Centers, 55
empowerment, 22, 23, 70, 97, 105, 106, 107, 138, 140, 170
engagement, 97, 214, 229; dimensions of, 51; future, 23; intellectual, 103; intentional, 74–75; learning and, 236; metacognitive, 104; online, 117; scholars, 82; student, 11, 113, 114. *See also* community engagement
English, academic, 219
English Department (FIU), 167
English studies, 7, 38, 49, 224
Enos, Theresa J., 129
Eodice, Michele, 196, 206n2; coauthoring and, 7–8, 16, 147; collaboration and, 6, 14, 147
Erickson, Kresten, 43
ethics, 45, 69, 80, 85, 145, 150, 155, 159, 190, 209; research, 50–53
experiences: activism/agency and, 121; coauthoring, 19, 21, 22, 23, 45, 87, 96, 99, 112, 115, 118, 120, 124, 139, 160, 163, 168–69, 198, 203, 204–5, 219–20, 224, 225, 229, 230, 231, 235, 236–37; collaborative, 57, 91, 113, 235; immersive, 136, 213; learning, 124, 132, 202; personal, 104, 113, 114, 132, 202, 227, 229; reflecting on, 236–37; research, 14, 106, 137; women's, 114; writing, 139, 211–12, 213
expertise, 5, 14, 21, 65, 85, 105, 106, 112, 113, 115, 119, 123, 130, 131, 137, 147, 149, 152; building, 122; distributed, 123; experience and, 131; forms of, 88, 89; knowledge and, 128, 161–62; notions of, 127, 129; professional, 186; realigning, 13; reinforcing, 124; shared, 117; student, 75; writing process and, 88
Expressionists (Pepperdine University), 66

faculty, 163; evaluating, 18; redefining, 10–14
Faculty Code (USU), 37
Faculty-Student Partnerships for Diversifying Courses (Pepperdine), 64, 67
Fallon, Brian, 16
Fay, Nicolas, 19, 22, 224, 225; experiences of, 226, 227, 228
feedback, 106, 122, 132, 183, 213, 214, 215; communication and, 137; iterative, 137; seeking, 134, 184
Felten, Peter, 17
feminist framework, 57, 96
feminist groups, 115, 170
feminist theory, 60, 123, 220
Ferriero, David S., 149–50
(First Person): A Study of Co-Authoring in the Academy (Day and Eodice), 6, 147, 152, 154
Fishman, Jenn, 3, 164
FIU. *See* Florida International University
FIU Undergraduate Research Journal, 168, 171
Flint, Abbi, 11
Florida International University (FIU), 164, 167; CoPs at, 168, 171; demographic disparities at, 160
Foss, Sonja K., 163
Freire, Paolo, 64, 73, 198
French, Warren, 4–5
Funda, Evelyn, 42
funding, 61, 109, 139, 167, 183, 185

Gaillet, Lynée Lewis, 13, 19, 20, 21, 149, 151, 152
Gale, Ken, 6
Garcia, Larisa, 57
gatekeeping, 17, 131–32, 136, 181
gender, 97, 148, 182; role differences, 60; writing/rhetoric and, 113
Gender and Communication (course), 178, 182
Gender and Women's Studies (GWST), 121
General Education Committee (USU), 42
genres, 132, 135, 136, 161; academic, 137, 140; gate-kept, 132, 139; multi-source, 180; multiple, 128; traditional, 123
Georgia State University (GSU), 148–49
Gerard, Morna, 148, 149
Giuliano, Traci A., 212, 213, 218, 220
Go Online!: Reconfiguring Writing Courses for the New Virtual World (Gray-Rosendale and Rosendale), 151
Godbee, Beth, 165

Goldman, William, 231
Google Docs, 75, 80, 82, 91, 134, 224
Gordjin, Bert, 45
Graban, Tarez, 143, 152
Graham, Morgan Sanford, 39, 43
Gray-Rosendale, Laura, 151
Greer, Jane, 5, 23, 40, 210
Gregory, Natalie Hatch, 42–43
Griffin, Cindy L., 163
Grobman, Laurie, 11, 40, 178, 210; academic authority and, 5; coauthoring and, 23; on methodology of inquiry, 156
guidelines, 7, 85, 152–53, 214, 218, 226
"Guiding Undergraduates through the Process of First Authorship" (Giuliano), 212
Guido, Nick, 53, 54
Gutman, Ellen E., 67

Hamlet, 231
Haney, Cameron, 41
Harrington, Kathy, 11
Harris, Joseph, 3, 4, 10
Hart, D. Alexis, 24n2
"Haul, Parody, Remix: Mobilizing Feminist Rhetorical Criticism with Video" (Dubisar et al.), 180
Haverford College, 12, 204
Hawisher, Gail, 4
Hayden, Wendy, 143, 152
HBCUs. *See* historically Black colleges and universities
Healey, Mick, 11
"Heart Beats" (exhibition), 40–41
Heilbrun, Carolyn, 129
Hernandez, Paola, 151
Hidden Figures (movie), 89
hierarchies: academic, 186; coauthorship, 178–80; destabilizing, 177–78, 191; epistemological, 88; faculty-student, 185; institutional, 194; research, 185; student-teacher, 180, 181
high-impact practices (HIPs), 21, 120, 121, 190; access to, 42; implementation of, 37; institutionalizing, 189
Hispanic-serving institutions (HSIs), 4, 159, 160, 167
historically Black colleges and universities (HBCUs), 4, 15, 22, 207, 208, 216
history: alternate, 150; archival, 145, 148–50; oral, 146, 150, 151, 156
Hochstetler, Sarah, 162
hooks, bell, 113, 198
Hosseini, Mohammad, 45
Howes, Emma, 50, 51

HSIs. *See* Hispanic-serving institutions
Hughes, Langston, 34
Humanities, Arts, Science and Technology Alliance and Collaboratory (HASTAC), 196
identities, 10–14, 59, 68, 133, 140, 169, 204, 219; academic, 14, 18, 128, 130; authorial, 16; collective, 128; cultural, 159, 163; development of, 91, 129, 131, 163, 166; intersectional, 22, 165–66; linguistic, 159, 163; multifaceted, 86; personal, 130; professional, 9, 159, 162, 163; racialized, 16; scholarly, 90; undergraduate, 85; writerly, 117, 128, 131
IMRaD. *See* introduction, methods, results and discussion
Inclusive College Classrooms: Teaching Methods for Diverse Learners (Cardon), 193, 196
indexing process, 35–36
infrastructure, 151, 171, 204; feminist, 96–97
institutional frameworks, 19, 65
instructional activities, 17, 18, 37, 202, 219
instructional texts, coauthoring, 19
Integrative Arts (course), 231–32
International English Honor Society, 33
internships, 104, 109
Intersection: A Journal at the Intersection of Assessment and Learning, 127–28
interviews, 89, 183; conducting, 146; mock, 213
introduction, methods, results and discussion, 132, 137
Introduction to Writing Studies (course), 101

Jack, Jordynn, 5
Jensen, Phebe, 40
Jiang, Xuan, 15, 21, 159, 160; authorship and, 165–66; collaboration by, 170, 171; CoP and, 18, 165, 168; writing center and, 164–65
Johnson, Brian, 87
Johnson, Kristine, 51, 52, 56
Journal of Advanced Composition, 3
Journal of Arts and Letters, 231
Journal for Undergraduate Multimedia Projects, 186
journalism, 230–31
journals, 4, 12, 39, 41, 68, 134, 169, 185, 196, 197; peer-reviewed, 20, 22, 117, 139, 171; rise of, 11, 44; writing center, 61n3, 159
Jump+, The, 11, 186, 187–88

Kairos: A Journal of Rhetoric, Technology, and Pedagogy, 12, 98, 104
Kinkead, Joyce, 11, 19, 20, 39, 41, 42, 44, 178; literary tourism and, 43; on methodology of inquiry, 156

knowledge, 100, 107, 108, 137, 143, 198, 211, 219, 225, 232; academic, 78–79, 97; cocreating, 20, 50, 51, 56, 59, 115; community, 78–79, 89, 148; constructing, 52, 53–60, 61, 112, 124; coproducers of, 7, 10–14; cultural, 82–83; expertise and, 128; pedagogical, 75; production of, 114, 123; rhetorical, 102; shared, 122
knowledge-making, 16, 21, 100, 109, 116, 121, 122, 124, 185, 189, 191
Kuh, George, 11, 129, 189

Ladson-Billings, Gloria, 197
Langston Hughes and the South African Drum Generation: The Correspondence (Graham and Walters), 34
language, 161, 169; justice, 24n2; theory, 66
Language Theory (course), 66
Larracey, Caitlin, 160, 161, 165, 171
Lave, Jean, 160, 161
leadership, 209, 218; fostering, 212, 213
Leal, Casidy, 57
learning, 108, 117, 232; collaboration and, 145, 238; collective, 114; engagement and, 236; participatory, 236; personal, 113; practices, 72, 131; trial-and-error, 137; two-way, 148
Learning Assistance Review, The, 128, 134
Lee, Joua, 84, 86
LGBTQ+ perspectives, 64
Licona, Adela C., 113, 122
linguistics, 232, 235, 236, 237
listening: feminist, 50; importance of, 50–51; lingering on, 53–60
"Listening to Research as a Feminist Ethos of Presentation" (Rosenberg and Howes), 50
literacy: Black, 83; digital, 39, 187; migrations/mutations of, 224; practices, 98, 122
literature, 32, 226; academic evaluation of, 235; advancing, 163; applied psychology and, 231; teaching, 223; utility of, 230
literature review, 129–30, 134, 135
Lockett, Alexandria, 24n2
London, Jack, 40
Lonesome Dove (McMurtry), 231–32
Long 19th Amendment Project, 148
Lott, Jessica, 16
Lueck, Amy, 148
Lunsford, Andrea, 3, 21, 23, 149, 157; coauthoring and, 144–45; on cognitive/rhetorical strategies, 155; on creativity/originality, 147; on group-authorship, 150

MacVicar, Margaret, 32
Malcolm (Purdy), 4

Martinez, Aja Y., 99, 197
Martinson, Tracie, 188
Massagee, Lucy, 5
Mathews, Elizabeth, 16
May Swenson Poetry Path, 43
McGregor, Beth, 3
McKee, Heidi, 190
McLeod, Faith, 24n1
McMillan, Laurie, 8
McMurtry, Larry, 231–32
McPhearson, Dominique, 120
Meader, Mica: video by, 186–87, 188
meaning-making, 21, 114–15, 140, 162; collective, 13, 112, 117, 118, 119, 120, 122, 123
mentoring, 37, 38, 99, 104, 137, 165, 166, 170; Black women, 210; coauthoring and, 129, 163, 218; coauthors and, 106, 178; editing and, 154; faculty, 164, 177; intergenerational, 13, 17, 149; modeling, 130, 145; mutual, 13, 72; publication, 178; top-down, 128; undergraduate, 129
mentorship, 44, 96, 97, 103, 165, 166, 170; ad hoc, 129; building new relationships to, 135–36; collaborative, 168; definitional boundaries of, 72; equal playing field and, 130; horizontal, 130, 135; model for, 128, 129, 130; mutual, 73, 97, 107, 128, 130, 135, 139, 140; nested, 107, 108
Mercer-Mapstone, Lucy, 12, 65
Merchant of Venice, The (Shakespeare), 231
meta-analysis, 21, 119, 120, 121, 123, 124
metacognition, 96, 100, 103, 137, 164
methodology, 130, 147, 162–64, 208–10; quantitative, 212; research, 217, 223
Miller, Susan, 4
Milu, Esther, 24n2, 59
Mintie, Elizabeth, 16
Modern Language Association (MLA), 7, 224
Monk-Turner, Elizabeth, 214, 215
Moore, Jessie, 11
Morales, Alyssa, 57
Mullin, Charity, 15
Muwekma Ohlone Tribe, 17, 99, 103, 105, 110n2

Nagar, Richa, 78, 82
narratives, 89, 98–108, 120, 194, 195, 202, 205, 224, 228; border-crossing, 151; circulating, 196; DEI, 196, 197; individual, 113, 121, 123; original, 122; personal, 113, 124, 205, 235; polyvocal weave of, 98
Nasr, Nadia, 148
National Conference of Peer Tutors in Writing, 15, 52, 59

National Council of Teachers of English
    (NCTE), 39, 41
National Institute of Reproductive Health, 88
National Survey of Student Engagement, 11
N.C. A&T. *See* North Carolina Agricultural and
    Technical State University
NCCU. *See* North Carolina Central University
NCTE. *See* National Council of Teachers of
    English
Neruda, Pablo, 43
nest-building, 95–96, 99; how-to for, 108–9;
    methods/methodology and, 97–98; relationships and, 97
nesting, stories of, 98–108
neurodiversity, 16, 53, 64
New Yorker, The, 231
1984 (Orwell), 230–31
Nora Eccles Harrison Museum of Arts (USU),
    40–41
North Carolina Agricultural and Technical
    State University (N.C. A&T), 208, 209
North Carolina Central University (NCCU),
    207, 209, 217; mission statement of, 208
Northway, Kara, 51

O'Connor, Elizabeth, 88
O'Donnell, Ken, 189
Office of Equity (USU), SAAVI and, 41
opportunities: coauthoring, 19, 20, 108, 150–53, 156, 162, 181, 188, 204, 207; curricular/extracurricular, 96; publishing, 204, 208, 211–12; seeing/situating, 38–43; undergraduate, 144
Orwell, George, 230–31
Oswald Review, 11
Othering, 10, 201
othermother, 210
Otuteye, Mark, 3

Palermo, Gregory J., 16
Palgrave Macmillan, 34, 35–36
Palmer, Ruth J., 161, 166, 170
Paradise Lost (Milton), 235–36
participation, 153; audience, 201; legitimate peripheral, 97; research, 51
partnerships, 6, 78, 82, 84, 90, 177; agreements for, 44; coauthoring, 36, 38; faculty-student, 65–66; forming, 79, 81, 213; graduate-student, 132; mentoring, 89; mutualism in, 75–76; pedagogy and, 71; student-faculty, 66–71, 75–76; transactional nature of, 69; undergraduate, 73, 131, 132, 145; university-community, 83; writing, 128, 177

Passionate Humanities, 224
Payne, Brian, 214, 215
Pedagogical Partnership program at University of Alabama, 204
pedagogy, 75, 81, 108, 146, 149, 156, 182, 203, 208–10, 222, 223, 228; approaches to, 20, 31, 50, 84, 236; changes in, 153; critical, 198; critical creative, 224–25; DEI, 193, 194–95, 196; engaged, 233; feminist, 10, 21, 112, 113–14, 115–23, 124; partnership and, 71
Pedagogy, 11
Peer Educator, role of, 103
peer review, 35–36, 117, 136–37, 139, 177, 179, 197, 232–33
Penn State Berks, 229
Pepperdine University, 15, 64, 66, 67, 74
"Performing Writing, Performing Literacy" (Fishman, Lunsford, and McGregor), 3
Perspectives on Undergraduate Research and Mentoring (PURM), 41, 42
persuasion brief, 182, 183
Plakhotnik, Maria, 216–17
Plato, 225, 237, 238
PLC. *See* professional learning communities
Poe, Mya, 17
poetry, 41, 43, 201, 225
positionality, 78, 96, 113, 129, 131, 135; multifacted, 86
power, 68–71, 161; distribution of, 71; imbalances in, 88
Power of Partnership: Students, Staff, and Faculty Revolutionizing Higher Education, The (Mercer-Mapstone and Abbot), 12
predominantly white institution (PWI), 198
presentations, 50, 61, 201–2; conference, 79, 100, 103, 121
presenters, audience and, 201–2
Primary Research and Writing: People, Places, and Spaces (Eble and Gaillet), 153, 155
Princess Bride, The, 231
principal investigator (PI), 44
Pritchard, Eric Darnell, 191
problem-solving, 209, 214, 226
professional learning communities (PLC), 39
professionalism, 12, 106, 107, 209
"Promises and Perils of Higher Education: Our Discipline's Commitment to Diversity, Equity, and Linguistic Justice, The" (conference), 74
prompts, 68, 89, 117, 216, 226, 227, 228, 229, 237
public memory, 23, 148
publication, 6, 50, 58, 105, 106, 118, 137, 152, 171, 179–81, 182, 189, 190, 203, 228; academic,

144, 181, 191, 196, 197, 217, 220; coauthoring and, 12, 43, 49, 92, 186–88; collaborative, 150, 156; conventions of, 153; digital, 20; faculty, 37; group, 152; mentoring, 178; opportunity for, 204, 208, 211–12; peer-reviewed, 179, 197; preparing for, 35, 186–87; process of, 59, 109, 164, 169, 188; professional, 13; revisions for, 134, 135, 154
Purdy, James, 4
Putala, Andrea, 123

Quality Enhancement Plan (QEP), 54, 61
Queen City Writers, 12

racism, 82, 197
reciprocity, 73, 75, 163; asymmetrical, 14; collaboration, 130
Reed, Cynthia J., 214
reflections, 21, 42, 106, 120, 121, 124, 214; drafting/sharing, 119; macro-level, 112; metacognitive, 96; polyvocal, 100; written, 89, 119
Reflections: A Journal of Public Rhetoric, Civic Writing, and Service-Learning, 5
Regan, Devon Skylar, 16, 17
relationships, 86, 89, 90, 98, 163, 204, 227; building, 45, 50, 57, 61, 72, 88, 95, 97, 106, 147; coauthoring, 7, 31, 56, 88, 104–5, 109, 167, 168–69, 191; collaborative, 55, 80; intellectual, 108; intentional, 129–30; lingering on, 50, 53–60; mentoring, 96, 104, 129, 170; nested, 97, 109; rhetorical, 150, 163; student-teacher, 17, 101, 104, 170, 203; writerly, 109
reports: coauthored, 85; faculty-student, 42; research, 50–53, 54, 56
representation, problem of, 195–97
reproductive justice work, 82, 88
research, 10, 32, 37, 50, 117, 127, 147, 151, 162, 194, 196, 201, 213, 214–17; agendas for, 179; archival, 103, 143, 144, 146, 149, 150, 153–54, 155; articles, 55, 136; autoethnographic, 229; coauthoring and, 38, 51, 52, 146, 178, 179, 182; collaborative, 38, 51, 178; community-based, 82; conducting, 59, 183, 191, 212; digital, 149, 150; faculty, 18, 177; graduate student, 40; higher education, 69; integrity practices for, 44–45; meaning-makers of, 140; mentored, 109; opportunities for, 139, 207; primary, 153, 154, 157; process of, 51–52, 65, 102, 115, 122, 130, 185; productive, 187; projects, 87, 108, 217; tools for, 223. *See also* undergraduate research
Research & Creativity Conference, 229
research assistants, 33–34, 100

Research Office (USU), 38
research, scholarship, and creative inquiry (RSCI), 36–37
resources, 61, 93, 167, 169; cultural, 170; intellectual, 98; linguistic, 170; social, 168, 170
revisions, 134, 181–82, 186, 196, 211; creative, 184–85, 224; processes of, 6, 71, 105, 122, 155, 228; requesting, 212; sharing, 58; writing and, 168–69
rhetoric, 32, 65, 66, 75, 85, 104, 123, 156, 163, 164, 183, 190, 229; cultural, 105; feminist, 114, 116–17, 118, 119, 120, 122, 180, 186; gender/writing and, 113; historians of, 143
"Rhetoric and Affect in Undergraduate Research: A Diary Study" (Johnson and Rifenburg), 51
Rhetoric of Health and Medicine (RHM), 13, 14, 182, 183, 184, 186
rhetorical space, 67, 119
Rifenburg, J. Michael, 44, 51, 52, 56
Rivera-Mueller, Jessica, 39, 43
Roberts-Miller, Patricia, 8
Robillard, Amy, 11
Roe v. Wade (1973), 186
Rose, Jessica, 148, 149
Rosenberg, Lauren, 50, 51
Rosenberg, Marc, 4–5
Rosendale, Steven, 151
Ross, Laurie, 79
Rounsaville, Angela, 24n2, 59

SACS. *See* Southern Association of Colleges and Schools
SAE. *See* Standard American English
Sandmann, Lorilee, 83
Santa Clara Archives, 104
Santa Clara University (SCU), 17, 98, 99, 101, 109, 110n1
SaP. *See* students as partners
Sapp, David Alan, 113
Schlesinger Library, 148, 149
Schneider, Carol Geary, 189
Schneier, Joel, 24n2, 59
Schoettler, Megan, 8
scholarship, 153, 156, 159, 168, 228; coauthored, 150, 163–64, 194; collaborative, 227; DEI, 204; literary, 222, 223; pedagogical, 146, 193, 194; public, 148; secondary, 154; student, 97; writing center, 164–65
scholarship of teaching and learning (SoTL), 124
Schonberg, Eliana, 51, 52
science, 44, 207; natural, 33

SCU. *See* Santa Clara University
self-confidence, 114, 200
self-identity, 22, 204, 210, 218
self-perception, 170, 211
self-reflection, 119, 120
Selfe, Cynthia, 4
Senatro, Leah, 21, 98, 99, 107; experiences of, 101–2, 103, 104–5, 106; nest of, 100*f*; writing/publication and, 109
Sexual Assault and Anti-Violence Information (SAAVI) Office (USU), 41
Shakespeare, William, 40, 231
Shanahan, Jenny Olin, 74
Sharing Pedagogies: Students and Teachers Write about Dialogic Practices (Feinstein et al.), 235
Short Term Course Redesign, 204
Shum, Andromeda, 83–84, 89, 90–91; theoretical framework and, 84; "university-community" dichotomy and, 84
Sigma Tau Delta, 33, 193, 195, 199, 200–201, 203, 204
Sinor, Jennifer, 43
Sketchnotes, 89, 91
skills, 227; information, 215; literacy, 215; research, 36; writing, 36, 152, 211, 212, 213, 234
Skinnell, Ryan, 143, 150
Smith, Linda Tuhiwai, 84
"social closeness" continuum, 83
social media, 58, 231
social science, 33, 44, 232
Socrates, Plato and, 237
software, plagiarism-detection, 16
Solorzano, Daniel, 197, 198
sources, 184, 215, 216; primary, 153, 154, 157; secondary, 73, 154; synthesizing, 136
South Atlantic Modern Language Association, 151–52
South Central Writing Centers, 56
Southern Association of Colleges and Schools (SACS), 54, 61
Southern Connecticut State University (SCSU), 53
stakeholders, 8, 13, 15, 88, 144, 149, 153; coauthoring with, 156; collaborating with, 155
Standard American English (SAE), 210, 216, 217; learning, 218–19
Standardized Academic English, 169
StARs (UC Davis). *See* student assessment researchers
Start by Believing Day, 41
STEM, 206*n*3, 207
sterilization. *See* elective sterilization
storytelling, 166, 195, 198, 205

strategies, 113; pedagogical, 217; research, 144, 146; writing, 131, 135
student assessment researchers (StARs), 127, 128, 130, 136, 138, 139, 140
Student Research Symposium, 33
Student-Faculty Partnerships for Diversifying Courses (Pepperdine University), 74
Students as Learners and Teachers (SaLT), 12
students as partners (SaP), 11, 12, 64, 70, 74, 75, 76; building, 66; coauthorship and, 71, 72; framework for, 66, 69; programs, 15, 17, 20, 73; research and, 65, 67, 68
students of color, 218; underrepresentation of, 208, 217
#SuffrageSyllabus, 148, 149
suggestions, 59, 75, 169, 189, 195, 226; revision, 187; sharing, 58
Sullivan, Colleen, 53–54
Summer Partnerships, 69
Sun, Lulu C. H., 10
Swenson, May, 40, 43
Symposium (Plato), 225, 237
synthesis, 81, 82, 88, 90, 214; bridging, 89; collaborative, 89

TAMUK. *See* Texas A&M University, Kingsville (TAMUK)
Teacher-Librarian, 43
teaching, 117; DEI, 195, 204; feminist transformative, 51; ideology of, 113; instructional activities and, 37; methods, 204; theories of, 143
Teaching through the Archives: Text, Collaboration, and Activism (Graban and Hayden), 143
Teaching to Transgress (hooks), 198
technology, 8, 105, 207, 215, 217; enhancing, 214; learning, 115
Texas A&M University, Kingsville (TAMUK), 49, 51, 57, 61
Text, 224
textbooks, 20; student work in, 153–55
theory of practice, feminist, 50–53
Thompson, Archer, 85, 87
tokenization, 22, 195, 197, 202, 203
Tolkien, J. R. R., 236
Trapp, Joonna Smitherman, 73
Traywick, Deaver, 44
Tribal Land Acknowledgment, 15, 106
Truman, Avery, 44
tutors, 16, 32, 39, 49, 54, 55, 57, 58; coauthoring and, 51; Hispanic, 15, 59; peer, 60; scholarship about, 60
Tutor's Column, 39

UC Davis, 127, 130, 139
undergraduate research (UR), 6, 11, 32, 44, 96, 97, 99, 109, 120, 121, 127, 144, 145; award for, 37–38, 182; culture of, 31; describing, 179; experiences with, 33, 36, 40, 41, 42; models, 171
undergraduate research fellows (URF), 42, 43
Undergraduate Research in English Studies (Grobman and Kinkead), 11
Undergraduate Research Poster Session at CCCC, 11
Undergraduate Research Program (USU), 32
undergraduate teaching fellows (UTF) (USU), 43
University of Alabama (UA), 193, 199
University Writing Center (TAMUK), 49
UR. *See* undergraduate research
URF. *See* undergraduate research fellows
U.S. Supreme Court, 186
Utah State Parks, 43
Utah State University (USU), 20, 31, 32, 36

Vara, Annette, 15, 20, 50, 55; story of, 56–60
voices: authentic, 13, 113, 120, 123, 124; authorial, 14; collective, 123; diverse, 21, 64; faculty, 12, 19; student, 14–16, 19, 22, 43, 65, 73, 109, 113, 115, 123, 124, 127, 128, 130; underrepresented, 7, 66, 104, 114; valuing, 130
vulnerability, embracing, 71–73

WAC. *See* writing across the curriculum
WAC Journal, 117
Wallace, David, 5
Walters, John: collaboration with, 34, 35, 36; Graham and, 34, 38
webpages/websites, 41, 102
Weerts, David J., 83
Weidenhaupt, Sonja, 8, 9
Wenger, Etienne, 160, 161, 218; communities of practice and, 21; on CoPs, 169–70
Wheatley, Rebecca, 43
Why Literature Matters (course), 224
"Why Write . . . Together?" (Lunsford and Ede), 144, 155
Wolfe, Keira, 81
Womack, Anne-Marie, 193, 196
Women Writers and Writing (course), 104, 105
"Wonderful Writing" sessions, 219
writers-in-process, 10–11
writing: academic, 60, 79, 135, 136–37, 138, 146, 152, 164, 216–17, 227, 228; building new relationships to, 135–36; challenges of, 211–12; collaborative, 23, 108, 129, 134, 136–37, 226; community, 78, 83, 100; creative, 164, 222, 223; demystifying, 136–37; organizing for, 214–17; professional, 23, 230; public, 6; reflecting on, 119; rhetoric/gender and, 113; scrutinizing, 212; style, 29, 219; transactional approach to, 138; workplace, 146, 157
writing across the curriculum (WAC), 116, 122
Writing Center (Pepperdine), 66
Writing Center (TAMUK), 51, 54, 56, 57, 59
Writing Center (USU), 31
Writing Center Journal, 12, 16
writing centers, 49, 50, 51, 60, 61, 103; coauthoring and, 52–53; course, 164–65
writing courses, 117, 154, 166, 223; community-engaged, 78, 83
Writing Lab Newsletter (WLN), 39
writing process, 6, 75, 79, 106, 107, 109, 115, 121, 122, 130, 155, 185, 193; academic, 132; expertise and, 88; meta-analysis in, 112; resources for, 170; shared labor of, 139; thinking about, 135; weaknesses/strengths in, 137
writing projects, 132, 135, 139, 219; collaborative, 130; individual/joint, 225; managing, 210
Writing Research Across Borders (WRAB), 128
writing studies, 4, 9, 10, 51, 70, 76, 113, 179, 189; concepts of, 228; scholar-teachers, 190–91
writing to engage (WTE), 116, 118, 121
writing to learn (WTL), 116, 118, 119, 121
Wyatt, Jonathan, 6

Xchanges, 11

Yancey, Kathleen Blake, 147, 148, 191
Yosso, Tara, 197, 198
young adult literature (YAL), 39
Young, Iris Marion, 14
Young Scholars in Writing (YSW), 11, 44

Zea, Santiago, 51, 52, 53, 55, 58, 60
Zendejas, Mía, 14, 20; brainstorming by, 68; coauthoring with, 15, 74; code-switching and, 15; experience of, 65–66; mentorship of, 73; research dynamics and, 16; Thomson-Bunn and, 66–67, 69–70, 71, 72, 75
Zhang-Wu, Qianqian, 16
Zoom meetings, 72, 79, 82, 85, 103, 209, 210, 215

About the Authors

Christian D. Brendel recently completed his PhD in linguistics at the University of California, Santa Barbara. In addition to his research as an NSF graduate fellow and Beinecke Scholar on the confluence of cognition, speech perception, and language evolution, he has taught (and learned from) undergraduates in experimental classes ranging from Animal Communication to Memelogy. He has published in *Transactions of the Philological Society*, and his collaborative work appears across diverse venues (and topics), including *The Proceedings of the Association for Computational Linguistics*, *Rendezvous*, and *Dictionaria*.

Jennifer Burke Reifman is an assistant professor in the Department of Rhetoric and Writing Studies and the director of lower-division writing at San Diego State University. Her research uses participant-centered methodologies to understand the experiences of undergraduate students and explore issues of equity in writing assessment and postsecondary writing programs. Her work can be found in a number of peer-reviewed publications, including *Assessing Writing*, *Journal of Basic Writing*, and *College Composition and Communication*.

Lauren S. Cardon is an associate professor of English and director of Graduate Studies at the University of Alabama, with a PhD from Tulane University. She has authored three academic monographs on American literature, most recently *Fashioning Character: Style, Performance, and Identity in Contemporary American Literature* with UVA Press. She also specializes in DEI pedagogy and recently coauthored a fourth monograph in this field, titled *Inclusive College Classrooms: Teaching Methods for Diverse Learners*, published by Routledge. In addition, she has published pedagogical articles in *South Atlantic Review*, *Change: The Magazine of Higher Learning*, and the collection *Quick Hits: Teaching with Digital Humanities* (University of Indiana Press).

Teresa Contino is a master's student in the Cognitive Psychology: User Experience Program at Claremont Graduate University, where she also works as a program assistant for the Division of Behavioral & Organizational Sciences and a research assistant for the Drucker School of Management. Last year, she served as a Fulbright English teaching assistant in the Czech Republic. Her research interests include psychology, user experience, rhetoric and composition, and product design. She earned her bachelor's degree in English and psychology from Santa Clara University in 2023.

Steven J. Corbett is a professor of composition & rhetoric; division head of Communication, Composition & Rhetoric; and writing program administrator at Methodist University in Fayetteville, NC. From 2016 to 2023 he was an associate professor of English and director of the QEP and University Writing Center at Texas A&M University, Kingsville. He is the author of *Beyond Dichotomy: Synergizing Writing Center and Classroom Pedagogies* (2015) and editor of *If at First You Don't Succeed? Writing, Rhetoric, and the Question of Failure* (2024). He is also coeditor of *Peer Pressure, Peer Power: Theory and Practice in Peer Review and Response for the Writing Classroom* (2014); *Student Peer Review and Response: A Critical Sourcebook* (2018); *Writing in and about the Performing and Visual Arts: Creating, Performing, and Teaching* (2019); and *Writing Centers and Learning Commons: Staying Centered While Sharing Common Ground* (2023). His articles on writing pedagogy have appeared in a variety of journals, periodicals, and collections, and his current project is the coedited (with Teagan Decker) collection *Honoring Student Writers: Studies and Stories of Writing in Honors Colleges and Programs*.

Dr. Abby M. Dubisar is an associate professor at Iowa State University. She teaches courses in critical and cultural theories of rhetoric and communication, popular culture analysis, proposal and report writing, and gender and communication. Her publications have appeared in *Quarterly Journal of Speech*; *Journal of Agriculture, Food Systems, and Community Development*; *Peitho*; *College English*; *Community Literacy Journal*; *Rhetoric Review*; *Rhetoric of Health and Medicine*; *Computers and Composition*; and other venues. https://orcid.org/0000-0003-3957-1540

Shirley E. Faulkner-Springfield is the director of the University Writing Center at North Carolina Agricultural and Technical State University. Her publications appear in *Serendipity in Rhetoric, Writing, and Literacy Research; Computers and Composition Online; Reflections: Writing, Service-Learning, and Community Literacy;* and *Feminist Rhetorical Practices: New Horizons for Rhetoric, Composition, and Literacy Studies*. She has edited a twenty-chapter book titled *Treating Black Women with Eating Disorders: A Clinicians Guide* and two chapters of the edited collection *Antiblackness and the Stories of Authentic Allies: Lived Experiences in the Fight Against Institutionalized Racism*.

Nicolas Fay is a first-year master's student at the University of North Carolina at Chapel Hill where he studies political science. His work has appeared in *SPUR* and *TEXT*.

Sandy Feinstein, a professor of English at Penn State Berks, has copublished with colleagues and undergraduates since 1996, most recently in *Text*. She has also published a medievalist article in a festshrift edited by one of her former students, now a distinguished professor. Her coauthored articles on pedagogy have appeared in *Pedagogy, Intraspection, SPUR, New Chaucer Society: Pedagogy and the Profession, CEA: The Critic*, and *What We Talk about When We Talk about Creative Writing* (ed. Anna Leahy), among others. As a poet, she is a Pushcart nominee; as a writer of creative nonfiction, she is a finalist in the Short Edition's Money Chronicles competition—along with one of her present students, a sophomore (two finalists from one institution!).

Lynée Lewis Gaillet, a Distinguished University Professor of English at Georgia State University, researches rhetorical history and composition pedagogy, mentoring issues and coauthoring, feminist activism, and archival research methodologies. A longtime collaborator, her book projects include *The Present State of Scholarship in the History of Rhetoric, Stories of Mentoring, Scholarly Publication in a Changing Academic Landscape, Primary Research and Writing*, and *Remembering Differently: Re-Figuring Women's Rhetorical Work*. Currently, she is investigating women's labor and academic careers in the wake of 2020 (*Blurred Boundaries*) and coauthoring a revised edition of *Primary Research and Writing*. Gaillet has served as English department chair, president of the National Coalition of Feminist Scholars, and executive director of the South Atlantic Modern Language Association.

Isabella Gomez is a sophomore at Santa Clara University, majoring in philosophy. Isabella has had an internship at Santa Clara University since high school, where she works alongside Professor Amy Lueck in community engaged writing research and cultural programming. Isabella's research and programming focuses on her tribal history and present-day Native youth. Part of Isabella's work on Santa Clara University's campus includes an augmented reality tour on Native history, an annual campout for Native youth, and a permanent Native history kiosk at the De Saisset museum.

Shane Graham is a professor of English at Utah State University and author of *Cultural Entanglements: Langston Hughes and the Rise of African and Caribbean Literature* (2020) and *South African Literature after the Truth Commission: Mapping Loss* (2009). He is coeditor, with former student John Walters, of *Langston Hughes and the South African Drum Generation: The Correspondence* (2010). His current research projects include a study of Langston Hughes's connections to various institutions in the "Cultural Cold War" of the 1950s and 1960s, a project he is undertaking with undergraduate research assistant Eden Marroquín.

Jane Greer is a Curators' Distinguished Teaching Professor of English and women's & gender studies at the University of Missouri, Kansas City, where she also serves as director of undergraduate research and creative scholarship. She is the editor of *Girls and Literacy in America: Historical Perspectives to the Present* (ABC-Clio, 2003) and coeditor of *Pedagogies of Public Memory: Teaching Writing and Rhetoric at Museums, Memorials, and Archives* (Routledge, 2015) and *The Naylor Report on Undergraduate Research in Writing Studies* (Parlor Press, 2020). She published *Unorganized Women: Repetitive Rhetorical Labor and Low-Wage Workers, 1834–1937* with University of Pittsburgh Press in 2023, and it received an honorable mention for the Winifred Bryan Horner Outstanding Book Award from the Coalition of Feminist Scholars in the History of Rhetoric and Composition. At UMKC, Professor Greer teaches courses ranging from sophomore-level composition to graduate seminars in feminist rhetoric, public memory, and archival methodologies.

Laurie Grobman is a distinguished professor of English and women's, gender, and sexuality studies at Penn State Berks. She is a social justice educator, regularly facilitating community-engaged scholarship and pedagogy to (re)write local histories of marginalized ethnic, racial, socioeconomic and cultural communities in Berks County and the city of Reading in Pennsylvania. Her article, "'Engaging Race': Critical Race Inquiry and Community-Engaged Scholarship," received the 2018 NCTE Richard C. Ohmann Outstanding Article in *College English* Award. Laurie is the 2014 Carnegie Foundation for the Advancement of Teaching, Outstanding Baccalaureate Colleges Professor of the Year. Her most recent publication is "Social Justice Pedagogy and Collaborative Counterstorytelling: We Are Reading," in *Social Justice in Action: Models for Campus and Community* (MLA 2024). She has published several books, including the coauthored *Major Decisions: College, Career, and the Case for the Humanities* (University of Pennsylvania Press, 2020). Laurie is currently facilitating a community-wide story project, "This is All of Us: A Community's Stories of Violence, Loss, and Love," as part of a $1,600,000 grant from the Pennsylvania Commission on Crime and Delinquency and is currently conducting research on narrative and community violence.

Letizia Guglielmo is a professor of English and interdisciplinary studies at Kennesaw State University (KSU), where she teaches courses in writing and rhetoric and gender and women's studies in a variety of course modalities, including online asynchronous environments. Her writing and research explore feminist rhetoric and pedagogy, gender and pop culture, and student and faculty professional development, and her work has appeared in a variety of peer-reviewed journals and edited collections. She is author and coeditor of *Immigrant Scholars in Rhetoric, Composition, and Communication: Memoirs of a First Generation*, author and editor of *Misogyny in American Culture: Causes, Trends, Solutions*, coauthor of *Scholarly Publication in a Changing Academic Landscape*, author and editor of *Contingent Faculty Publishing in Community: Case Studies for Successful Collaborations*, and author and editor of *MTV and Teen Pregnancy: Critical Essays on 16 and Pregnant and Teen Mom*. As a certified professional coach with the International Coaching Federation (ICF), Letizia also has served as a faculty success fellow and Coach with the Center for Excellence in Teaching and Learning (CETL) at KSU, where she facilitated faculty development workshops and offered one-to-one coaching for faculty on a variety of topics connected to faculty writing and publishing and career progression.

Faith Iseman, formerly Dalavai, graduated from Penn State Berks with a degree in communication arts and sciences. Presently she works for Ephrata National Bank as part of their trust and estate services.

Rachel Jensen recently completed her PhD in criminology, law, and society at George Mason University and works as a project manager at a policing nonprofit organization. Her research interests focus on policing and behavioral health crisis response, with a particular focus on intellectual and developmental disabilities. She has coauthored several publications that appear in *Victims and Offenders*, *Journal of Contemporary of Criminal Justice*, *Police Practice and Research*, and *Police Chief Magazine*.

Xuan Jiang has been the assistant director of Florida International University (FIU)'s writing center since 2018. During her term, she has coauthored with multiple tutors for ten publications of empirical and pedagogical studies: two articles in *Writing Center Journal*, two articles in *Praxis: A Writing Center Journal*, and two articles in *Peer Review*. Besides publishing in the three main writing center journals, Xuan has coauthored two language-teaching chapters published by Palgrave Macmillan and Routledge, one coauthored article in *Peitho*, and one coauthored article in *Global Education and Research*. In addition to copublications and long-term mentorship, Xuan has continued her research line in language teaching and published in journals and edited collections on education. Moreover, Xuan has been co-designing and delivering faculty workshops as a faculty fellow at FIU, which has given her a pragmatic and programmatic sense of feminism in implementation. Furthermore, in the establishment and execution of the *FIU Undergraduate Research Journal*, Xuan, working with Vanessa Sohan, expands the pracademic network and support from many FIU units and several grant projects. As a CCCC Dream Awardee in 2024, Xuan continues her dream as a member of the CCCC Accountability for Equity and Inclusion Committee (2024–2026).

Distinguished Professor Emeritus of English at Utah State University, **Joyce Kinkead** is the Carnegie Professor for Utah (2013), a CUR Fellow, and Thorne Career Researcher (USU). As associate vice president of research, she instituted Undergraduate Research Fellows, UR Day at the State Capitol, and the Utah Conference on Undergraduate Research. She has coauthored with or mentored nearly a hundred undergraduates. Several of more than a dozen books published focus on undergraduate research. Her most recent work, *A Writing Studies Primer*, is a five-thousand-year history of writing and its material culture.

Tina Le is a composition and rhetoric PhD student at the University of Nebraska–Lincoln, where she serves as a writing center assistant director and teaches writing and teacher education courses. With a background in teaching English at public high schools and juvenile detention, she is interested in the relationships between narrative identity, teacher development, and teacher well-being.

Amy Lueck is a professor of rhetoric and composition and associate provost for faculty development at Santa Clara University, where her research and teaching focus on histories of rhetorical instruction and practice, feminist historiography, cultural rhetorics, and rhetorical memory studies. Her book, *A Shared History: Writing in the High School, College, and University, 1856–1886* (SIU Press 2020), brings together several of these research threads, interrogating the ostensible high school–college divide and the role it has played in shaping writing instruction in the US. Her recent research builds on this work by attending to the cultural rhetorics shaping history and remembrance at various sites, from universities and the tribal homelands on which they are built to historic attractions like the Winchester Mystery House, examining the boundaries and rhetorics of containment that serve to isolate communities and their histories. Her work (most often coauthored, often with students) has appeared in *College Composition and Communication*, *Community Literacy Journal*, *Composition Studies*, *Pedagogy*, and elsewhere.

Brandy Martinez received her undergraduate degree in English with minors in psychology and interdisciplinary linguistics from The University of Alabama. She currently works at Turning Point. There, she advocates for the rights and protections of survivors of domestic violence and sexual assault at the medical and judicial level. Brandy focuses on assisting survivors living in rural communities of West

Alabama, providing the residents of this area with educational outreach and victim advocacy services. Additionally, she strives to promote language inclusivity for the wellbeing of the local immigrant population through her work.

Mikenna Leigh Modesto (née Sims) recently completed her PhD in education at the University of California, Davis, and is now a student services administrator with the Los Rios Community College District. Her research interests include writing assessment, multilingual writing instruction, and student support services. Her work has been published in *Assessing Writing*, *Journal of Second Language Writing*, and *The Learning Assistance Review*, among others.

Kayla Moore is an undergraduate honors student at North Carolina Central University. She is majoring in business administration with a concentration in entrepreneurial studies and minoring in biology. In 2024 she presented at the Conference on College Composition and Communication's "Teacher to Teacher" session, where she discussed the benefits and challenges of collaborating with writers from other disciplines to produce a manuscript.

Jennifer Muret-Bate completed her master's in restorative practices at the International Institute for Restorative Practices. She was a founding member of the Restorative Schools Initiative and continues to serve on that team through the Kansas Institute for Peace and Conflict Resolution. She has taught students aged kindergarten through adult during her career and specializes in at-risk students and any other learners who do not fit within the traditional educational system. She currently teaches at the Creative Learning Community program at Winfield High School in Winfield, Kansas.

Ashley Offenback is a data analyst with an undergraduate degree in professional writing from Penn State University. She is currently consulting on a project with the County of Chester while earning her graduate degree at West Chester University.

Jennifer Peña is a PhD candidate and research assistant at the University of Miami's School of Communication. She previously earned her master's degree in English from Florida International University. Jennifer's research interests include media studies, skill transfer within online communities and communities of practice, and intercultural communication and mentorship in educational contexts such as writing centers. Jennifer's work recently appeared in *In Media Res*, where she organized a Barbie theme week in 2024. She has co-authored articles about mentorship and intercultural communication that were published in *Writing Center Journal* in 2022 and *The Peer Review* in 2020. Jennifer's current research focuses on BookTube, the online reader community on YouTube. Her research investigates learning, community building, and social influence within online communities, as well as framing and modeling of behaviors on social media platforms.

Mik Penarroyo-Smith (née Penarroyo) received their undergraduate degree in sociology with a minor in history at the University of California Davis in 2023. Mik is currently a grants manager for nonprofits throughout Southern California. While at UC Davis, they worked as a student assessment researcher (StAR) for the Curious Aggies research initiative, which analyzed undergraduate students' perceptions of assessment practices on campus. Their work has been published in *The Learning Assistance Review* and *Peitho: Journal of the Coalition of Feminist Scholars in the History of Rhetoric & Composition*.

Charity Riddick-Mullen is a graduate of North Carolina Central University, where she earned a bachelor's degree in psychology. She works as an instructional assistant at Hillandale Elementary School, a part of Durham Public Schools.

Giovanna Rodriguez graduated from Florida International University in 2021. She continued her education and received her MBA with a concentration in data analytics from Florida Gulf Coast University in 2024 and is currently a behavioral therapist pursuing her BCBA certification at Florida Institute of Technology.

Leah Senatro is an English PhD candidate at University of California, Irvine, where she also provides administrative support for the Office of the Campus Writing and Communication Coordinator and the Writing Across Campus + Writing in the Disciplines program. Her research interests include rhetoric and composition, undergraduate research and pedagogy, rhetorical theory, and the medical humanities. Both her research and pedagogy seek to explore the rhetorical consequences of the body and sensorial experience. She earned her bachelor's degree in English and philosophy from Santa Clara University in 2019.

Rachael Shah is an associate professor of English at the University of Nebraska-Lincoln, where she directs the Nebraska Writing Project and teaches classes on community-based pedagogies, public rhetorics, collaborative learning, teacher education, and composition. She has coordinated community-based learning programs for over fifteen years, and she frequently cowrites with students and/or community partners. Her first book, *Rewriting Partnerships: Community Perspectives on Community-Based Learning*, won the IARSLCE Publication of the Year Award as well as the Coalition for Community Writing's Outstanding Book Award, and she is working on a new book on collaborative writing in community engagement.

Vanessa Kraemer Sohan is an associate professor of writing and rhetoric in the English Department at Florida International University (FIU) and director of the

FIU Liberal Studies and Interdisciplinary programs. Her research and teaching focus on translingual and transmodal approaches to literacy practice, feminist historiography, and material rhetorics. Her book, *Lives, Letters, and Quilts: Women and Everyday Rhetorics of Resistance* (University of Alabama Press, 2020), provides case studies of women activists and artists. Her scholarship has appeared in *College English, Pedagogy, JAC, Journal of College Literacy and Learning, Journal of Multimodal Rhetorics, Journal of Technical Writing and Communication*, and various edited collections.

Heather Thomson-Bunn is an associate professor of English and director of First-Year Writing at Pepperdine University, where she teaches courses in composition, rhetoric, language theory, professional writing, and creative writing. Her research focuses on religious rhetorics as they relate to academic norms, institutional values, and writing. Her work has appeared in *College English, Pedagogy*, and *Composition Forum*, as well as in *Mapping Christian Rhetorics* (Routledge Series in Rhetoric and Communication).

Loren Torres is a fifth-year undergraduate student at the University of California, Davis, studying sociology and anthropology. She plans to graduate in June 2025. Loren worked as a student assessment researcher (StAR) and, alongside her coauthors, has been published in *Learning Assistance Review* and *Peitho*.

Annette Vara holds a BA in marketing from Texas A&M University, Kingsville. Her work has appeared in *WPAing in a Pandemic and Beyond: Revision, Innovation, and Advocacy* (2025), and she is currently coauthoring chapters for two other collections. She was named Texas A&M University Kingsville's 2023 Student Employee of the Year.

Katherine Villarreal is a fifth-grade science teacher for the Alice Independent School District. She holds a BA from Texas A&M University, Kingsville, in education and interdisciplinary studies. Her work has appeared in the collections *Emotions and Affect in Writing Centers* (2022) and *WPAing in a Pandemic and Beyond: Revision, Innovation, and Advocacy* (2025), and she is currently coauthoring a chapter for another collection. She was named the 2020 South Central Writing Centers Association Outstanding Tutor of the Year.

Mía Zendejas is pursing an MFA in creative writing prose at the University of St Andrews in Scotland. In addition to focusing on her own writing, she teaches creative writing courses to undergraduates, is a bookseller at an independently owned bookstore that hosts author events, and attends international conferences, such as the 2024 Winter School: Ambivalence and Media in Lisbon, Portugal. Her research interests include postcolonialism, bilingualism in writing, and diasporic identity. Mía code-switches with Spanish in both her creative and academic writing and intentionally does not provide translations to rhetorically mimic the forced linguistic adoption and cultural erasure experienced by colonized peoples. She earned her BA in English, writing, and rhetoric along with two minors, great books and creative writing, at Pepperdine University Malibu and Florence. Her undergraduate thesis is titled "The Postcolonial Realidades of the Lone Star: Inconsistent Narrativas Nacionales in Puerto Rico-United States Relaciones." During her studies at Pepperdine, she served as the direct supporter of the English Program; editor of the university's literary and art journal, *Expressionists: Magazine of the Arts*; and diversified the Advanced Composition course with her coauthor, Dr. Heather Thomson-Bunn.

www.ingramcontent.com/pod-product-compliance
Lightning Source LLC
Chambersburg PA
CBHW060555080526
44585CB00013B/571